The **Brilliant Dot-to-Dot** *Book*
FOR GROWN-UPS

The *Brilliant* *Dot-to-Dot* Book

FOR GROWN-UPS

ARCTURUS

NOTES

Pages 20, 63, 109, 110, 154, 170, 173, 189, 194, 196, 247 and 265: These pictures are made from 2 continuous lines: a) numbers and b) lower case letters.

Pages 22, 94, 98, 153, 166 and 178: These pictures are made from 4 continuous lines: a) numbers, b) upper case letters, c) lower case letters and d) roman numerals

Pages 79, 103, 159, 162, 167, 183, 190 and 278: These pictures are made from 3 continuous lines: a) numbers, b) upper case letters and c) lower case letters

ARCTURUS

This edition published in 2016 by Arcturus Publishing Limited
26/27 Bickels Yard, 151–153 Bermondsey Street,
London SE1 3HA

ISBN: 978-1-78599-006-9
CH004768NT

Printed in China

CONTENTS

INTRODUCTION

Prepare to be hooked on these brilliant dot-to-dot puzzles! Get ready for a journey that will unlock famous works of art and scenes from the worlds of entertainment, sport, transport and the natural world. But don't expect an easy ride. Sometimes the next number may be difficult to find, but with patience, a pencil and a straight edge the final picture will be revealed. And if an image looks familiar, but you just can't remember its name, you'll find the answer at the back of the book.

Each of the 270 puzzles presented here contains up to 300 consecutively numbered dots, just waiting to be linked to reveal an exciting image. In a few cases, pictures are made from more than one continuous line. Check the Notes on page 4 to identify these.

As well as being immensely satisfying, dot-to-dot puzzles are proven to help improve short-term cognitive activity, hand-eye coordination and concentration skills. They are the perfect way to have fun while putting your brain to work. So, sharpen that pencil and get started!

Animal Kingdom

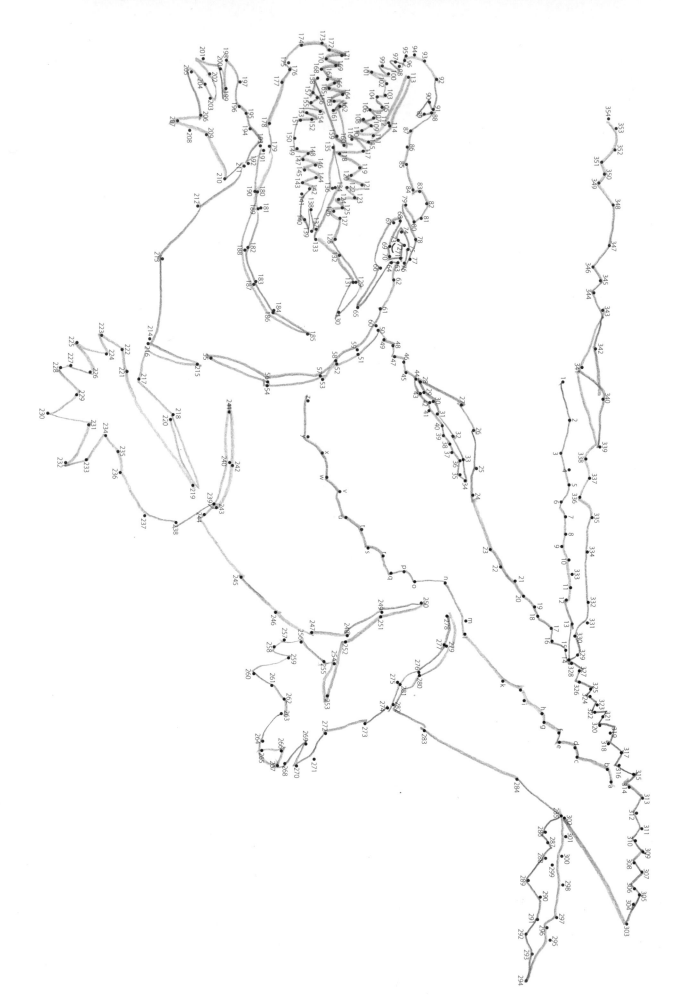

8

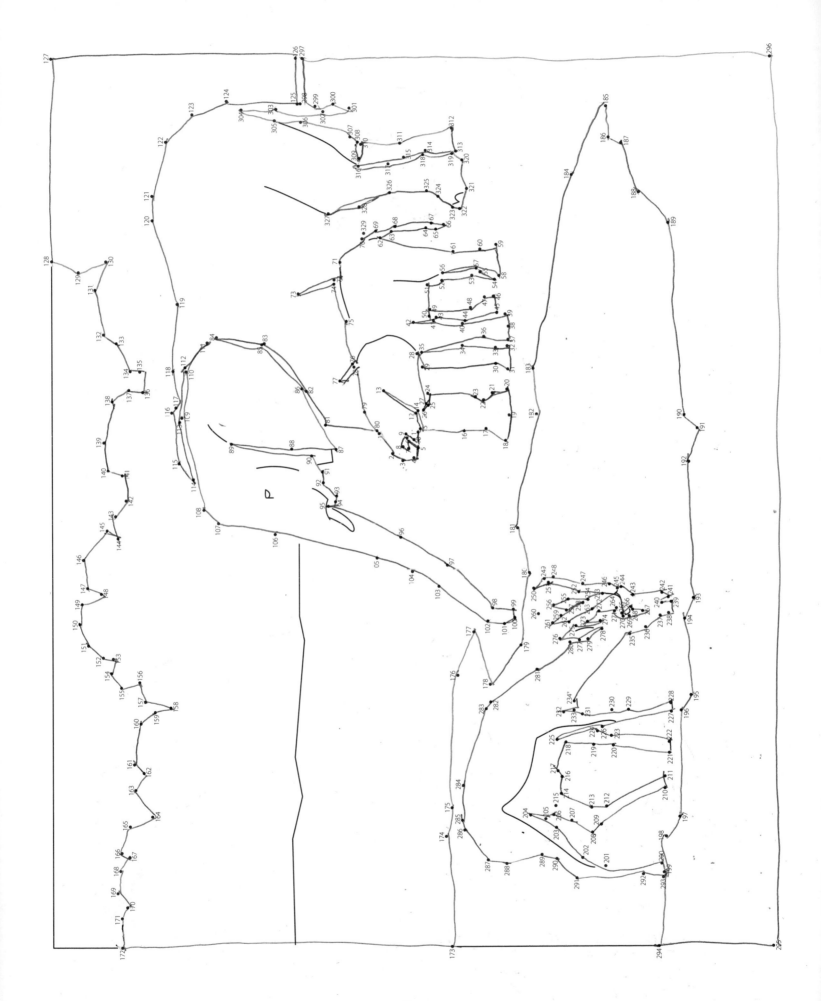

9

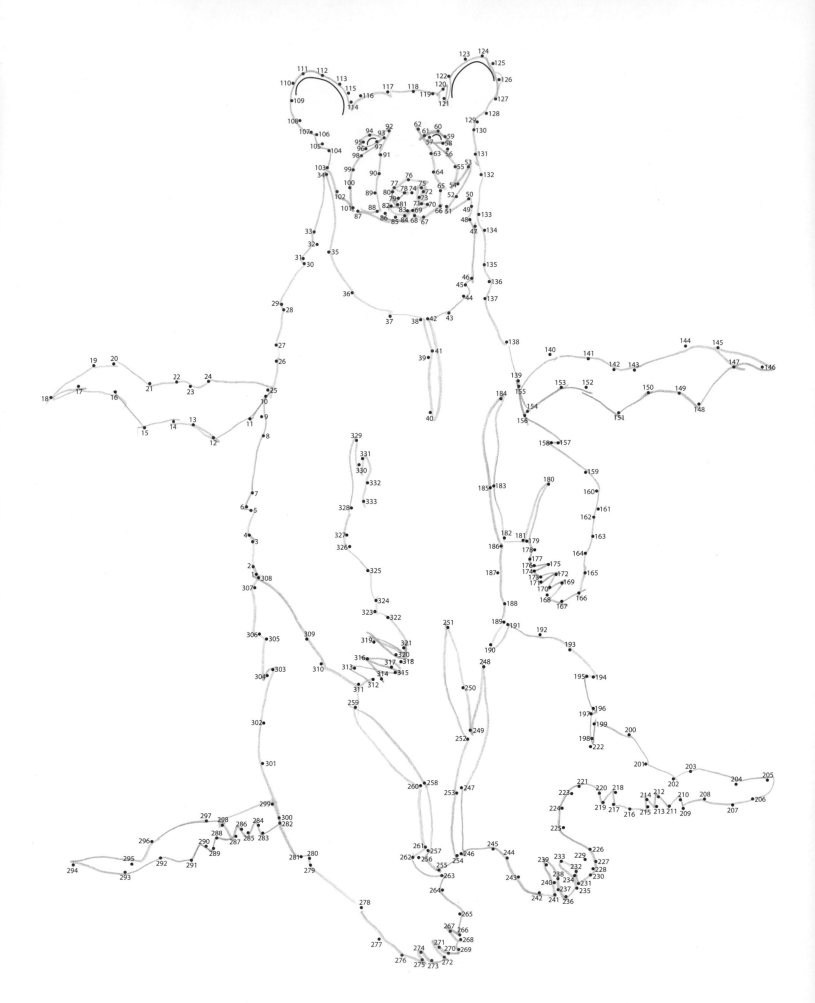

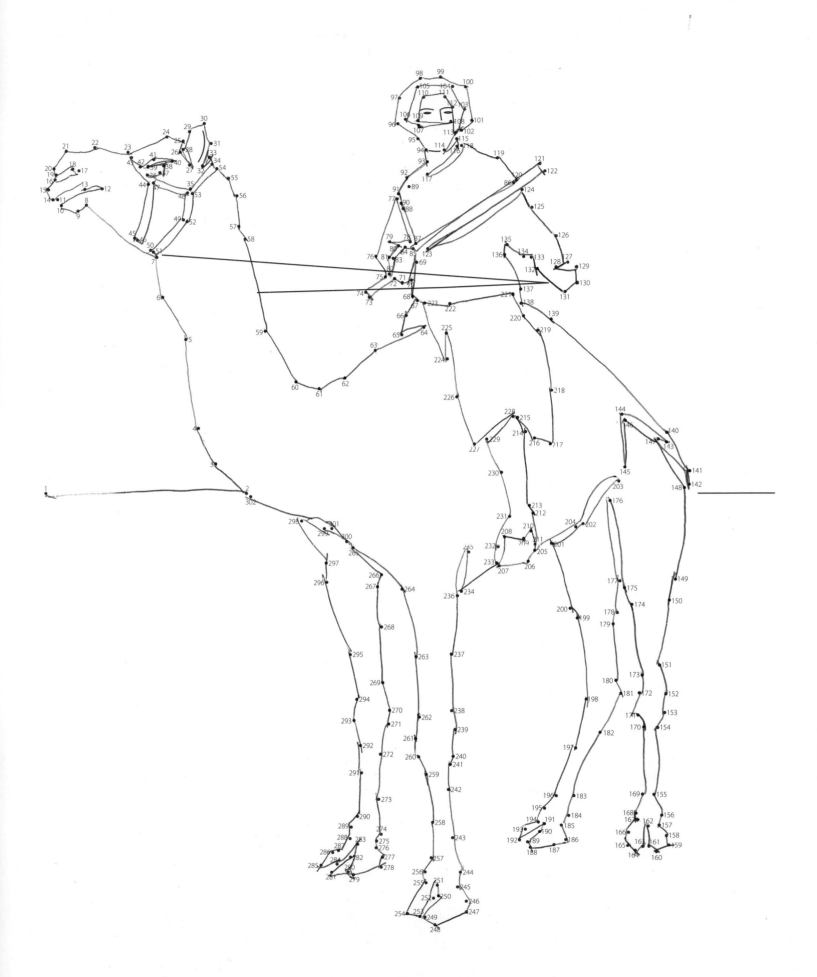

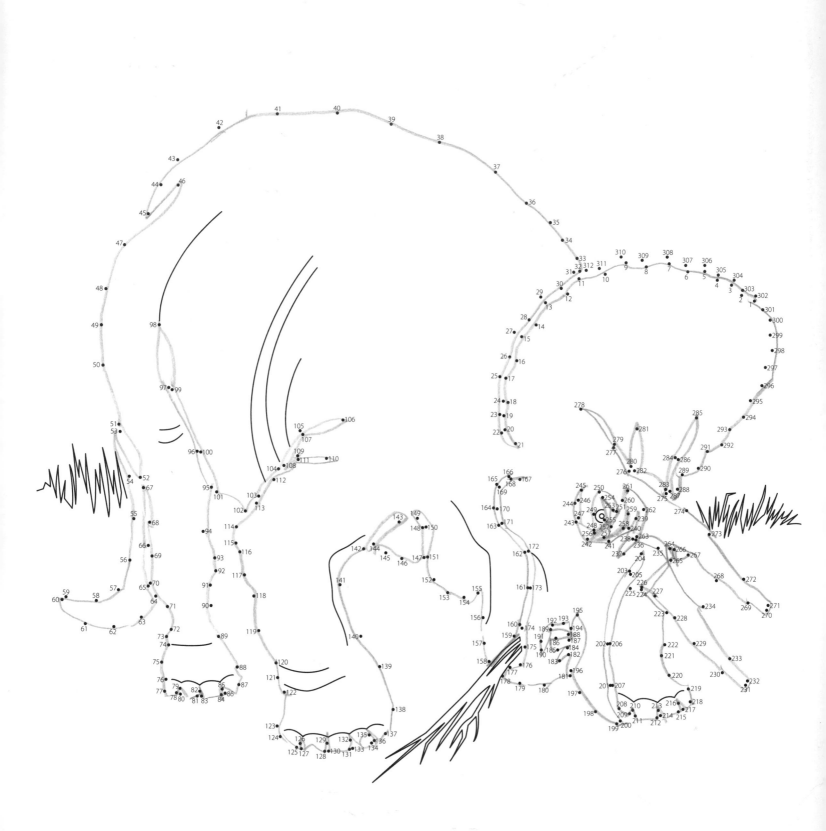

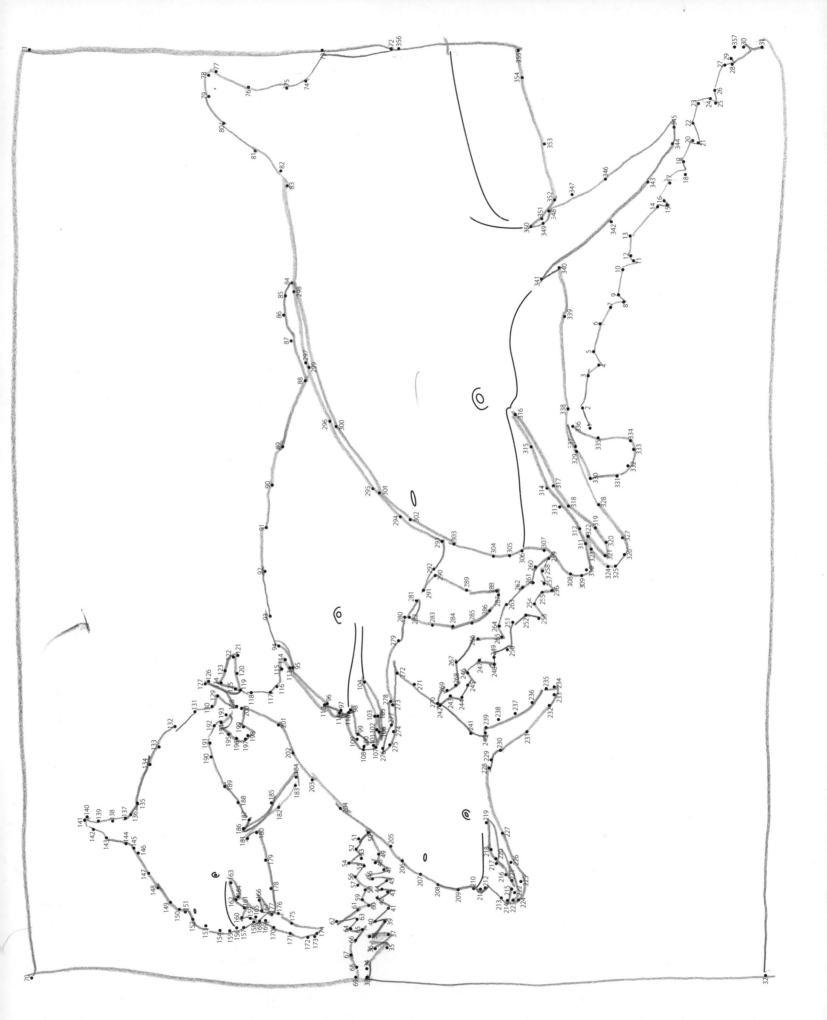

13

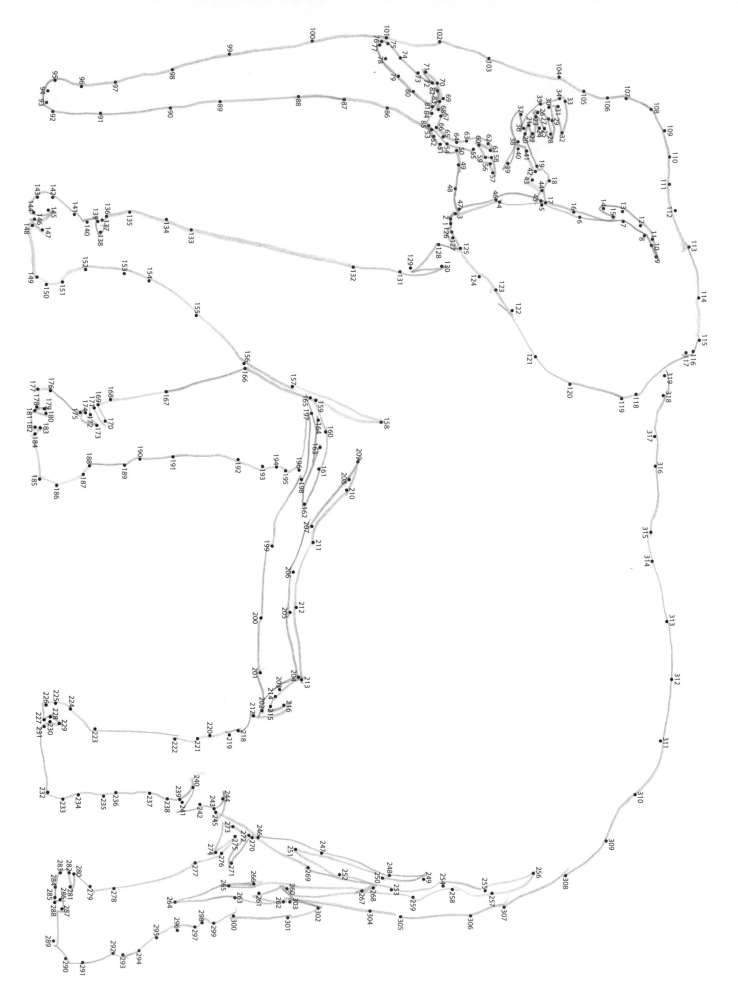

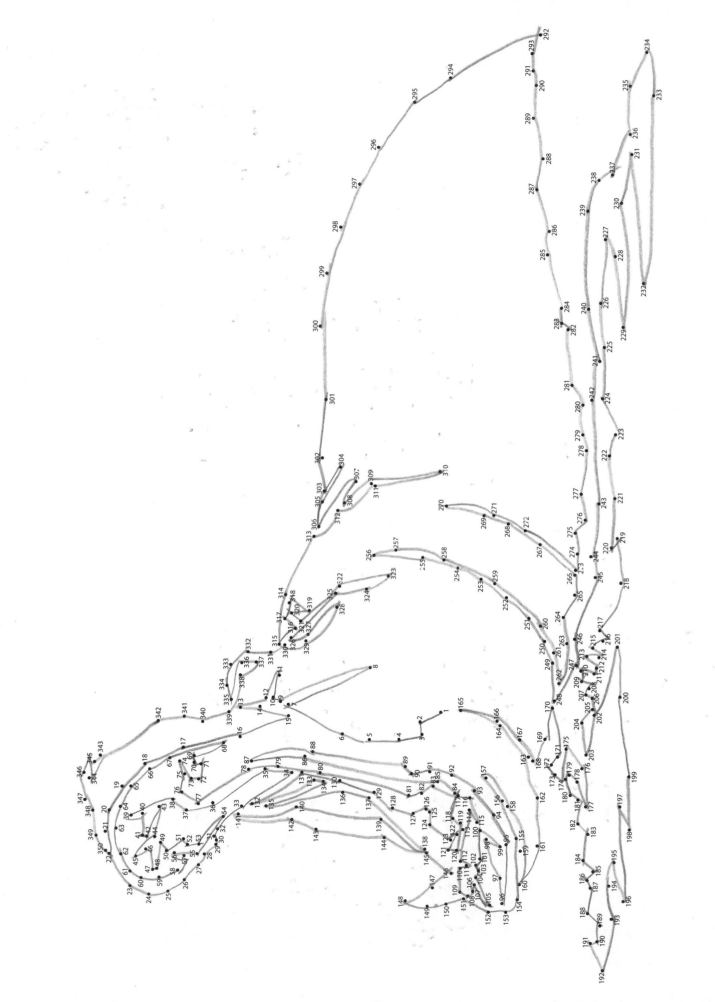

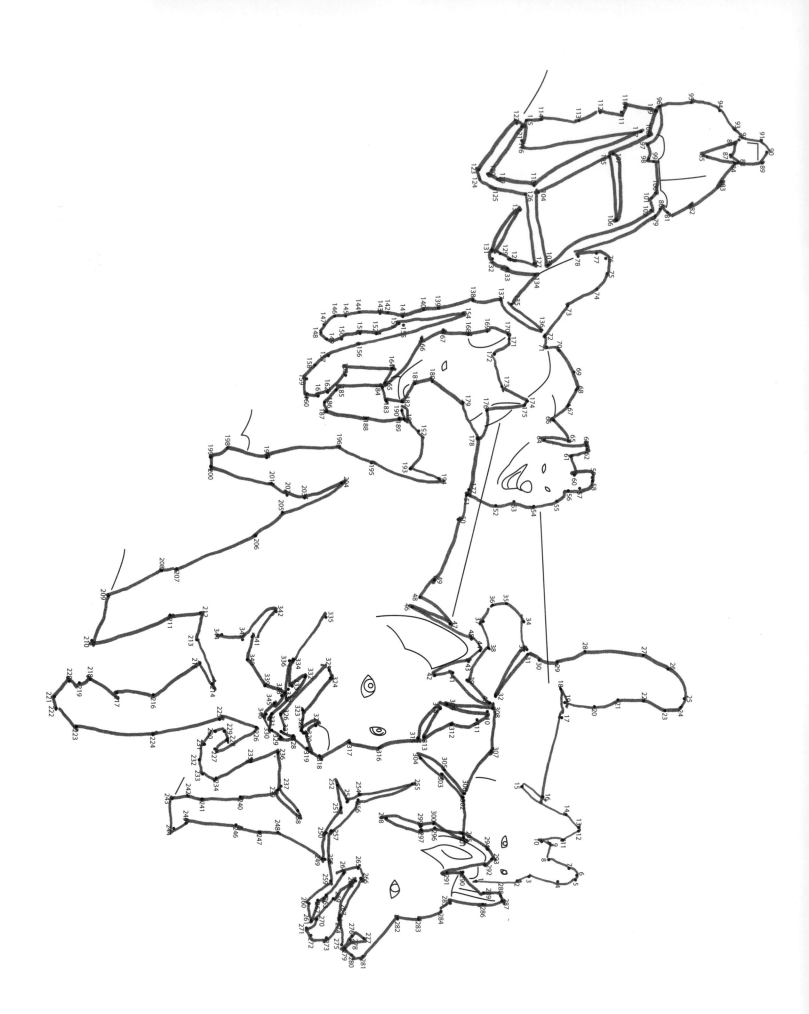

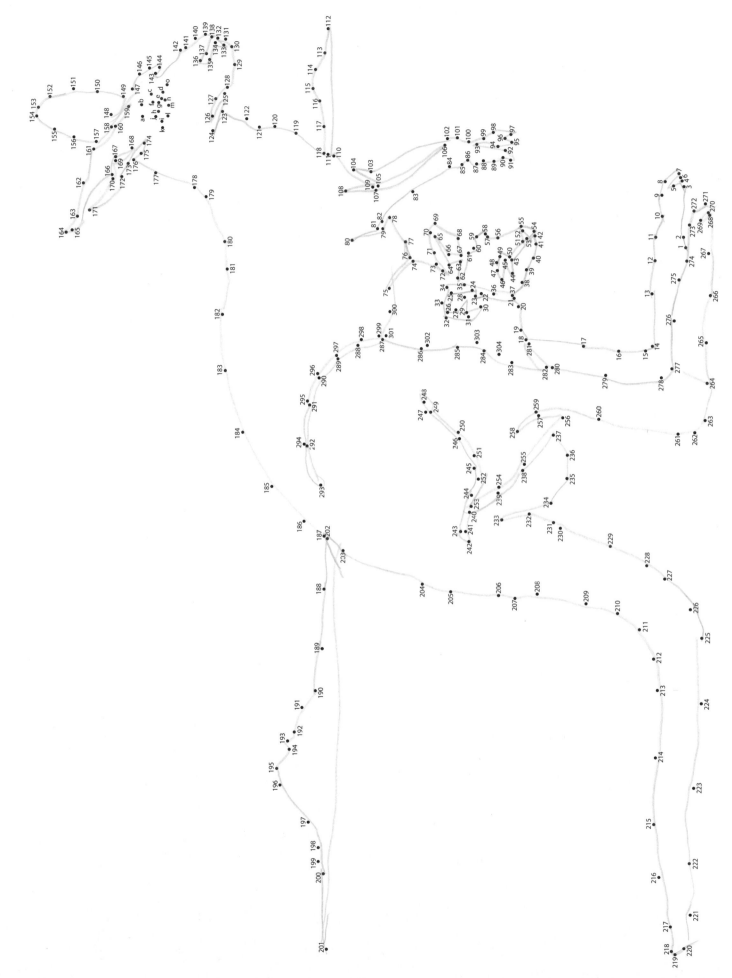

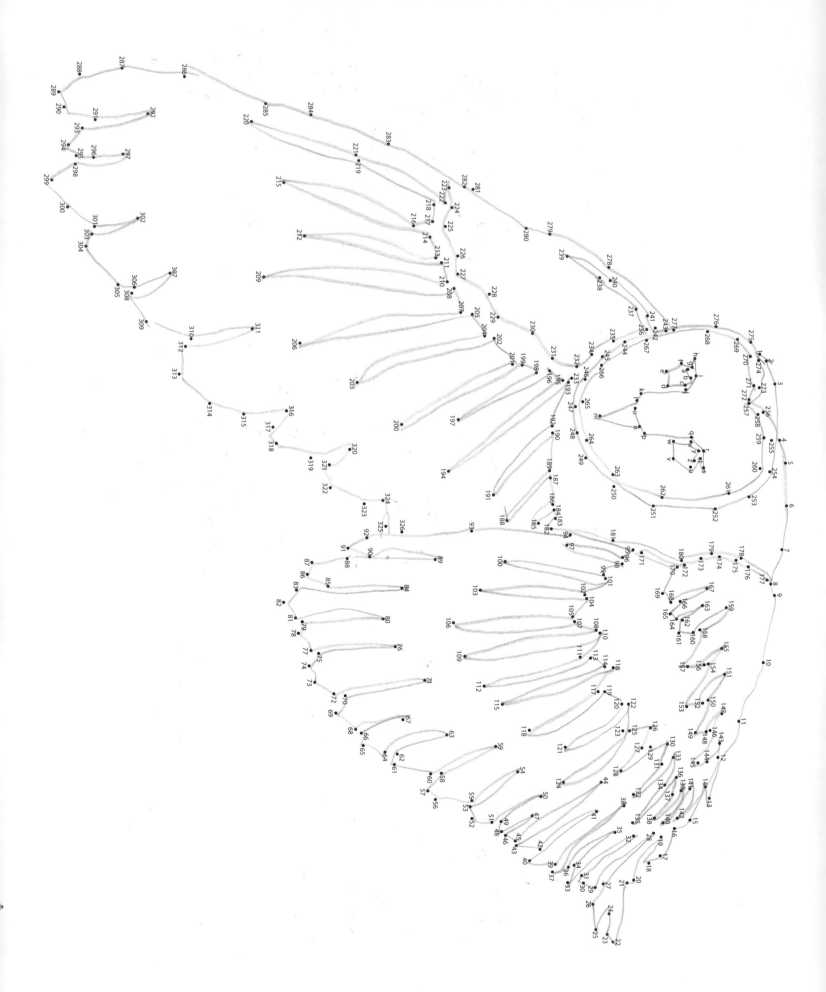

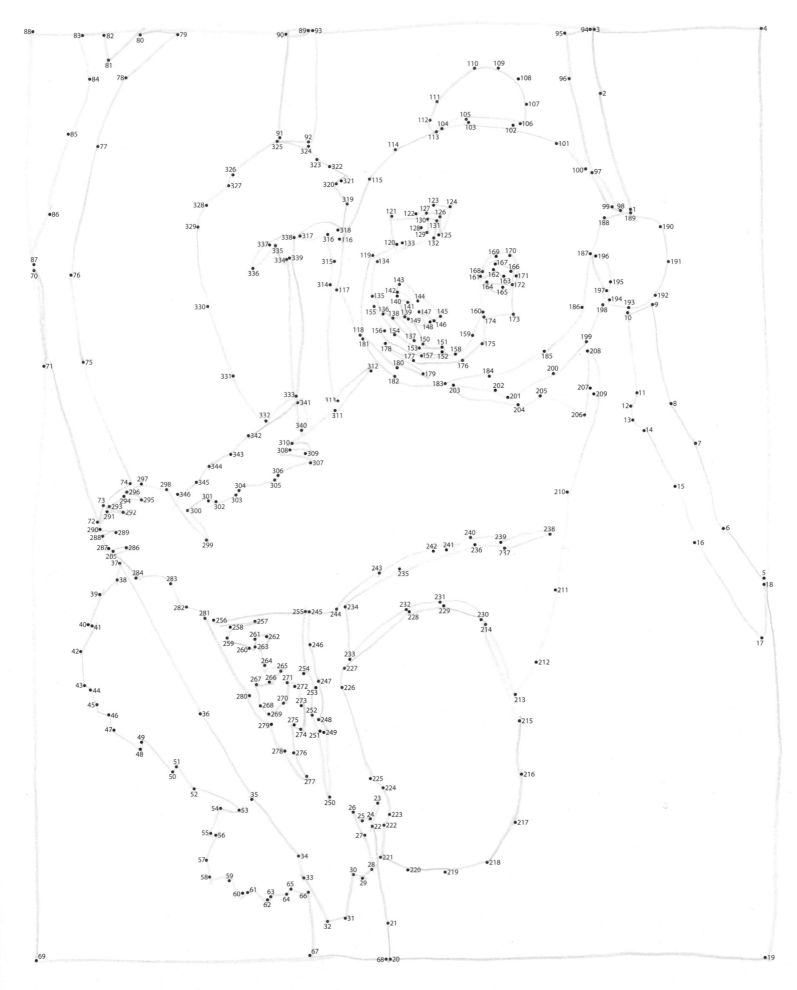

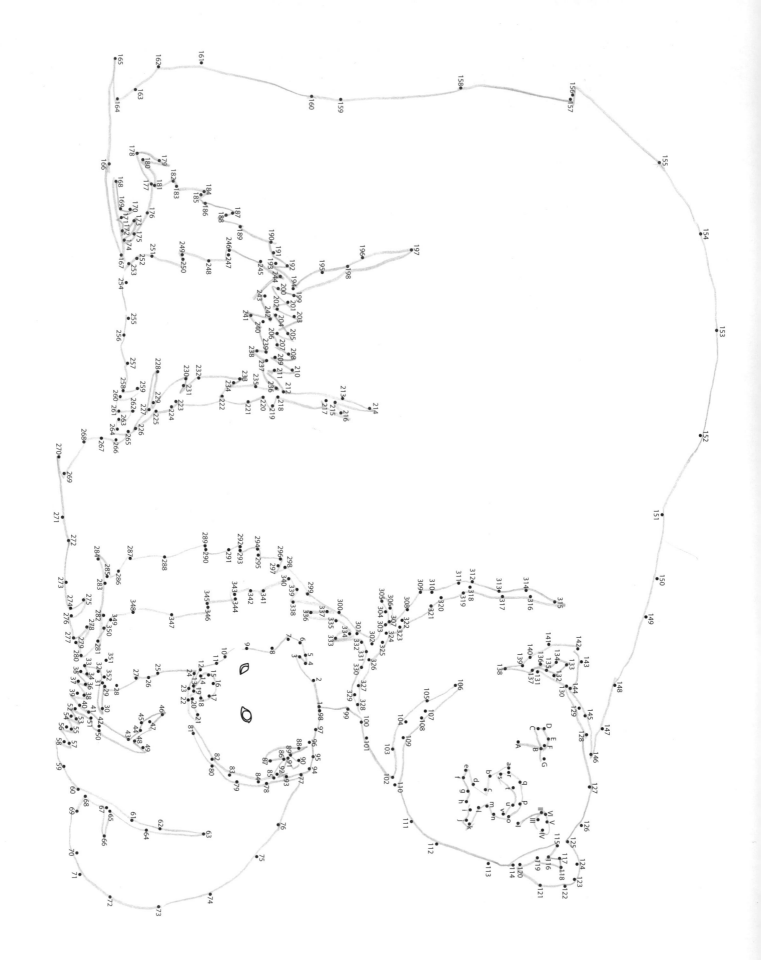

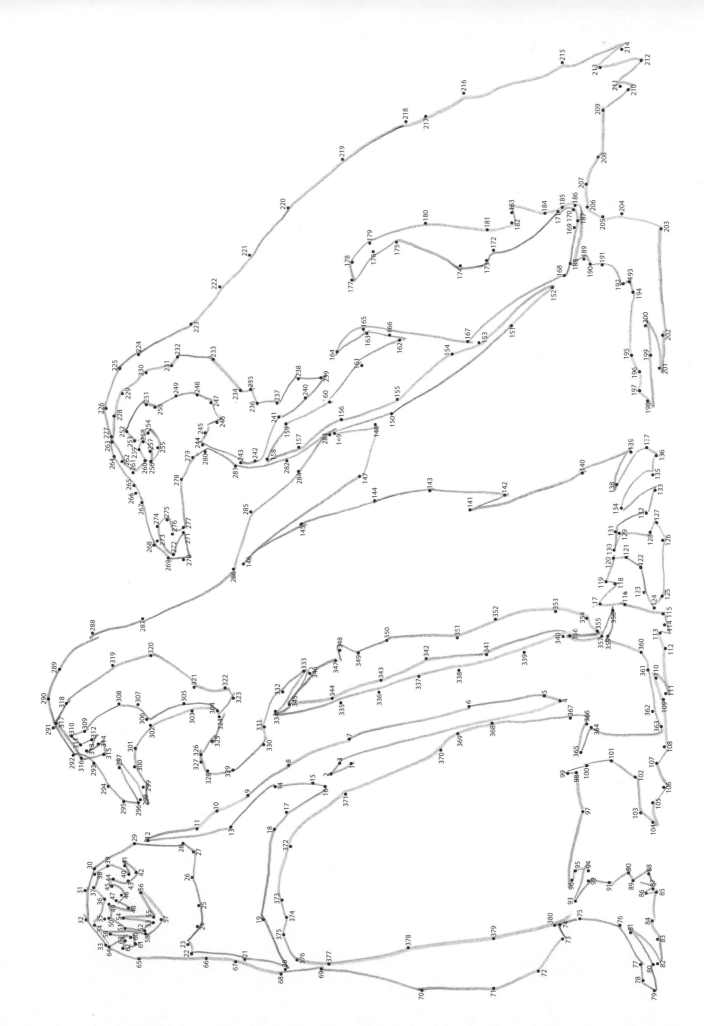

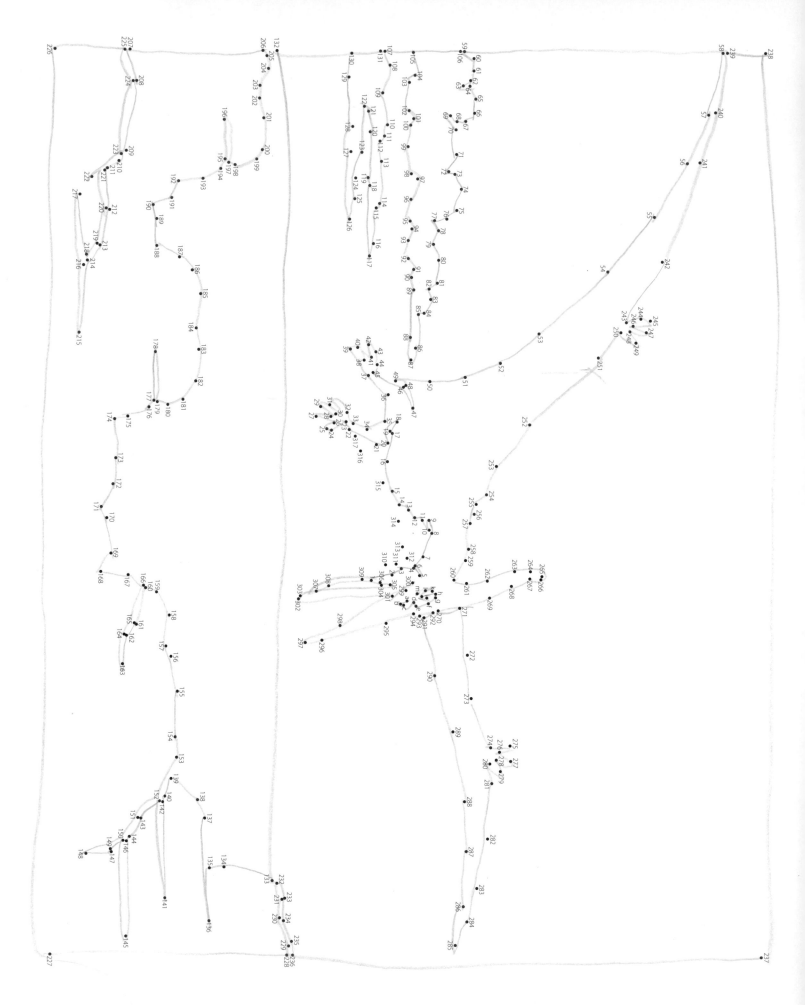

24

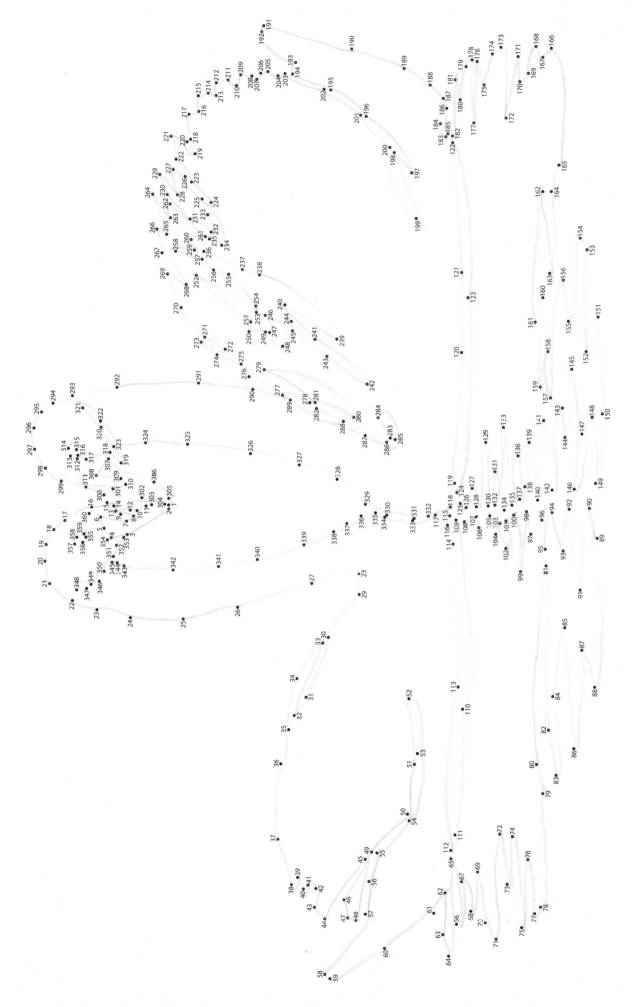

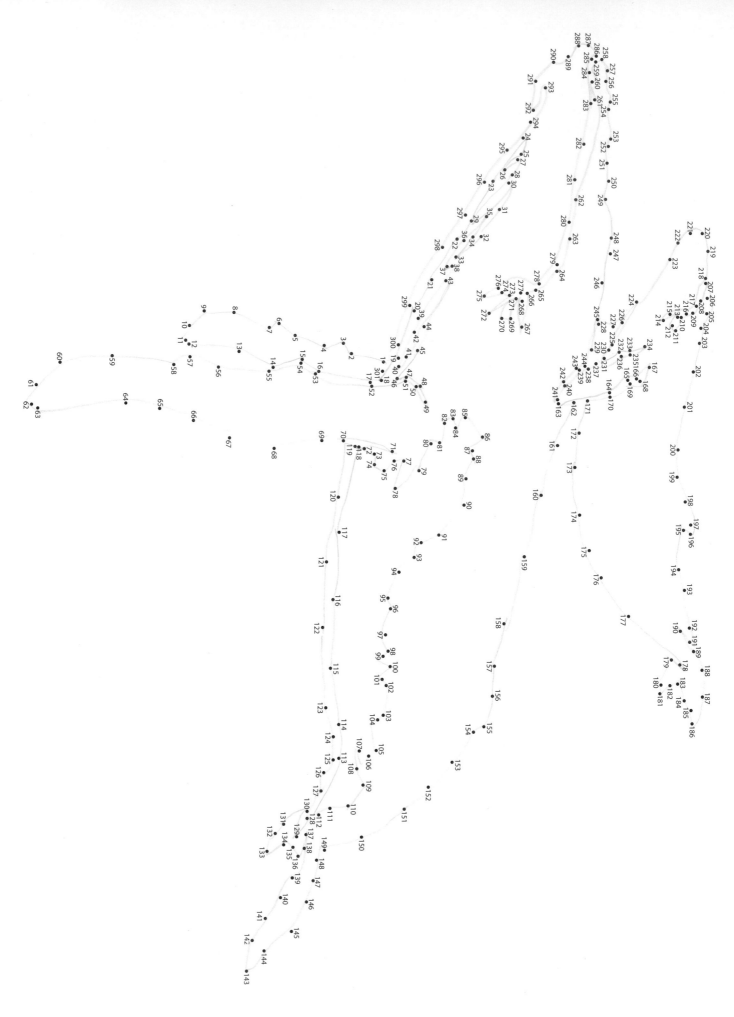

Landmarks

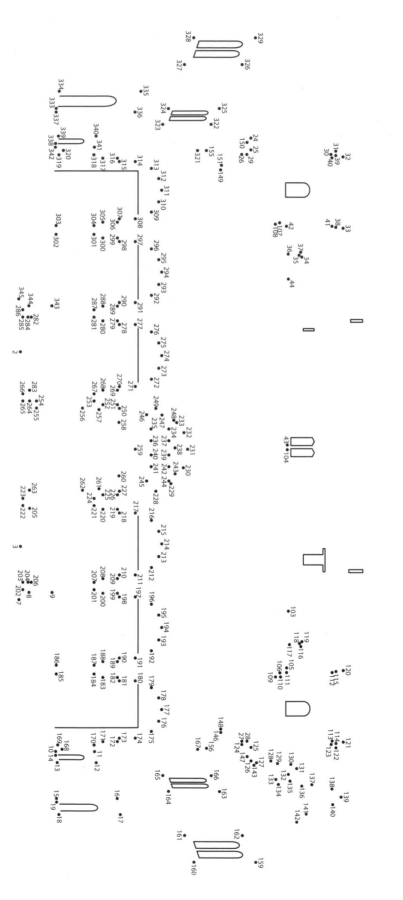

31

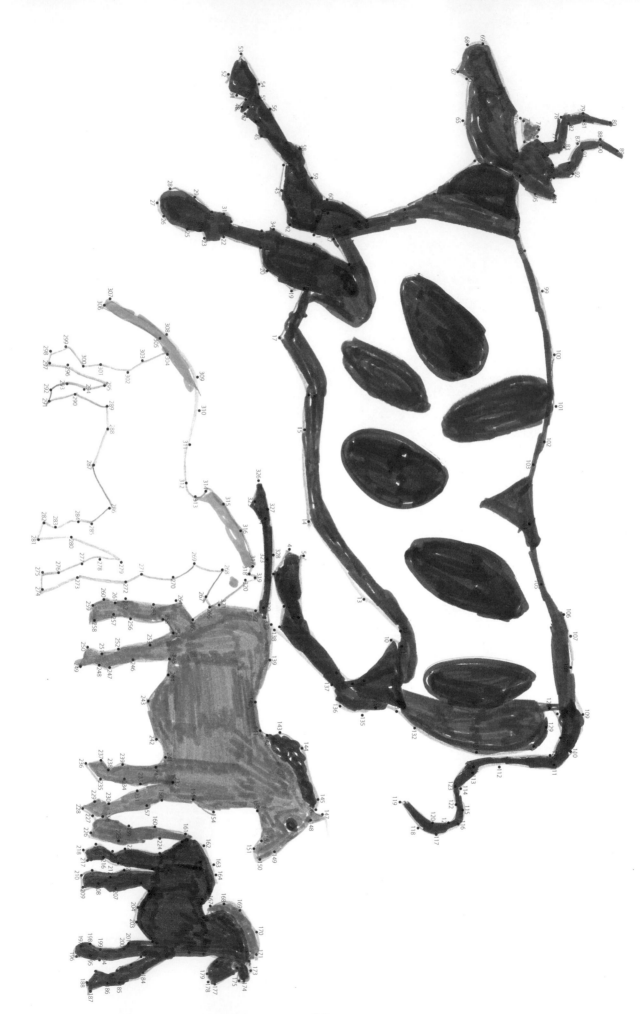

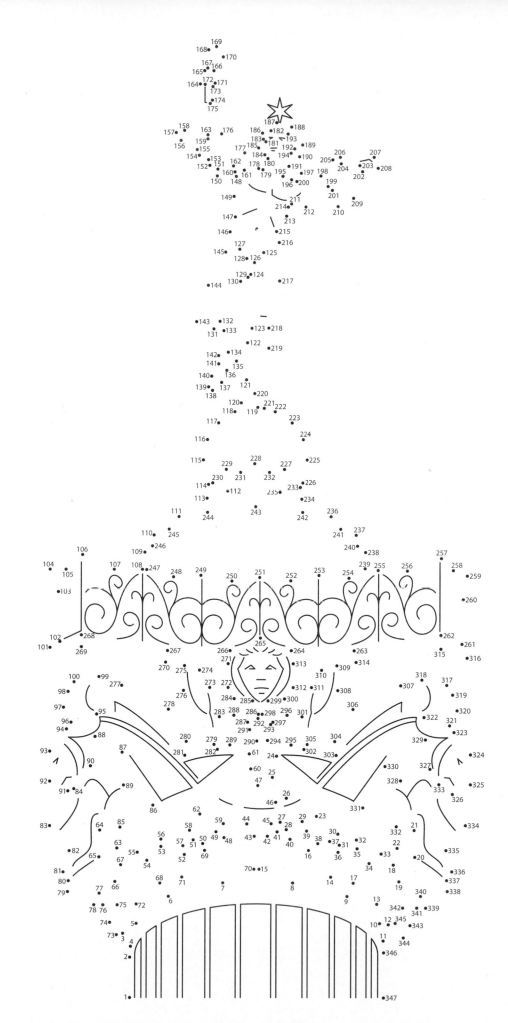

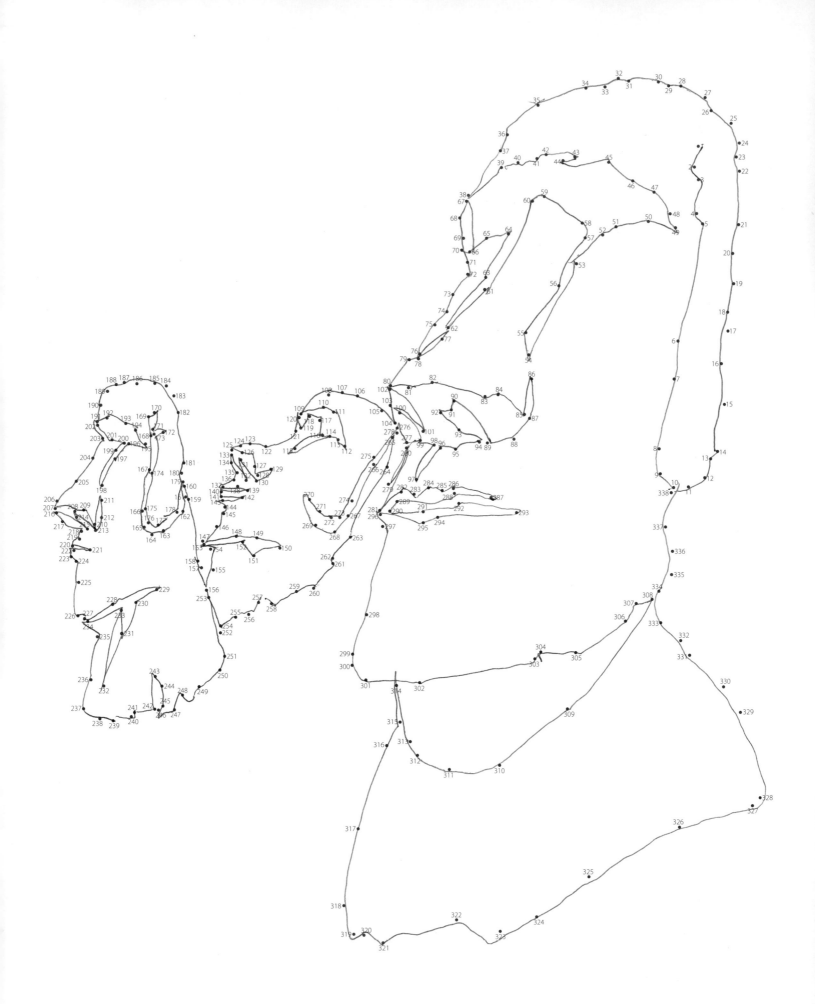

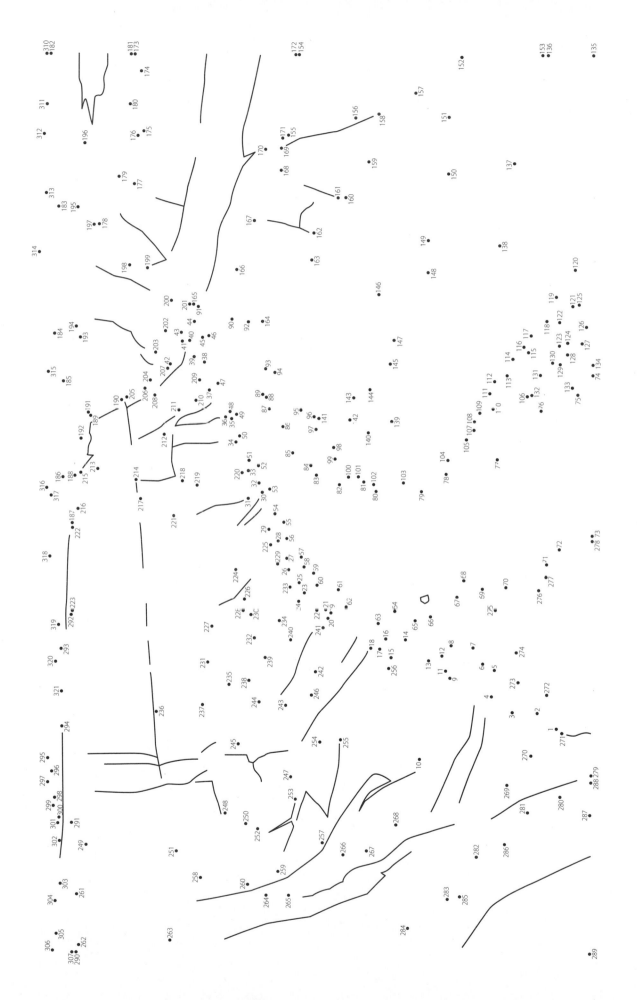

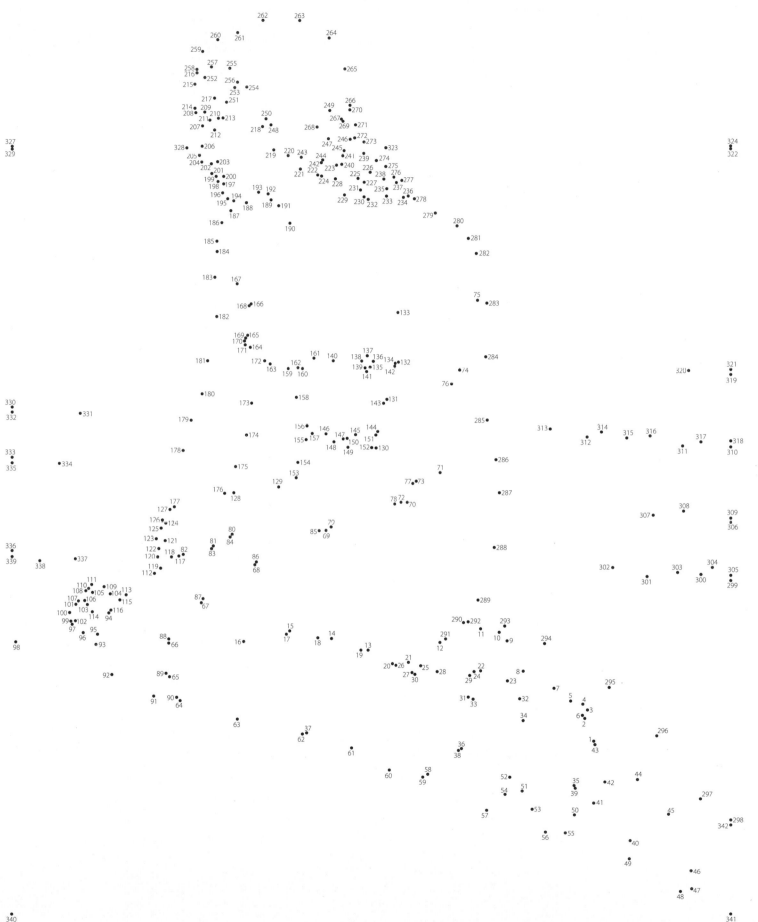

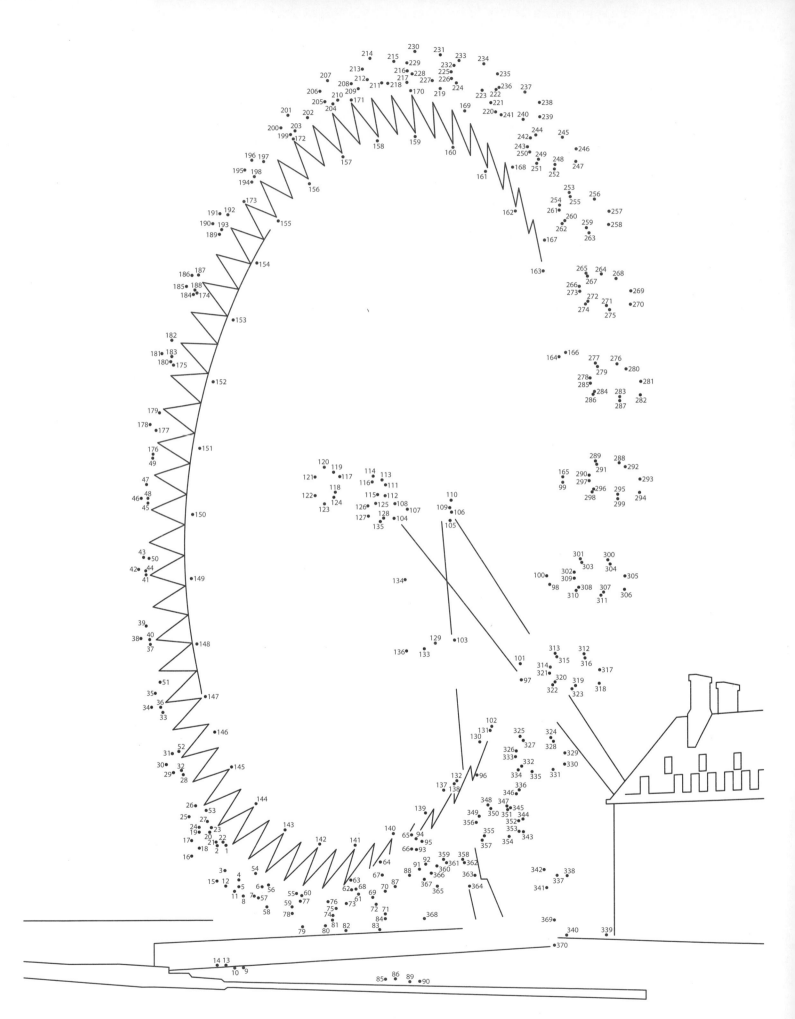

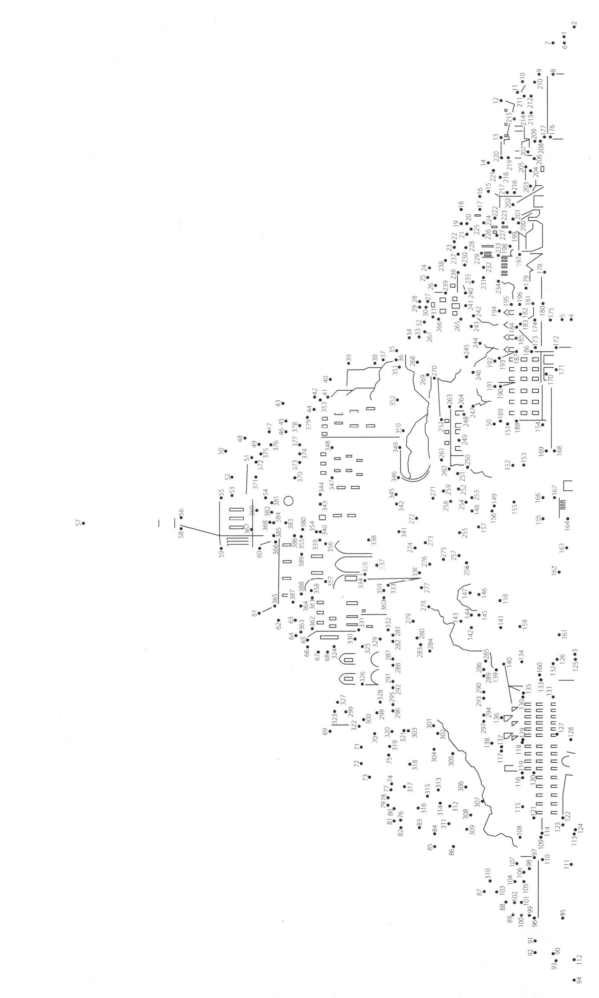

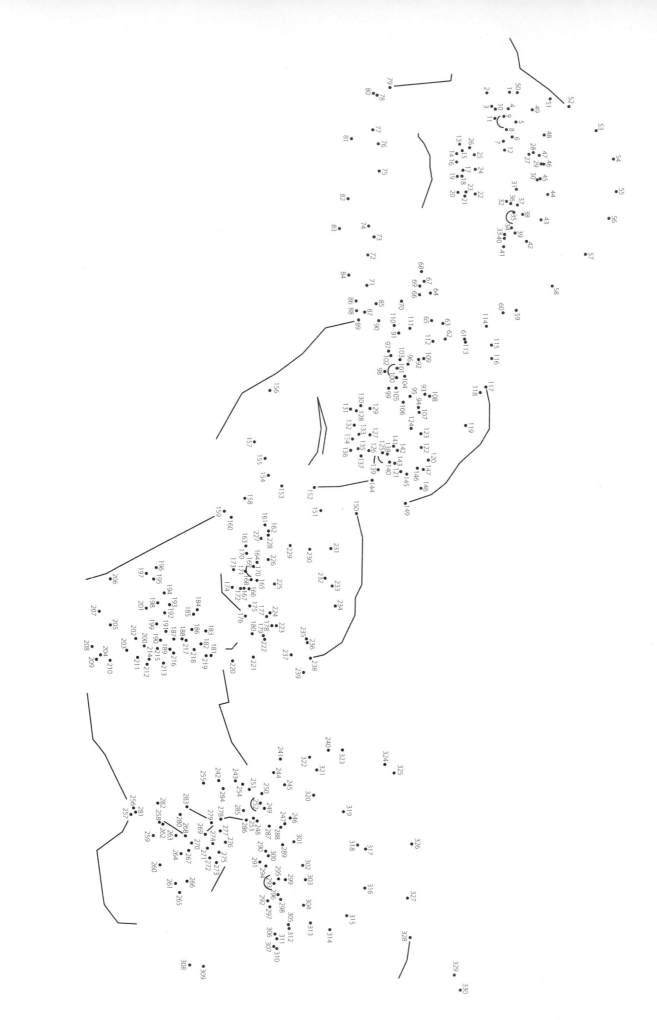

42

43

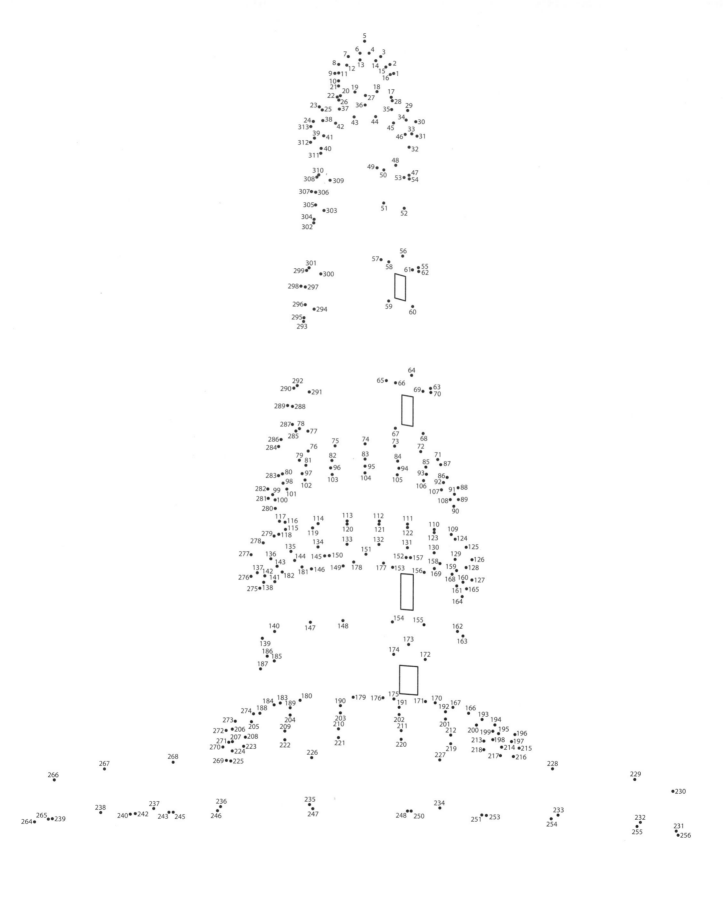

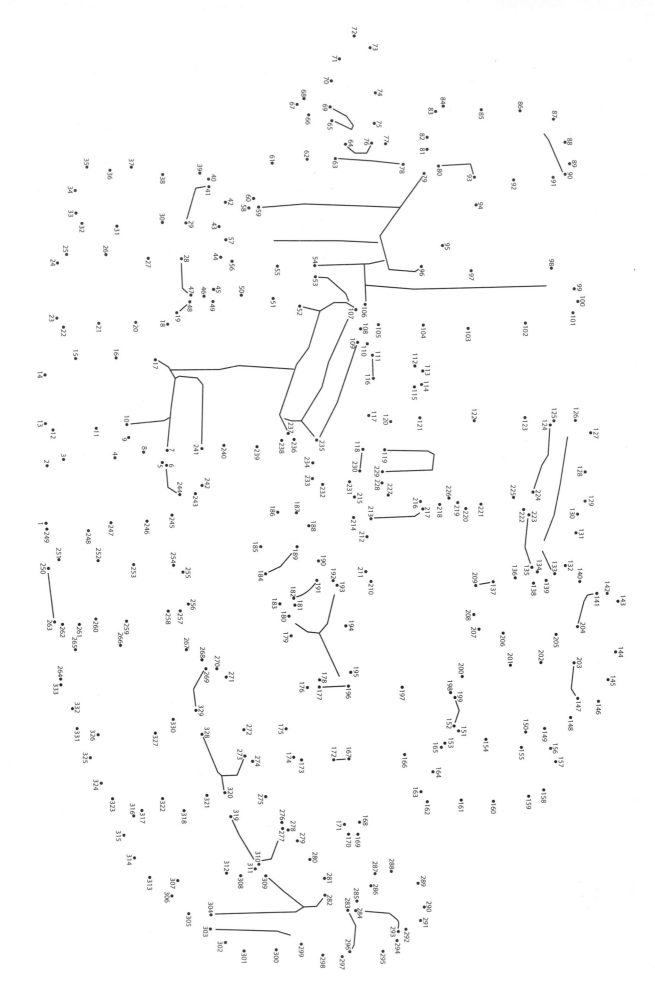

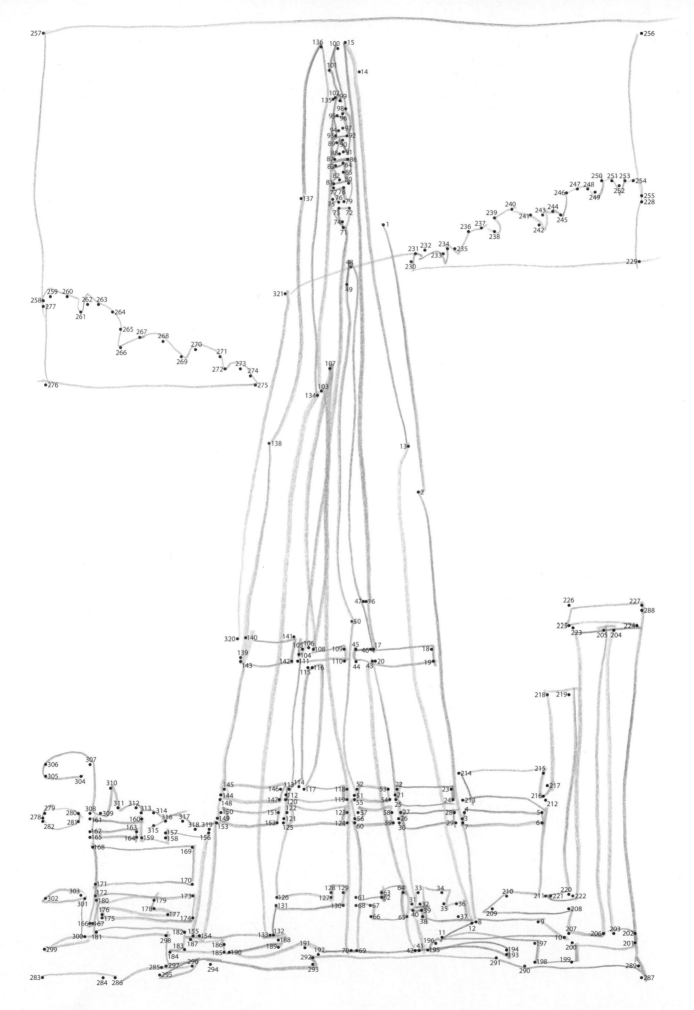

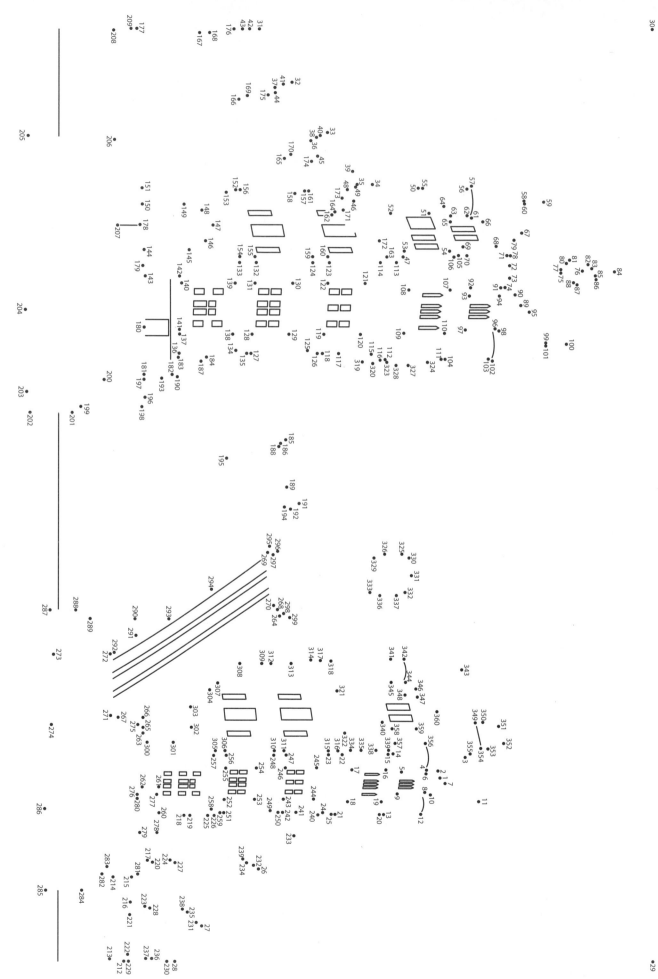

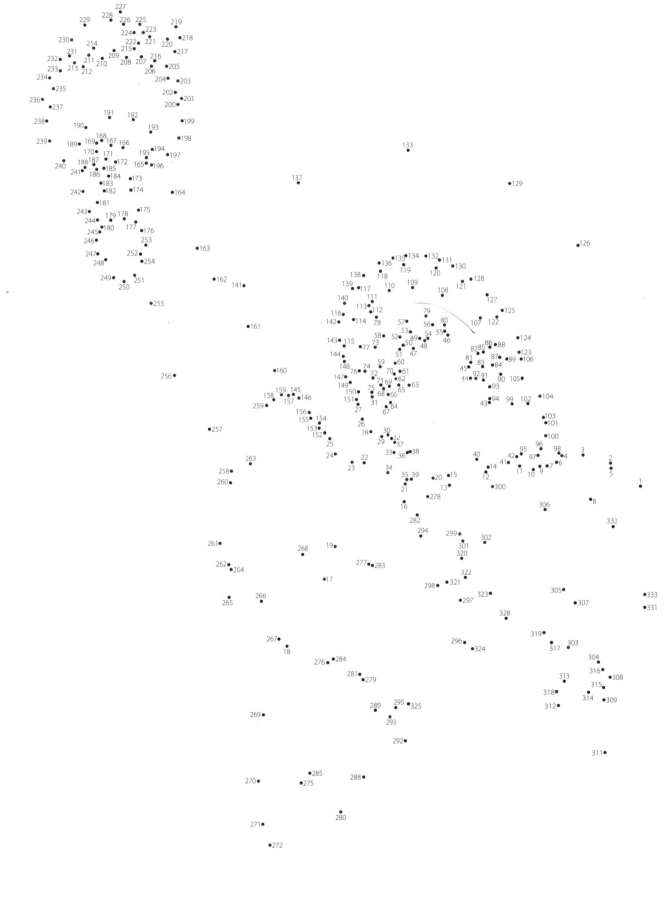

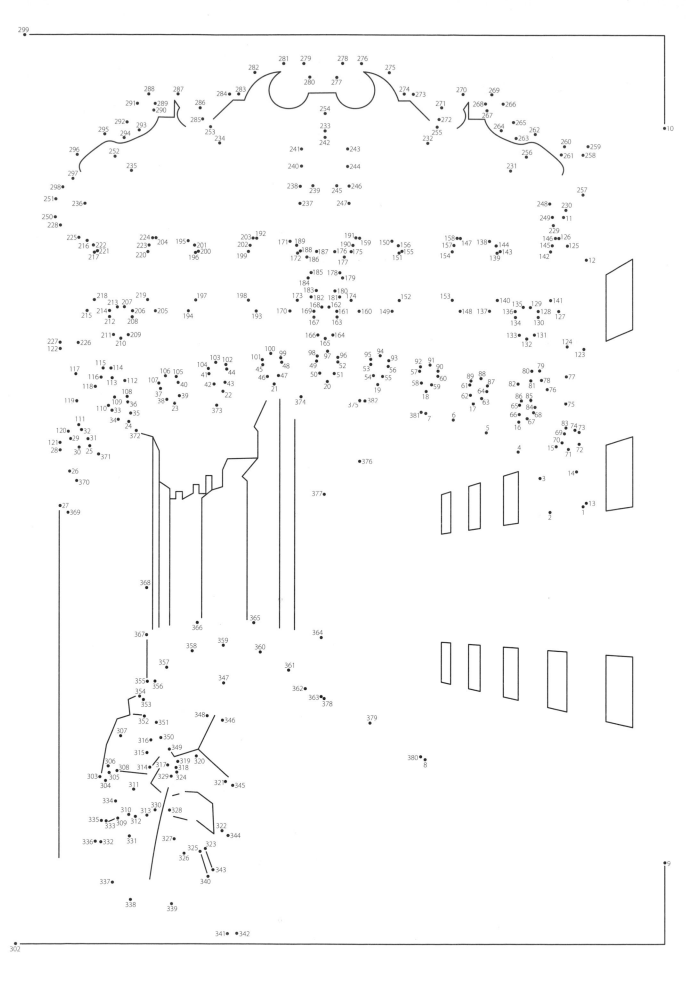

51

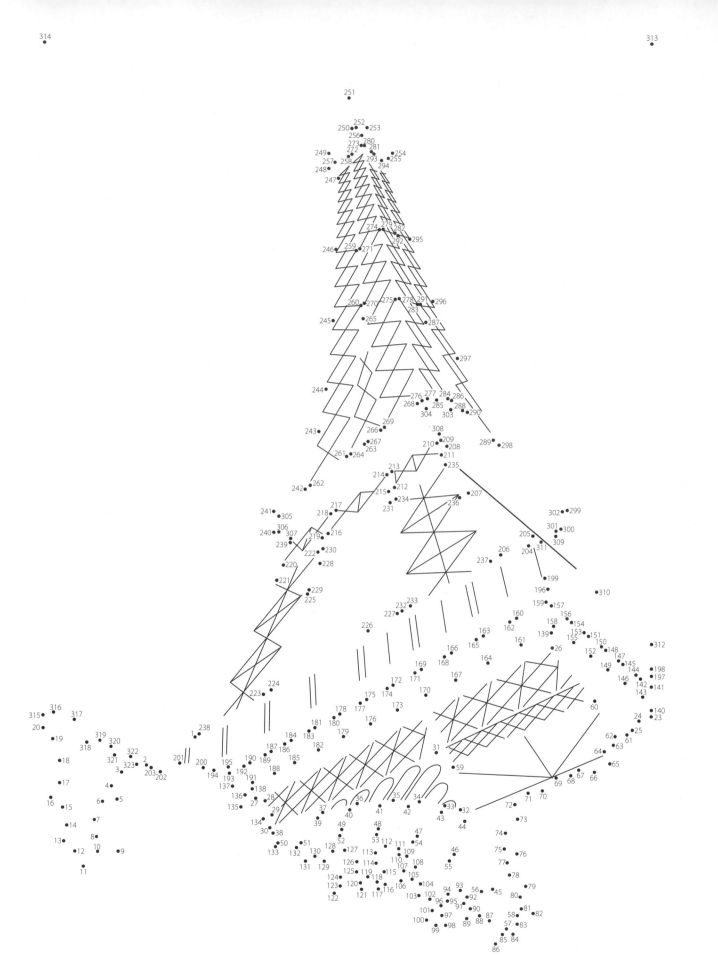

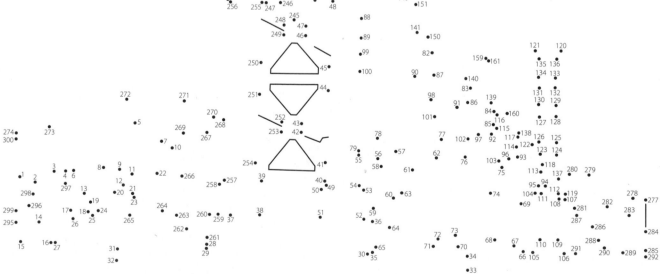

53

Iconic Buildings

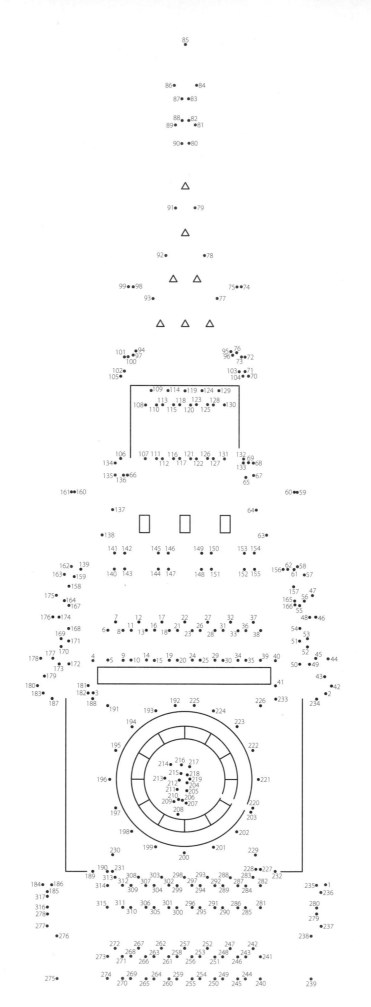

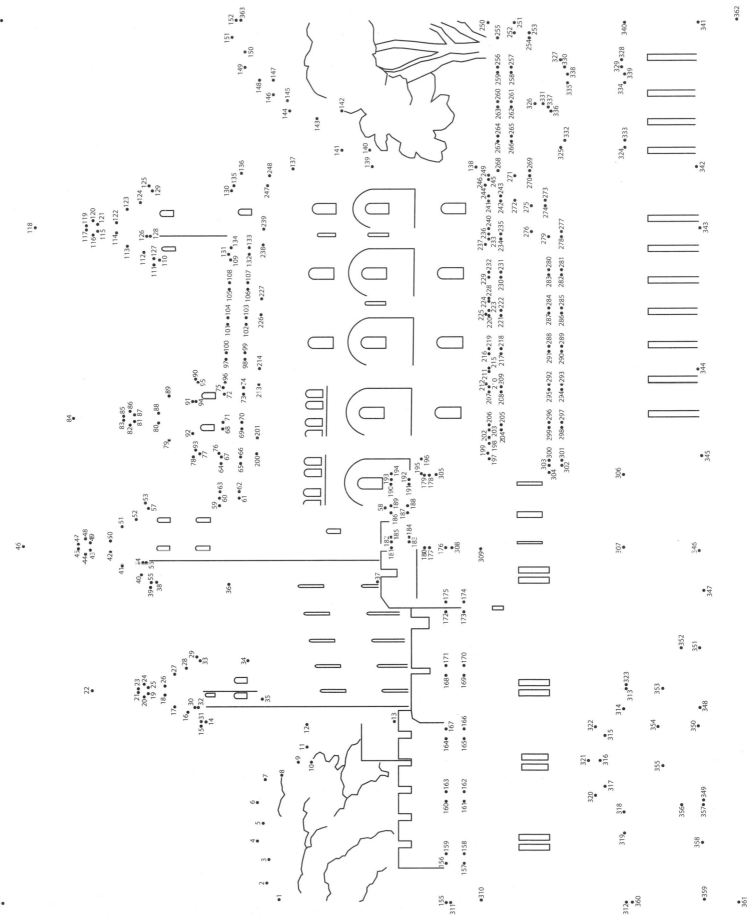

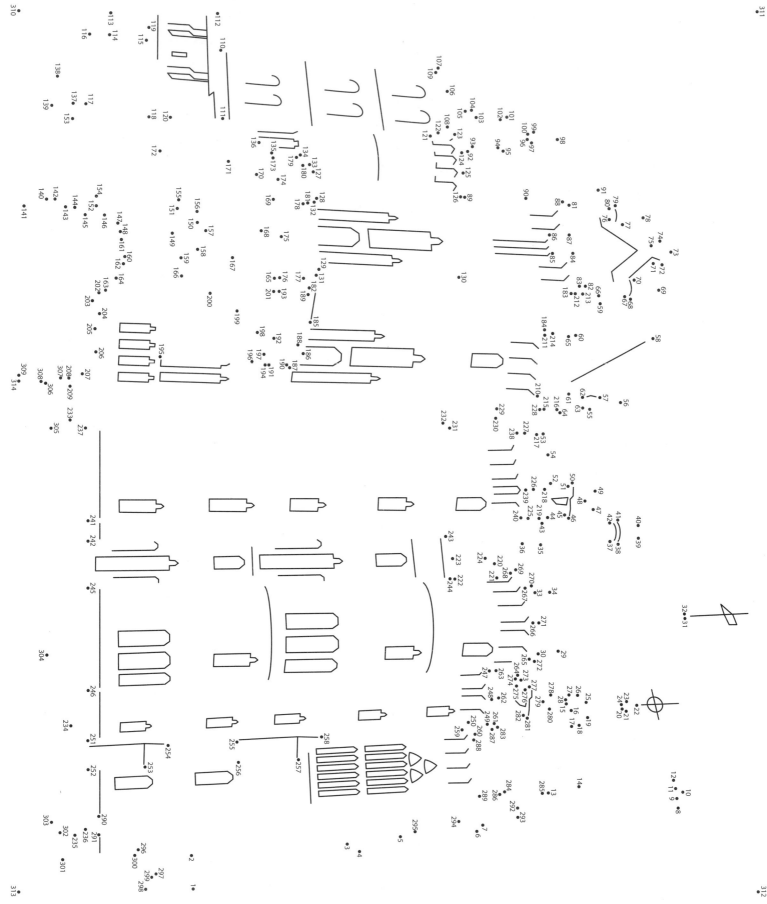

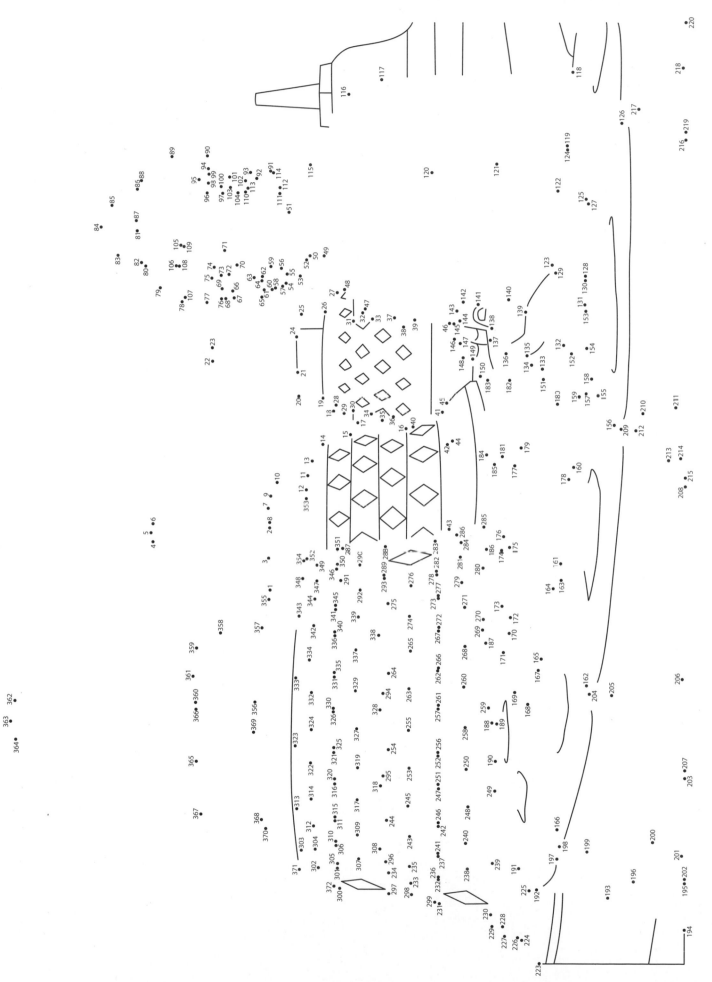

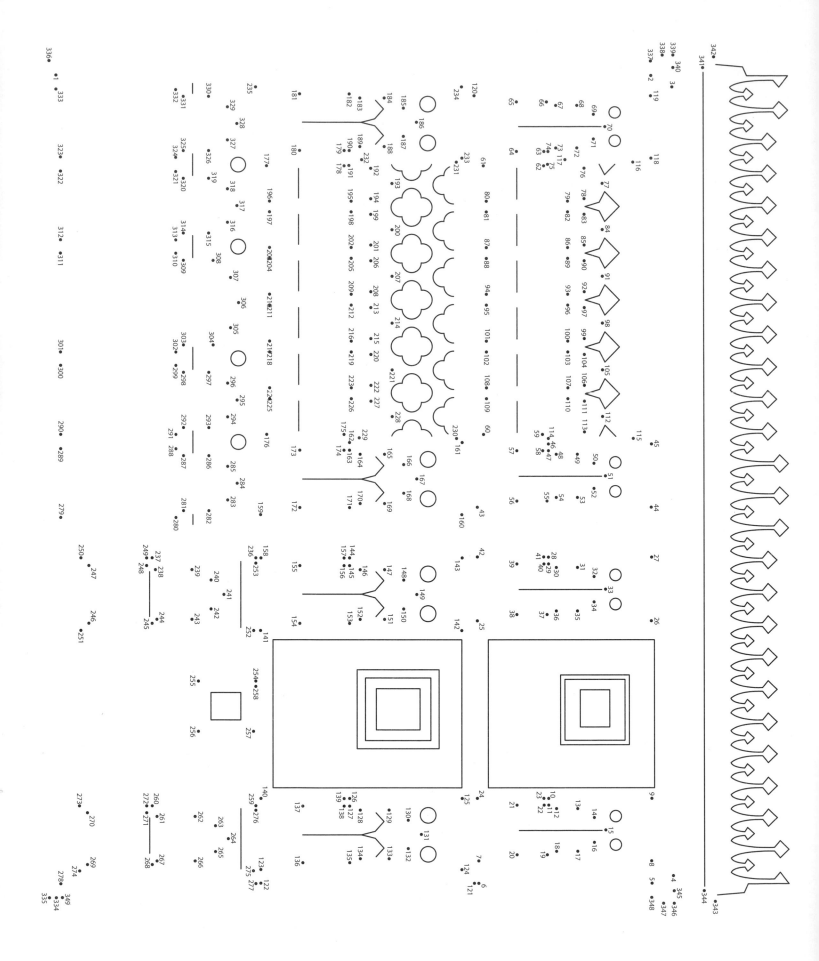

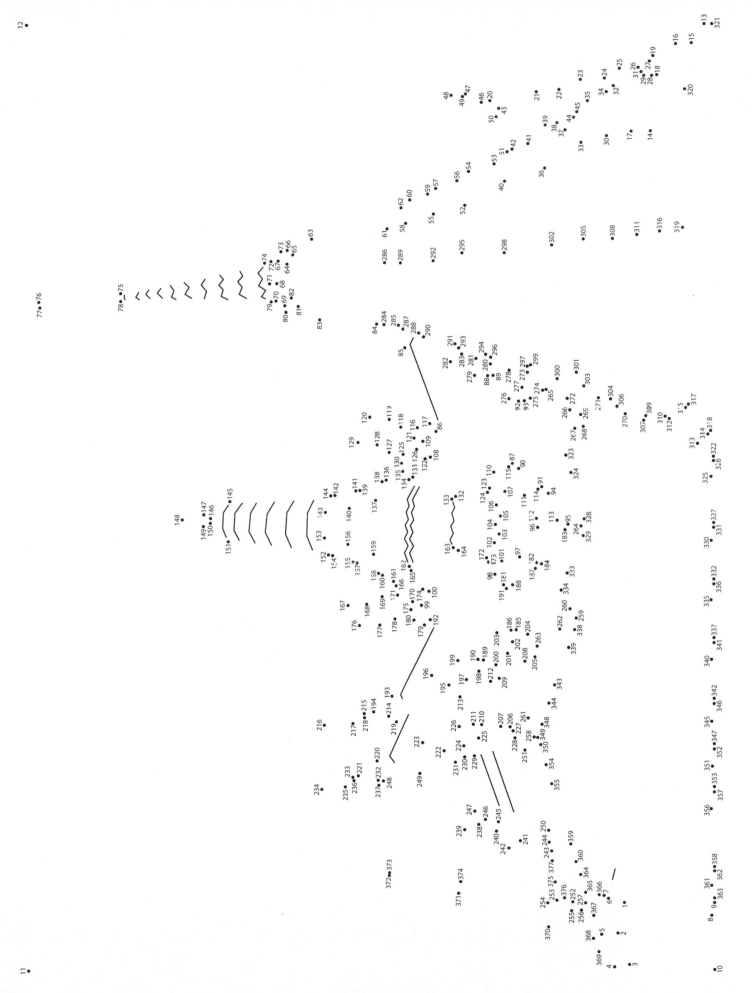

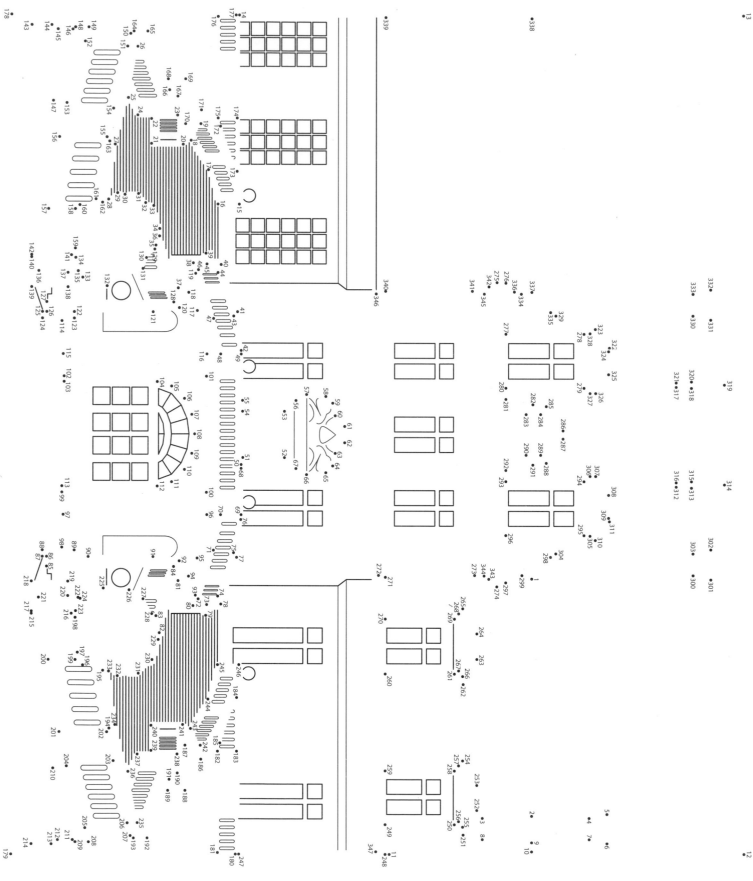

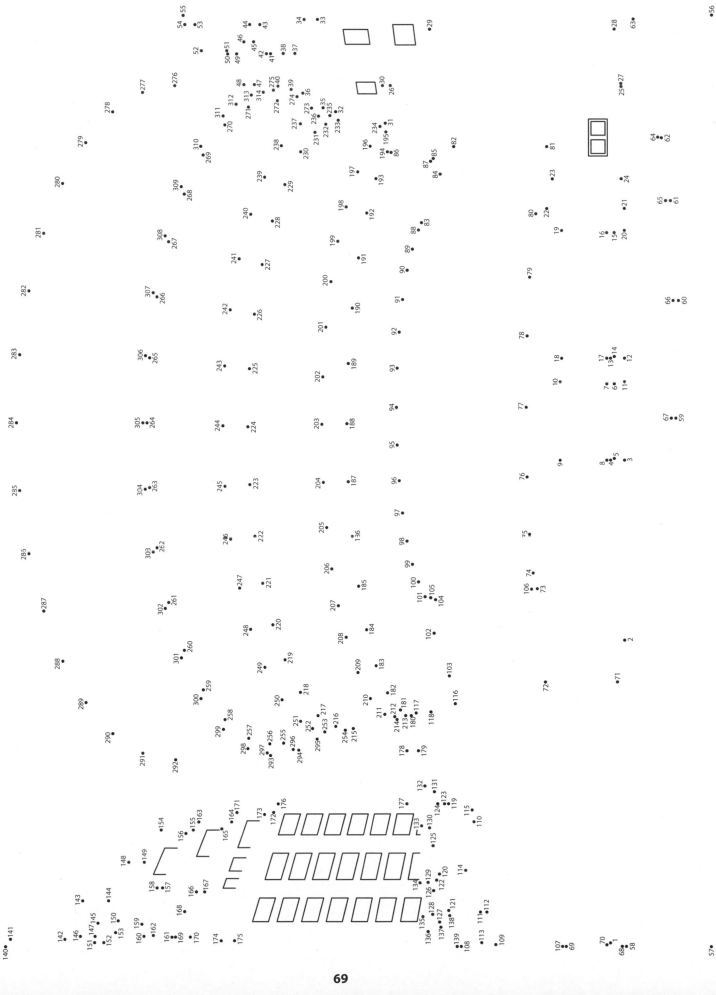

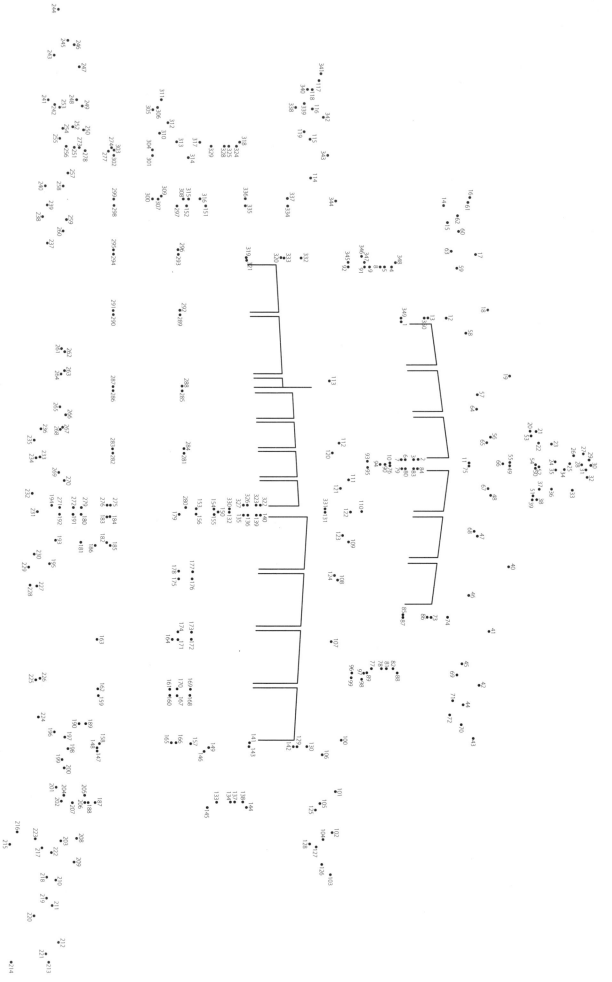

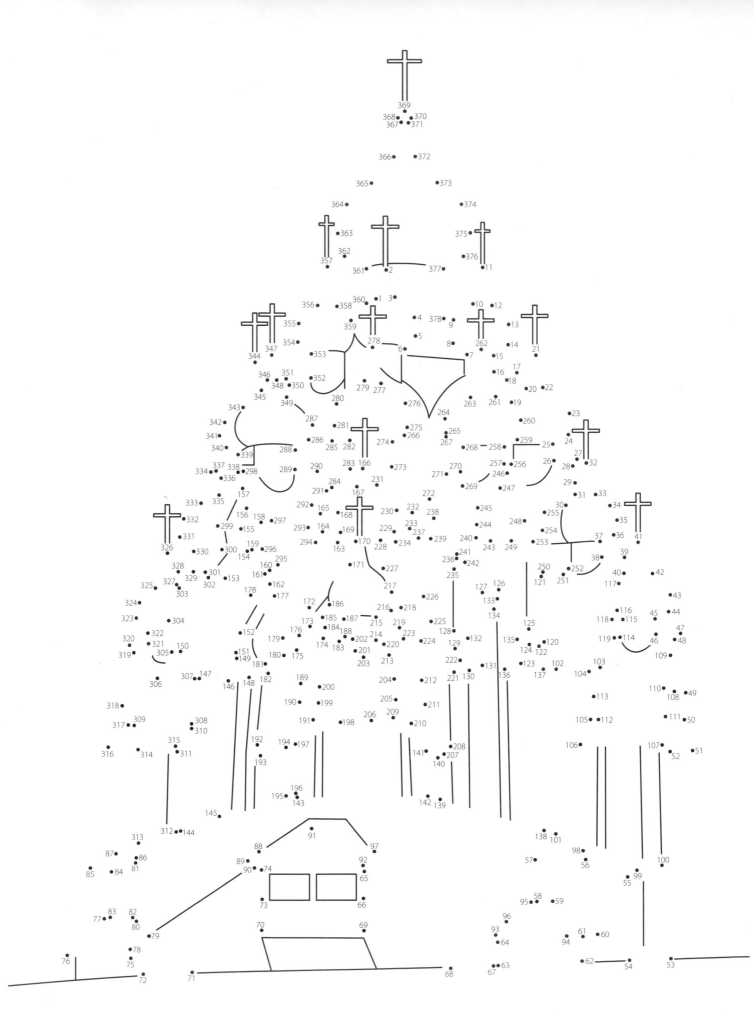

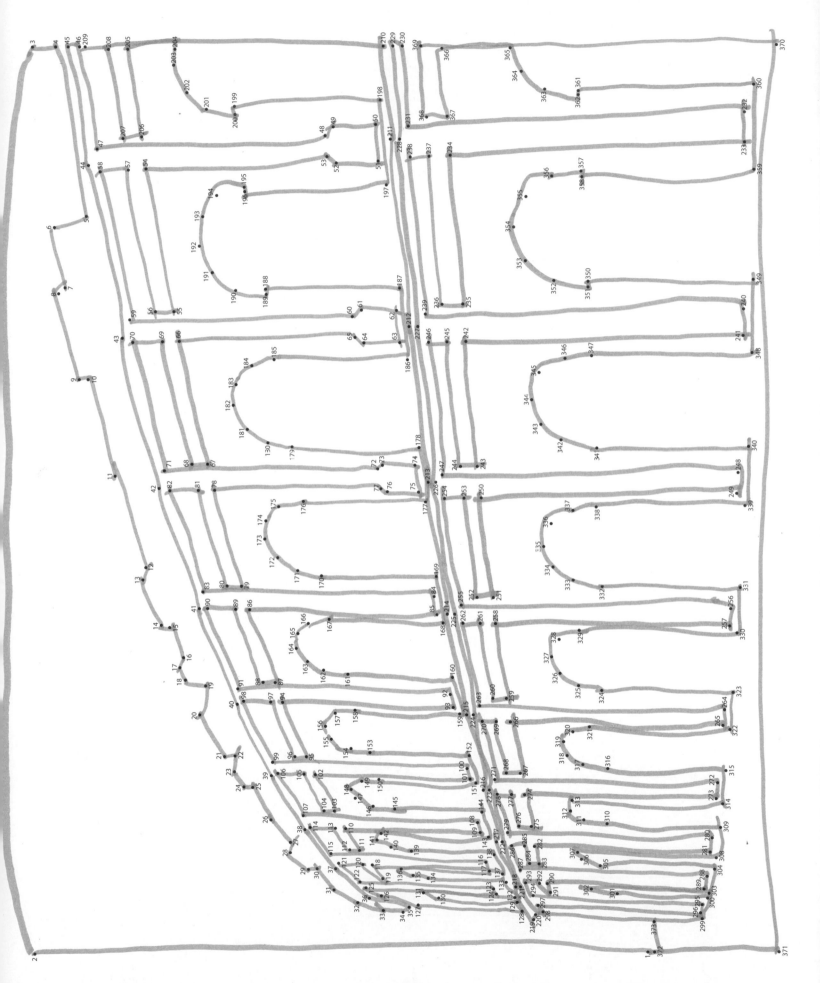

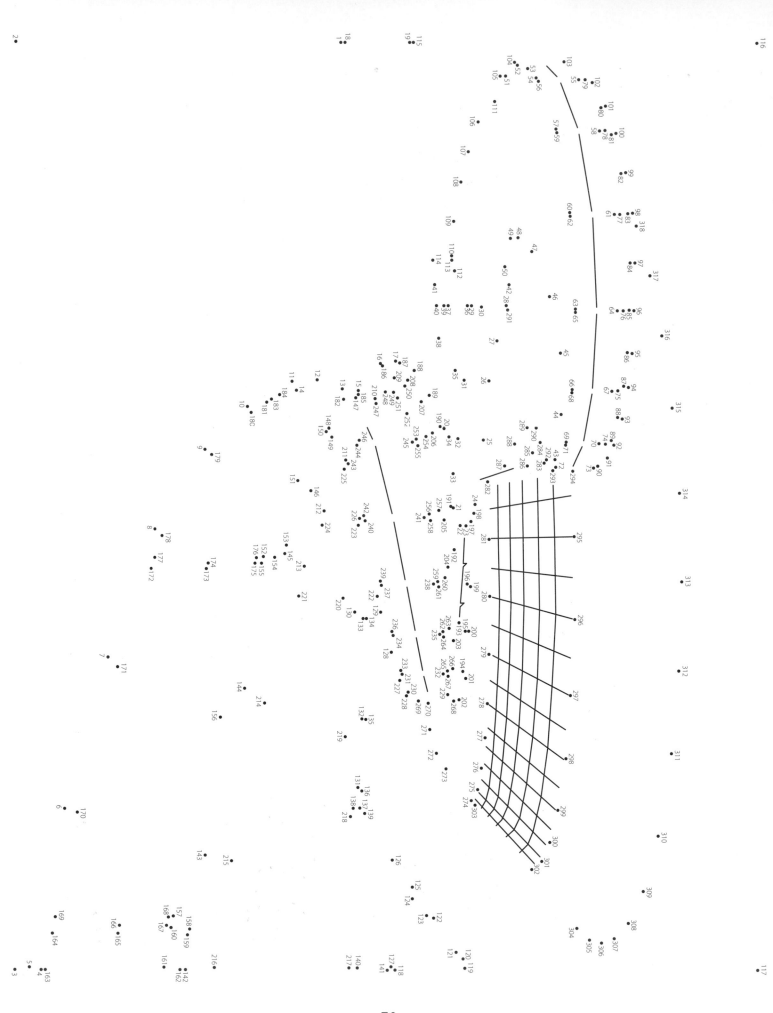

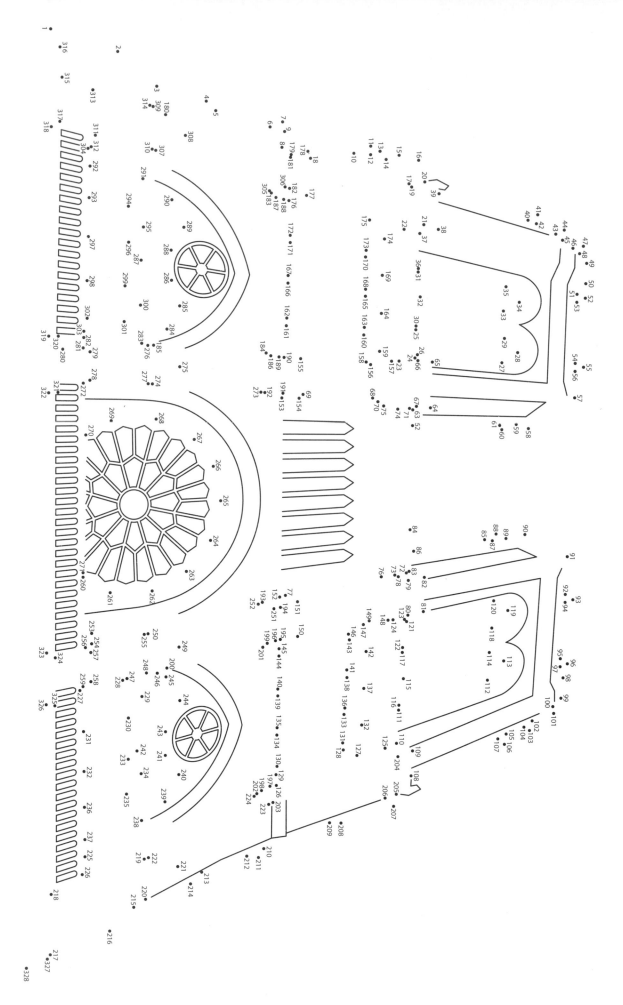

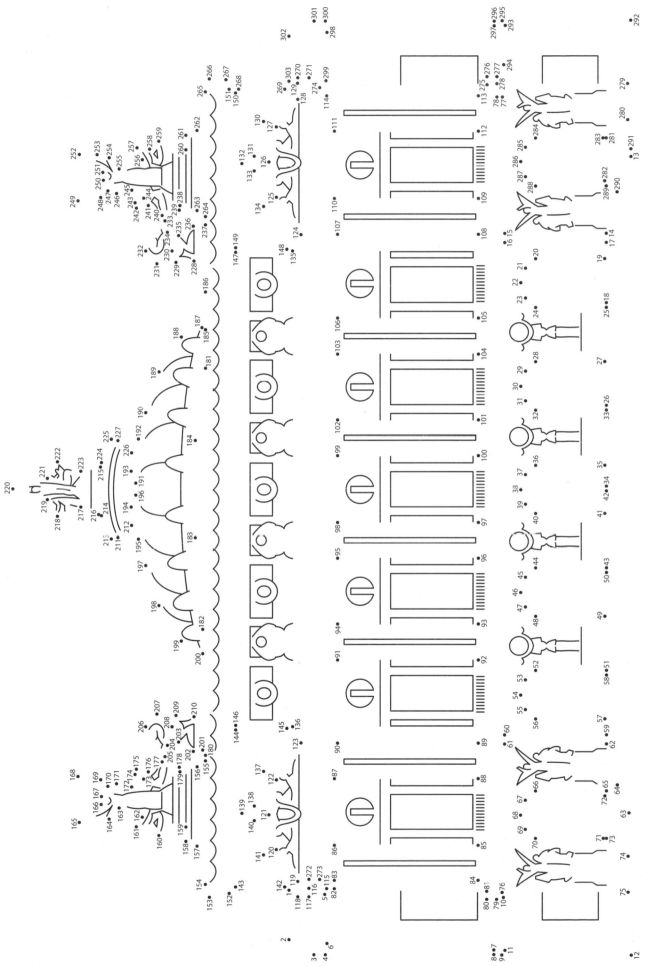

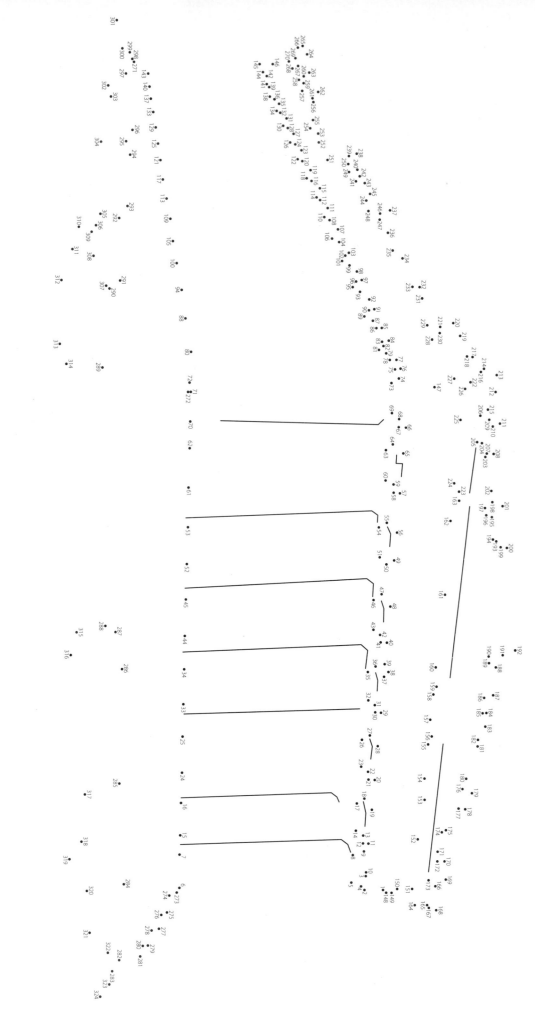

78

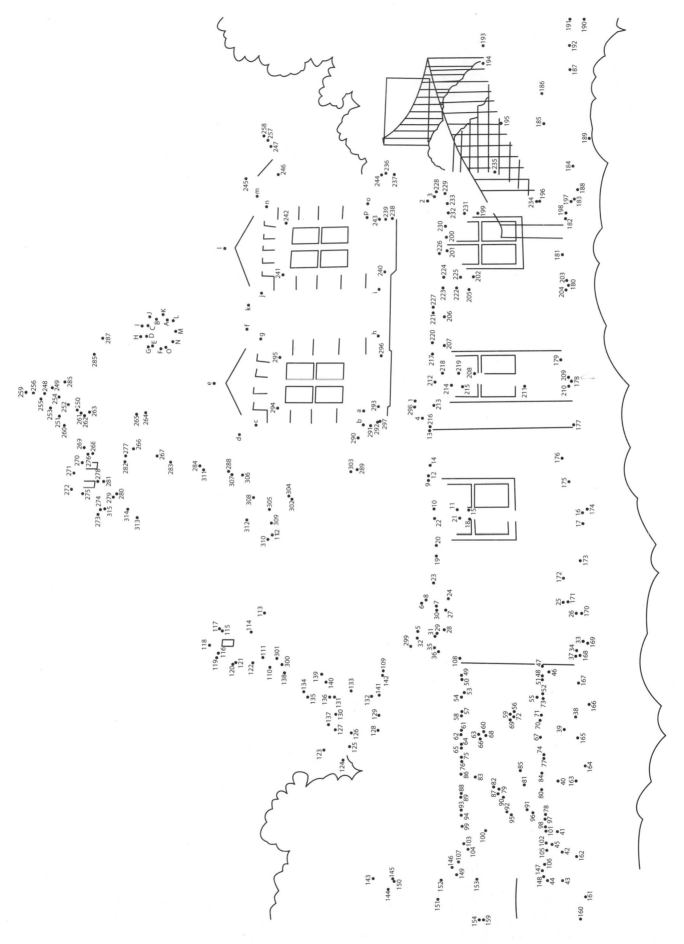

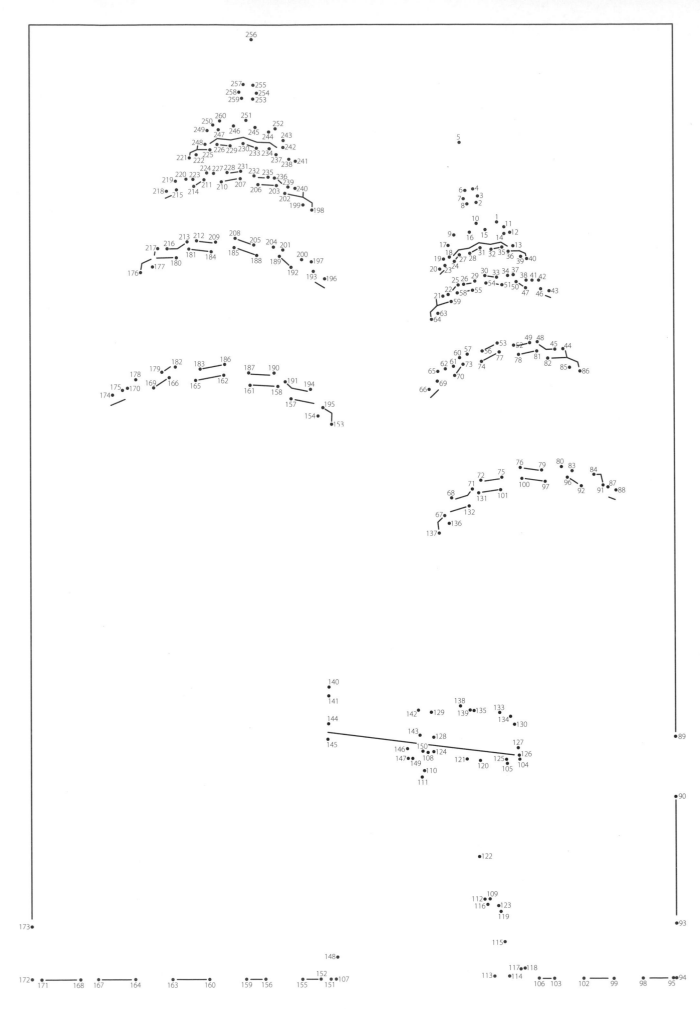

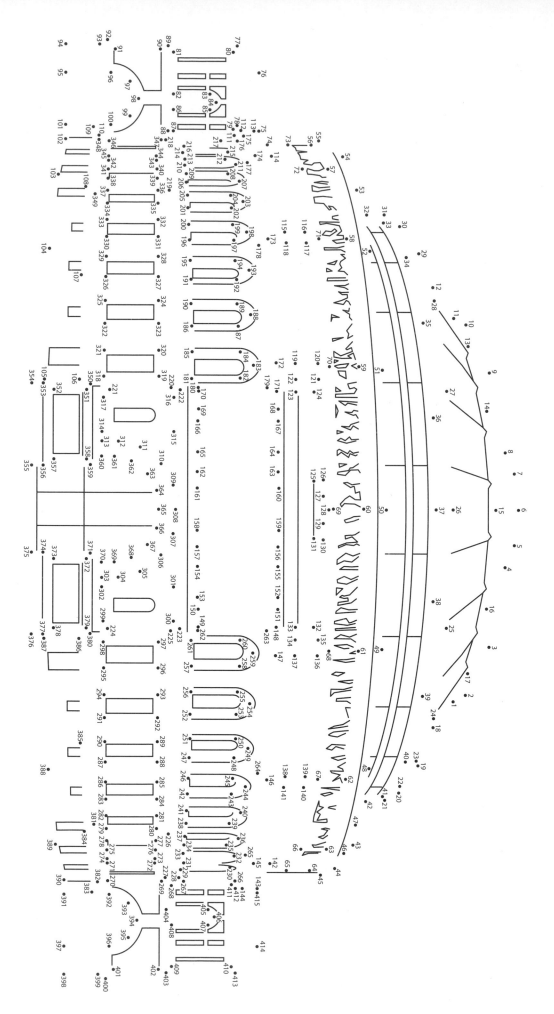

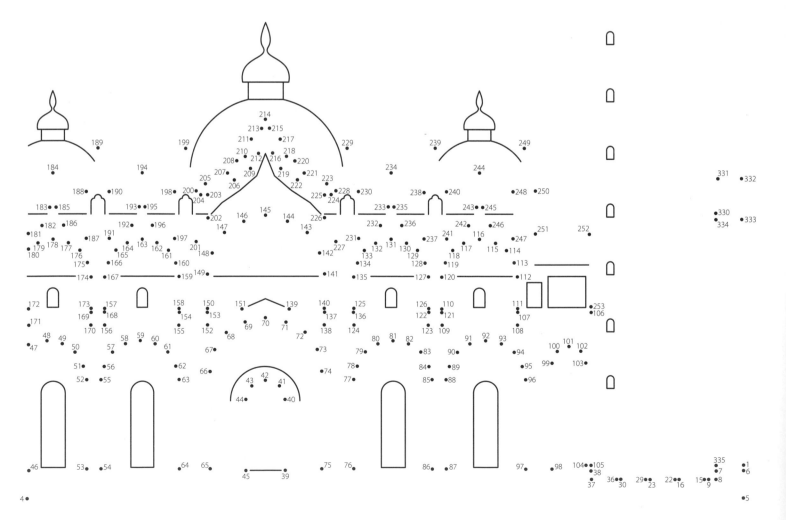
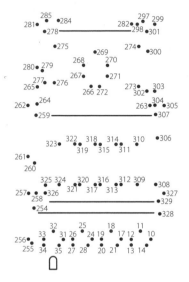

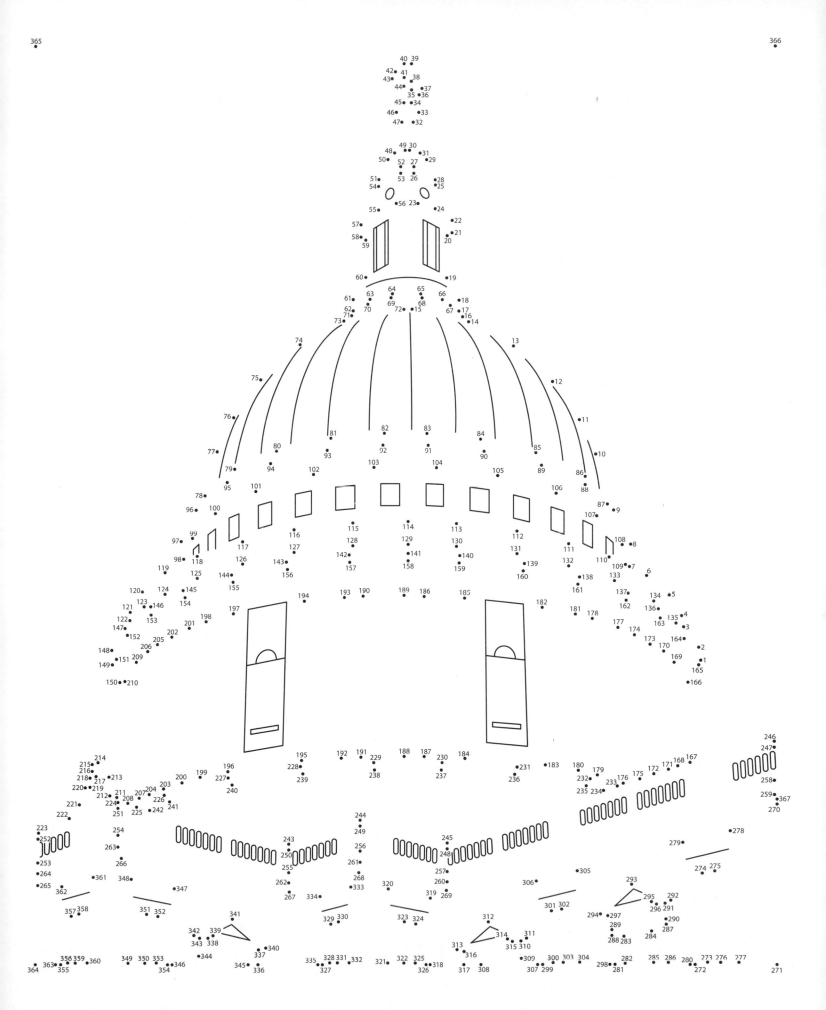

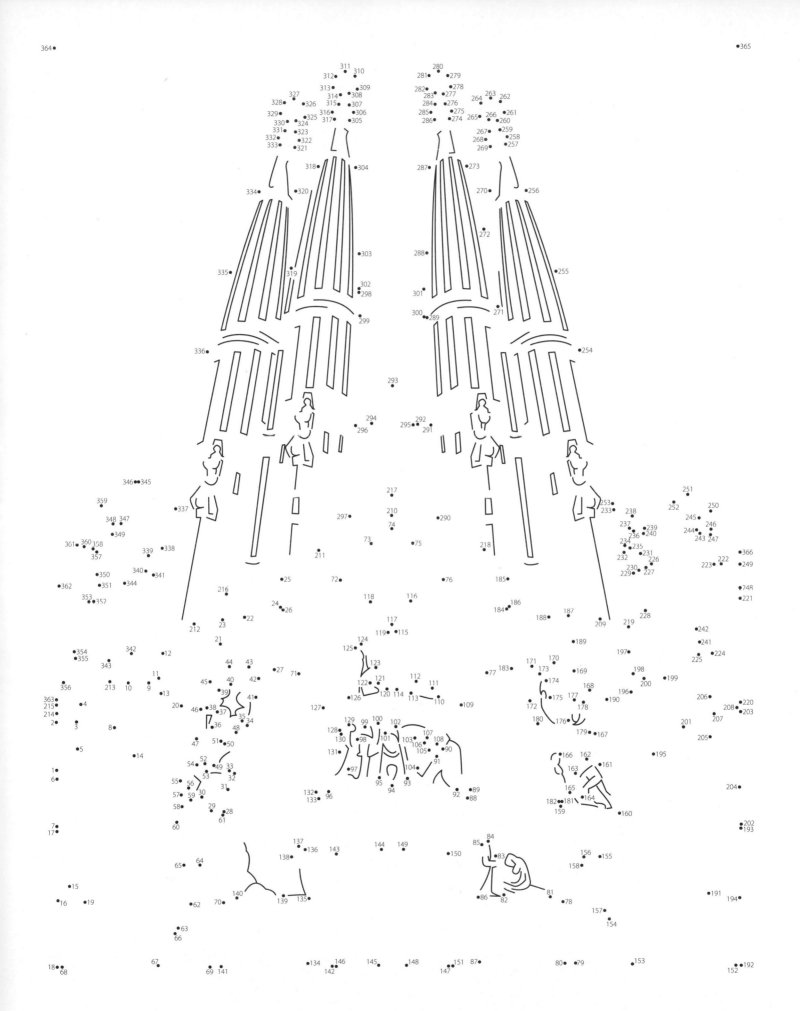

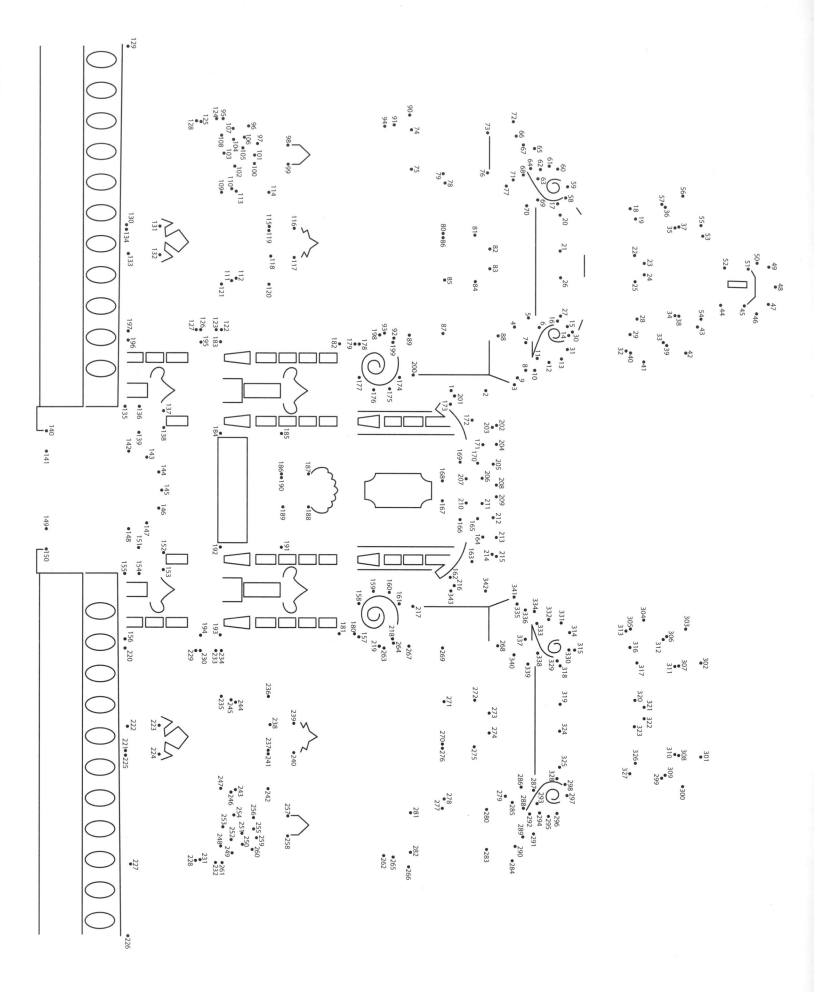

88

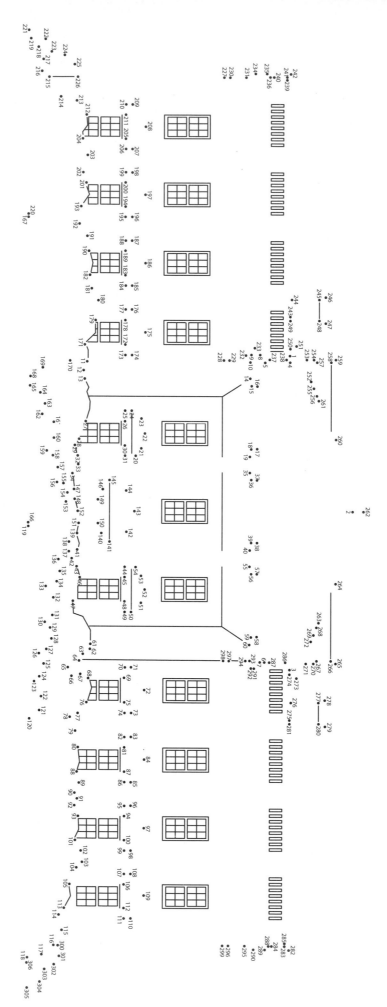

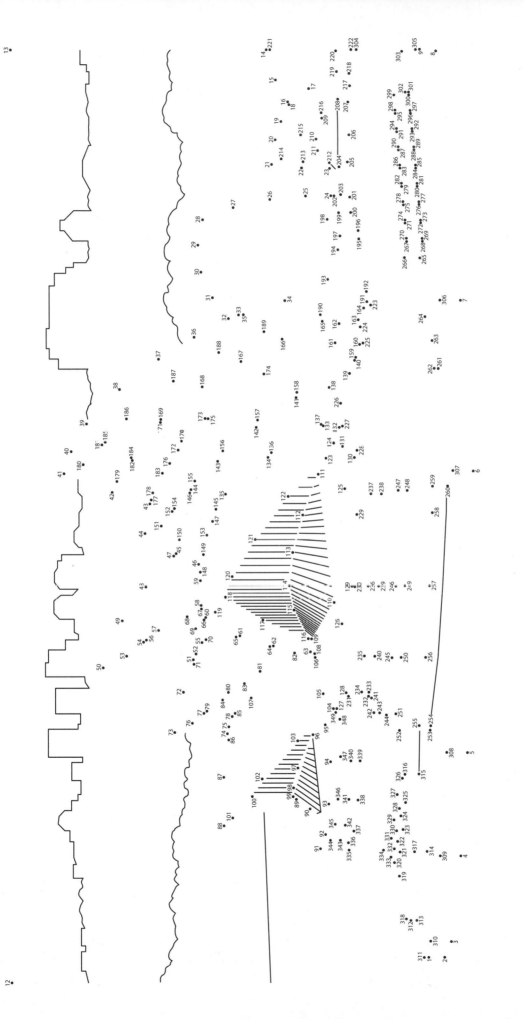

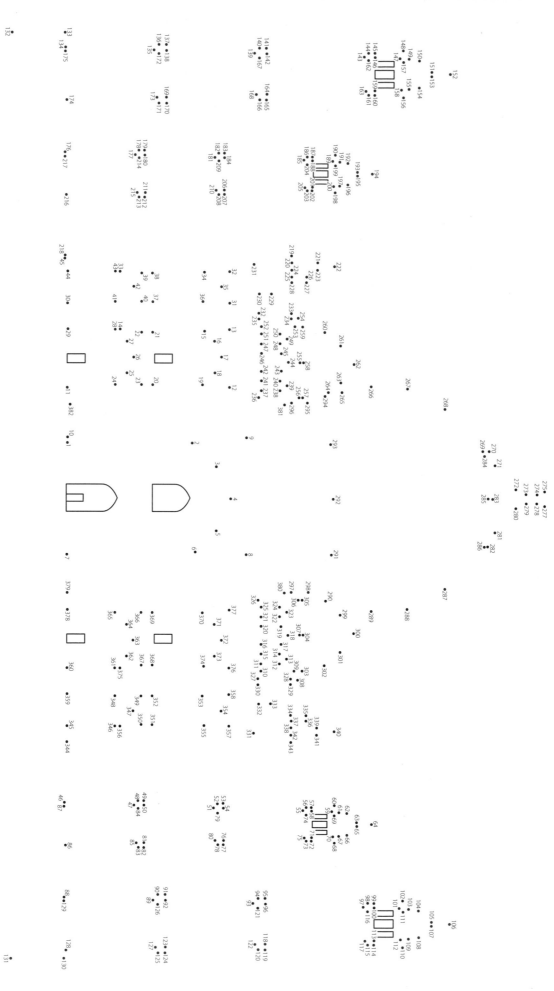

Works of Art

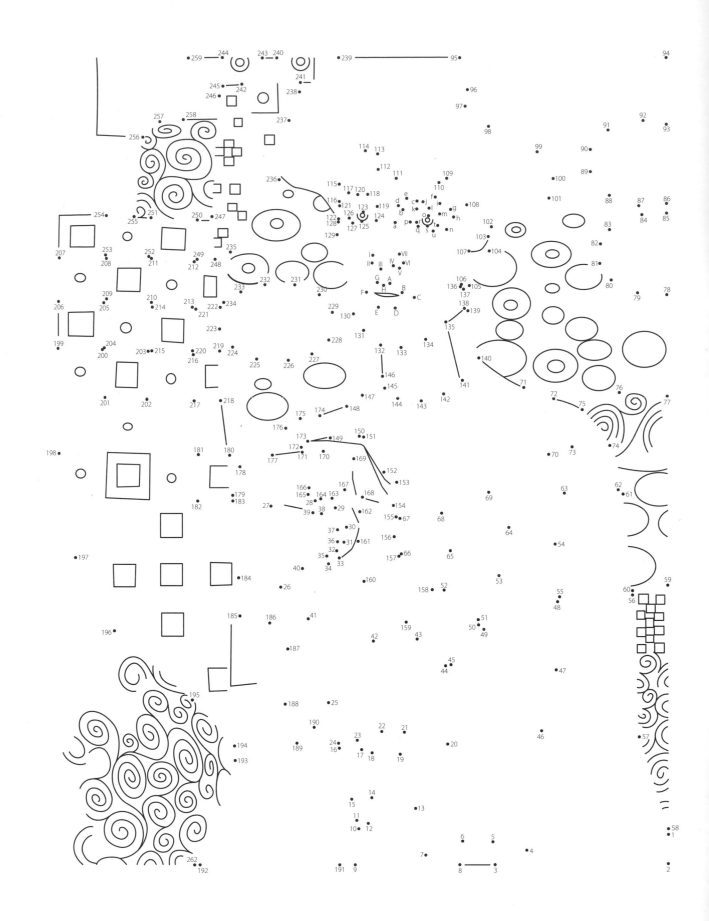

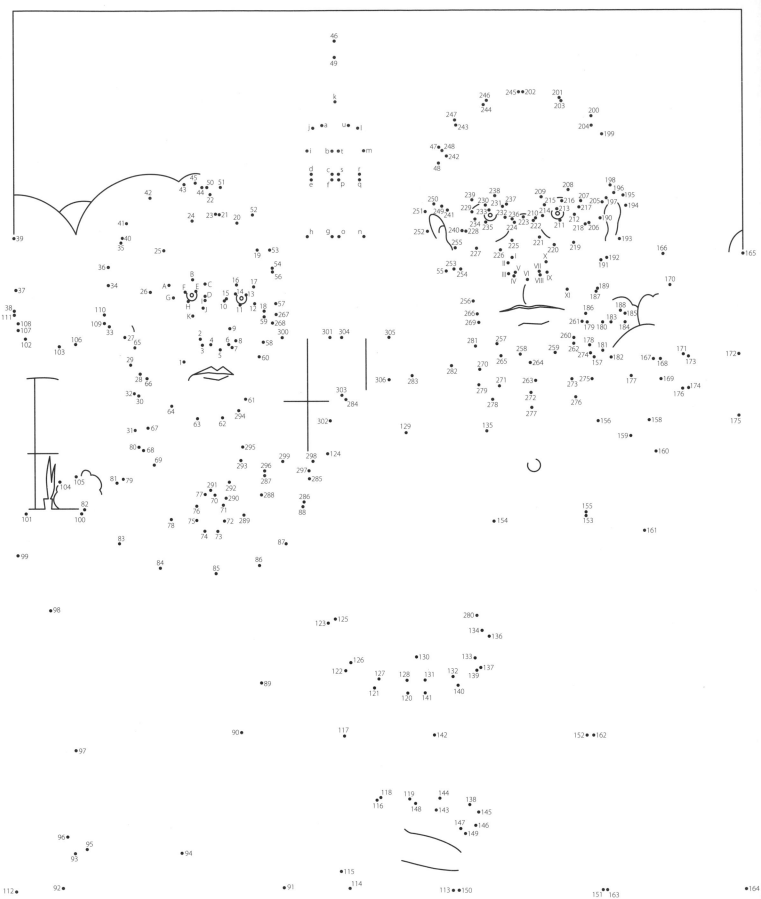

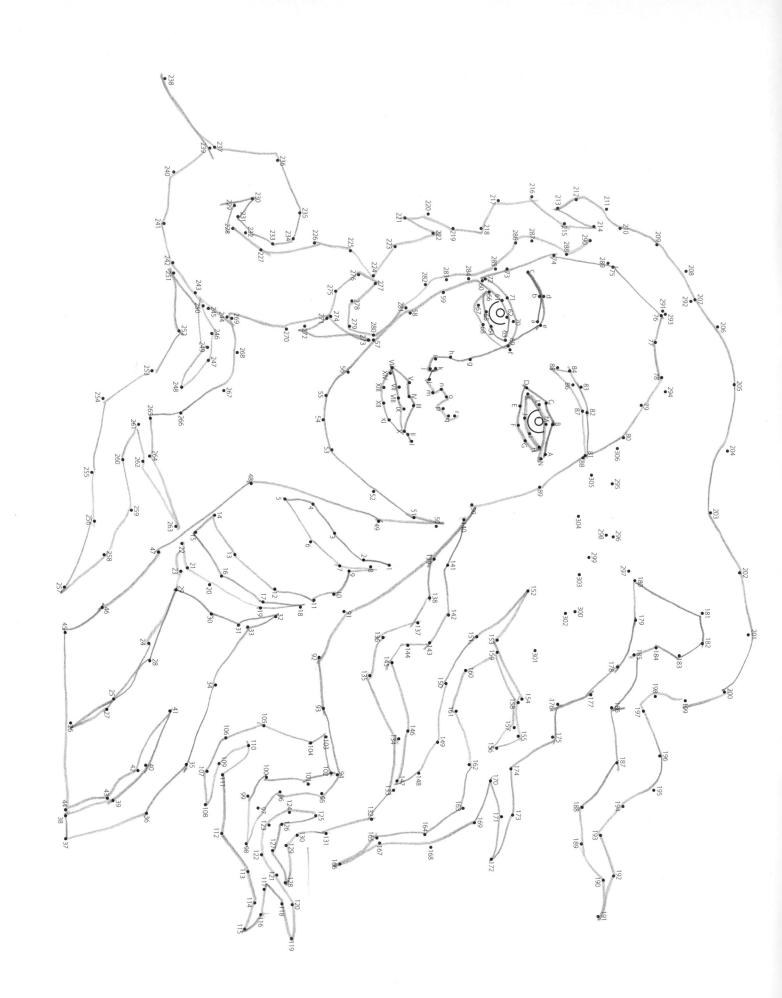

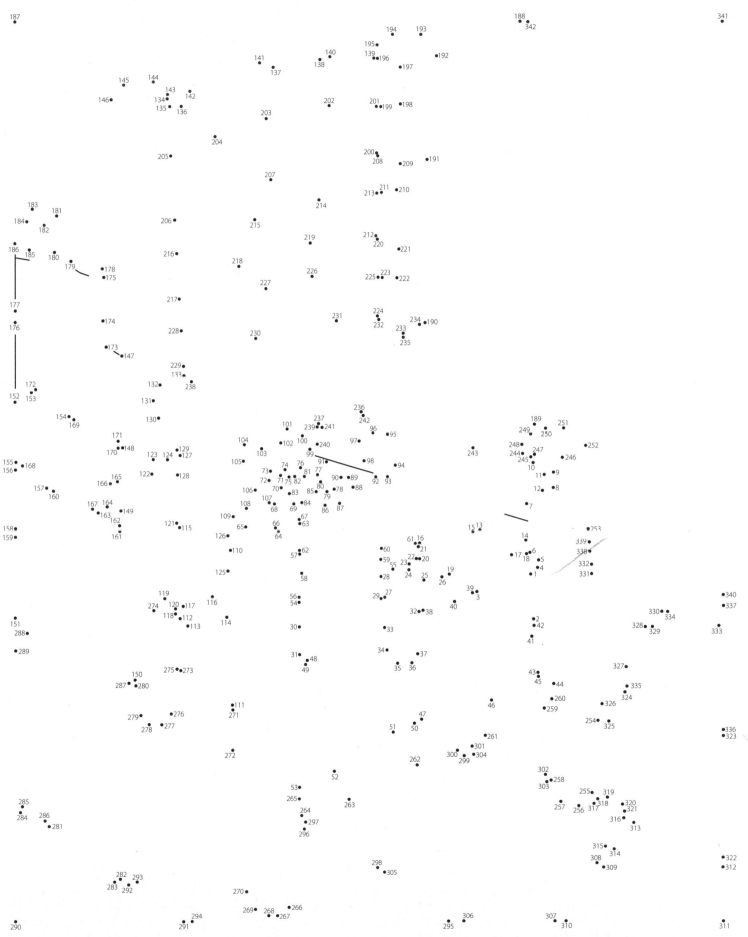

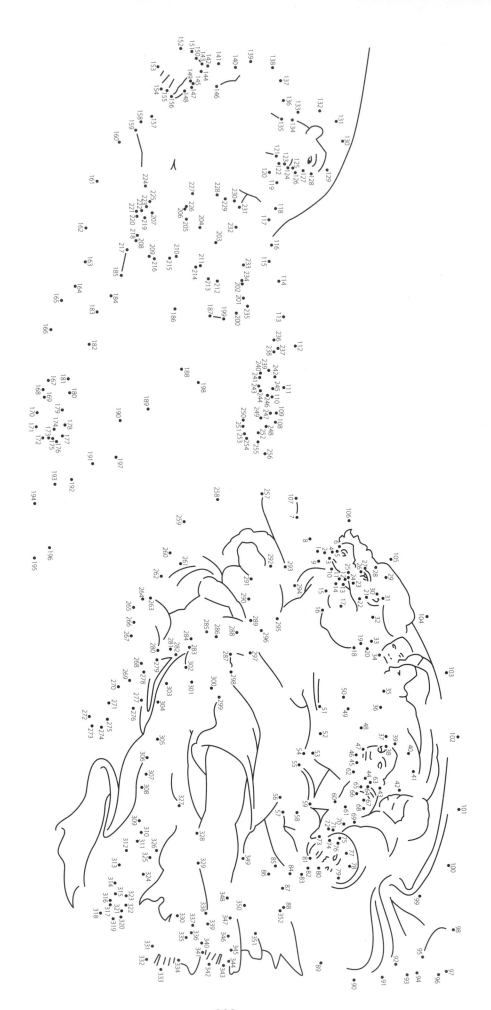

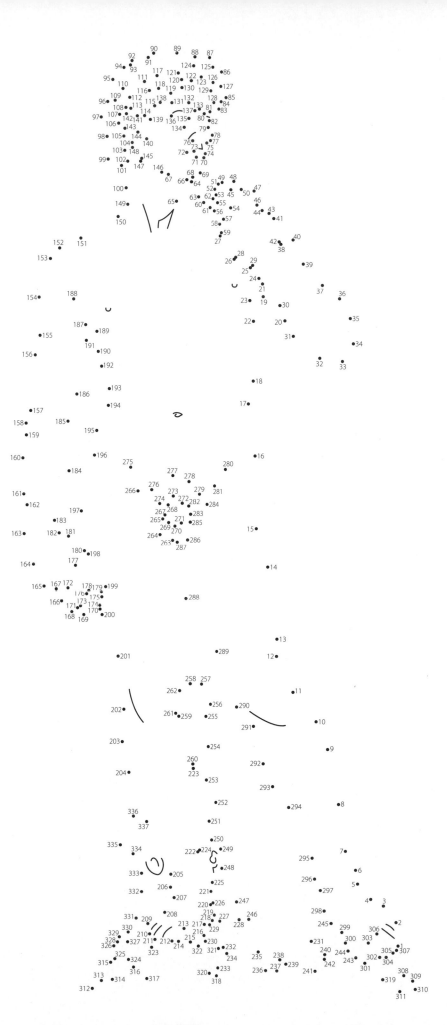

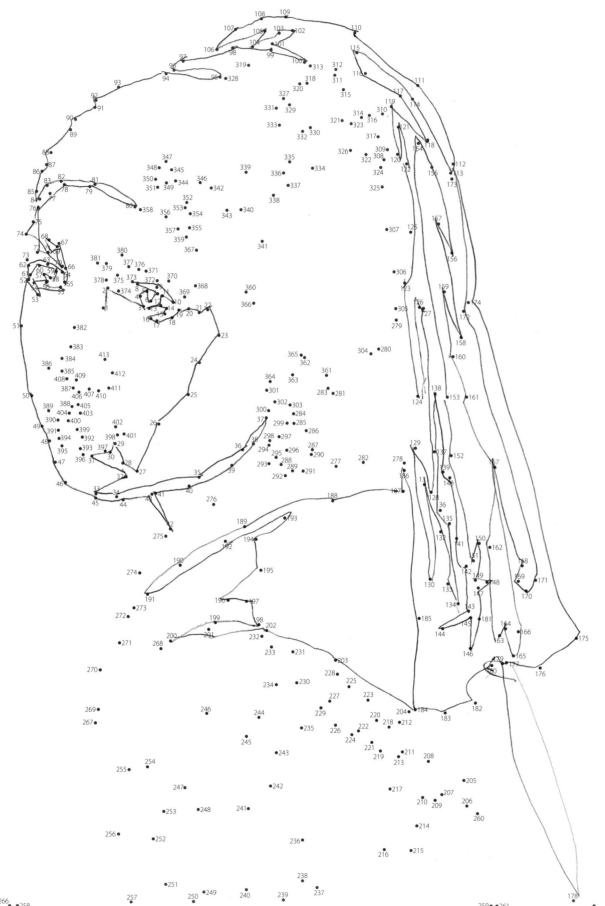

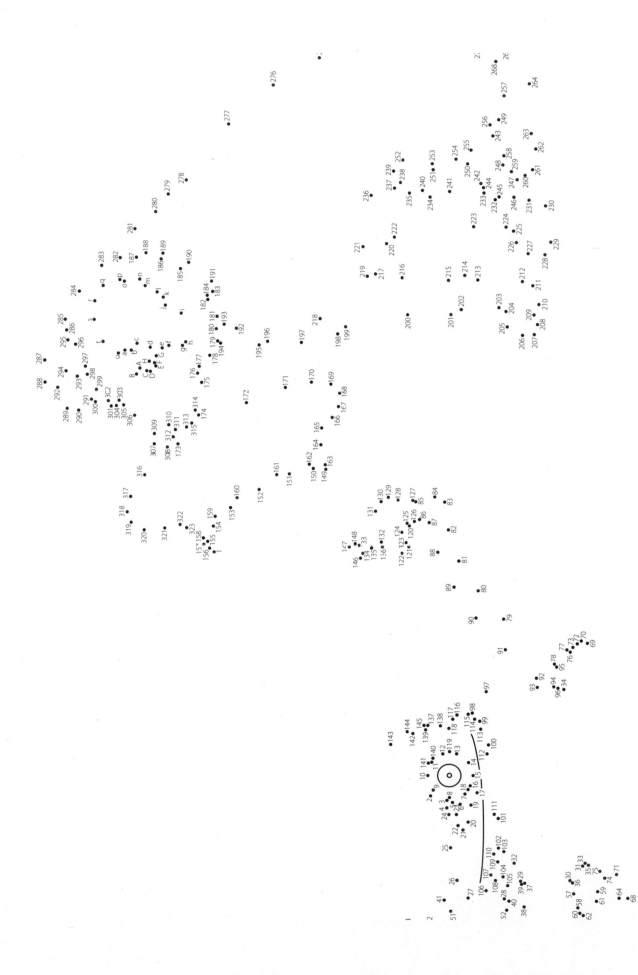

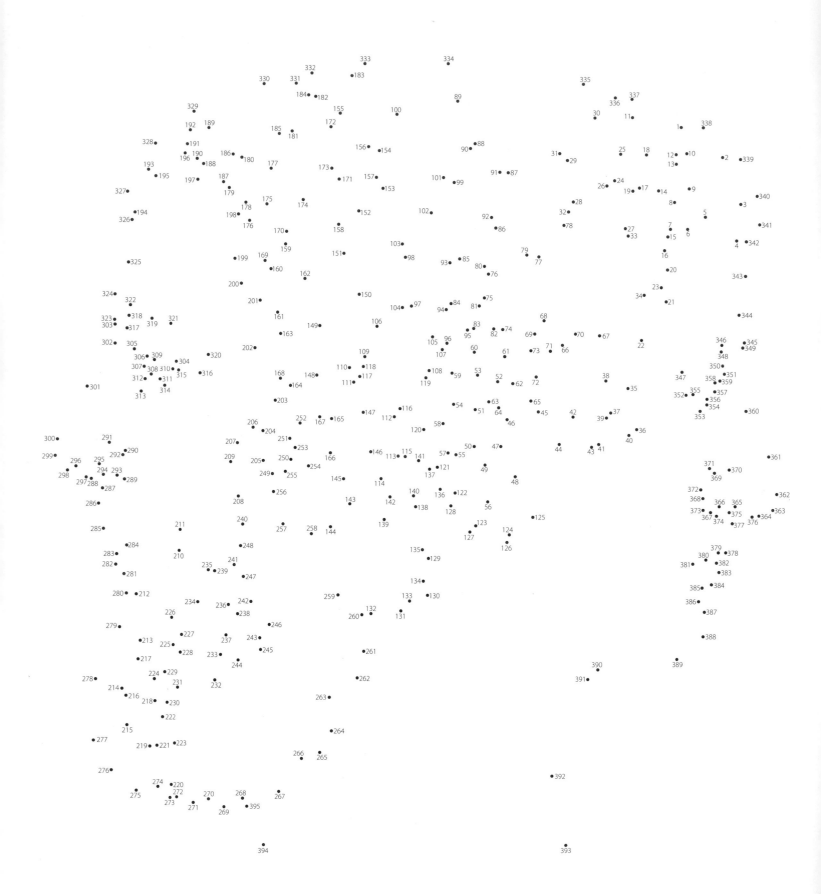

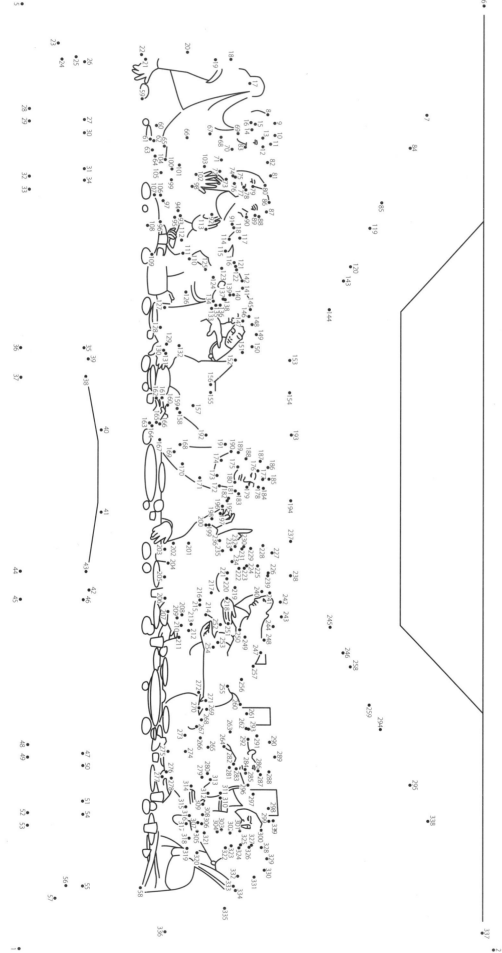

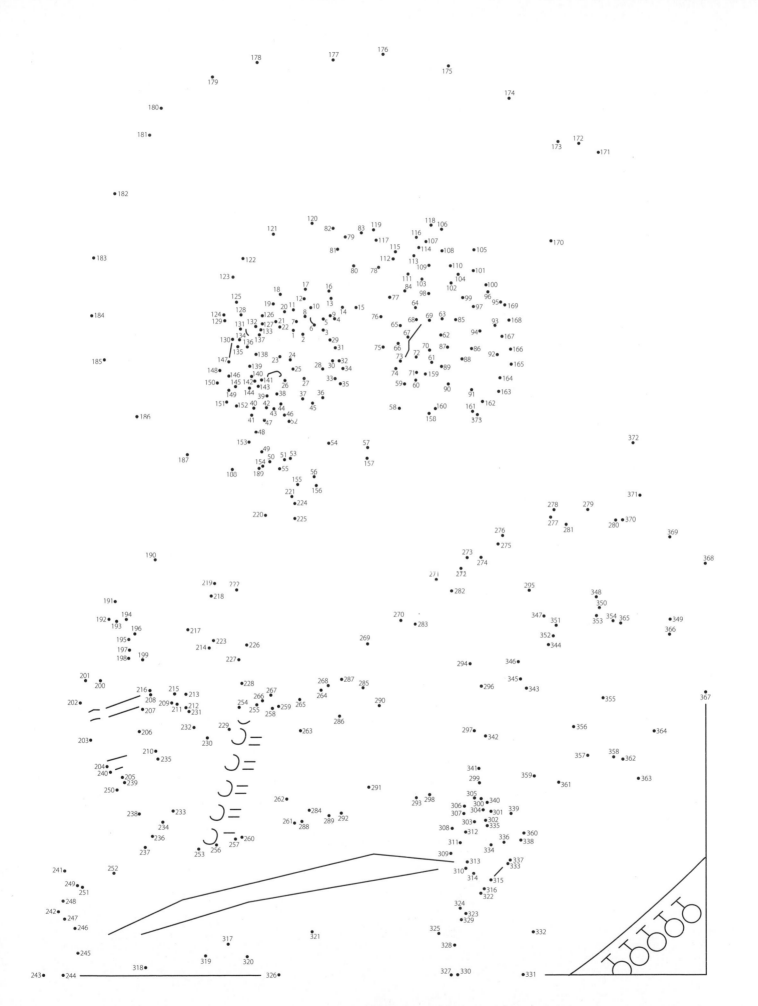

111

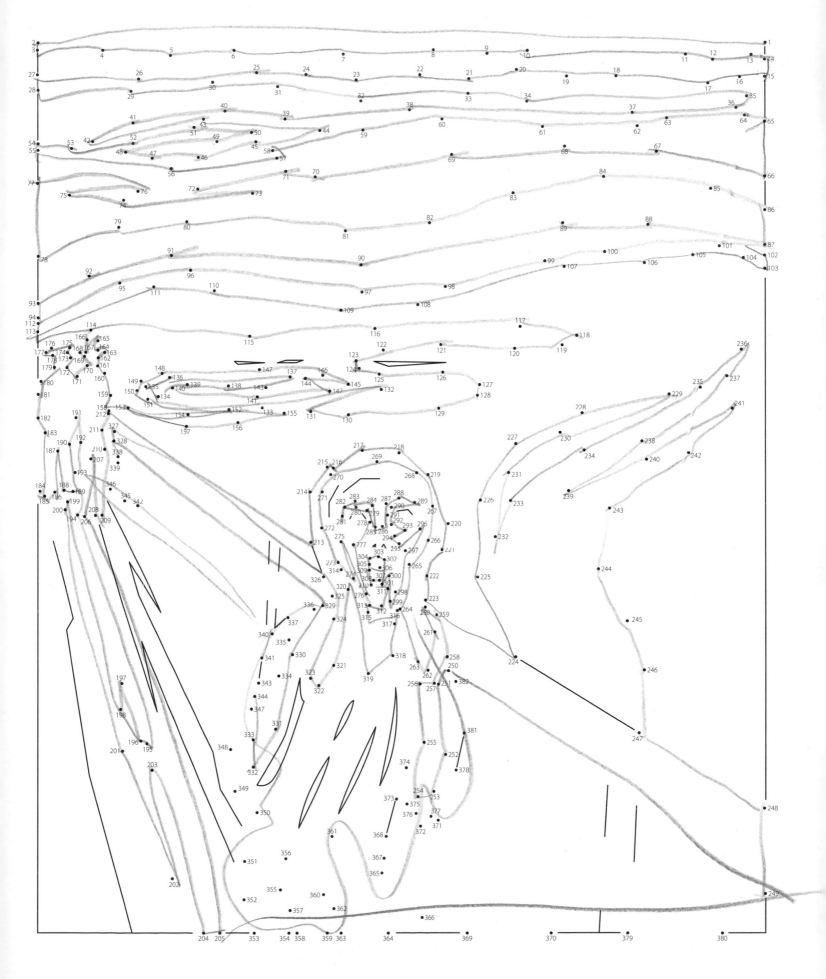

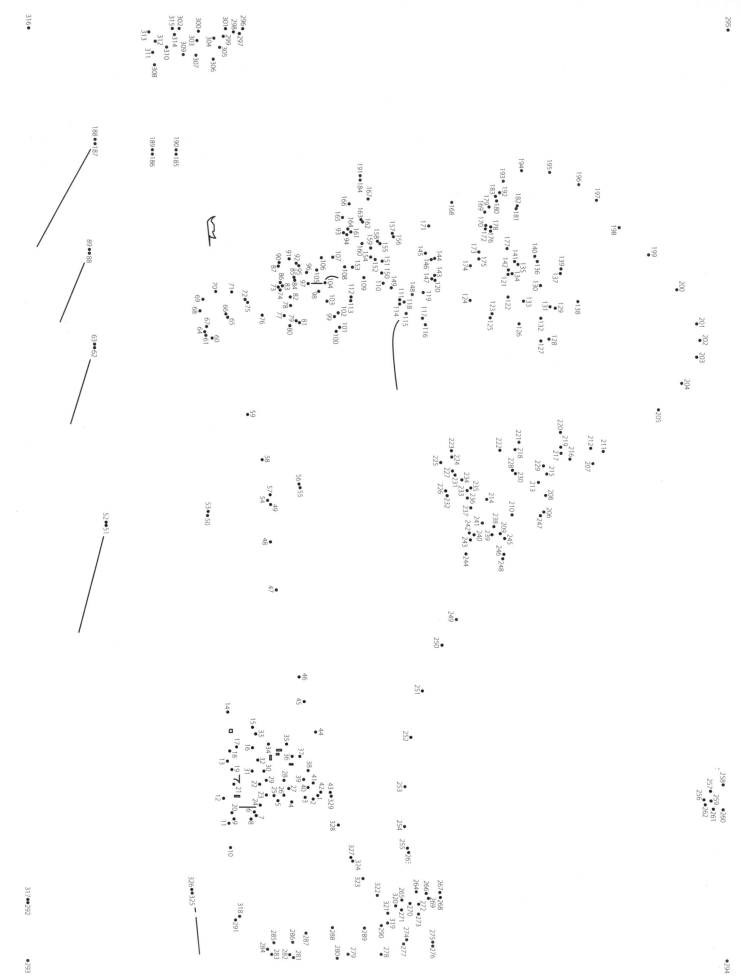

Vincent

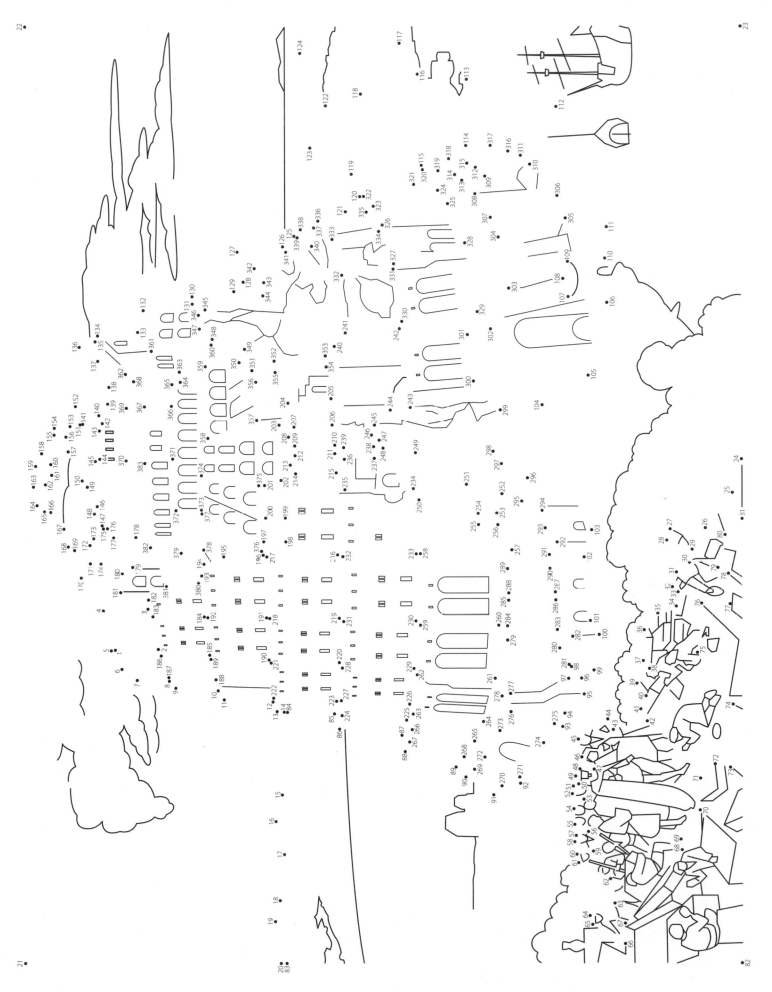

117

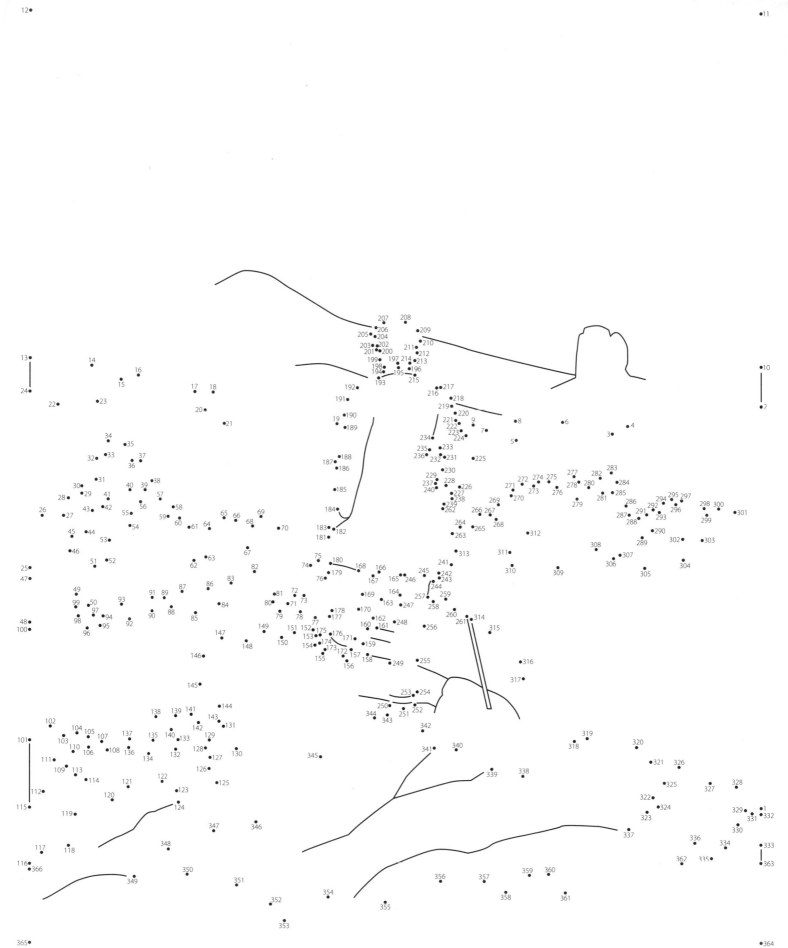

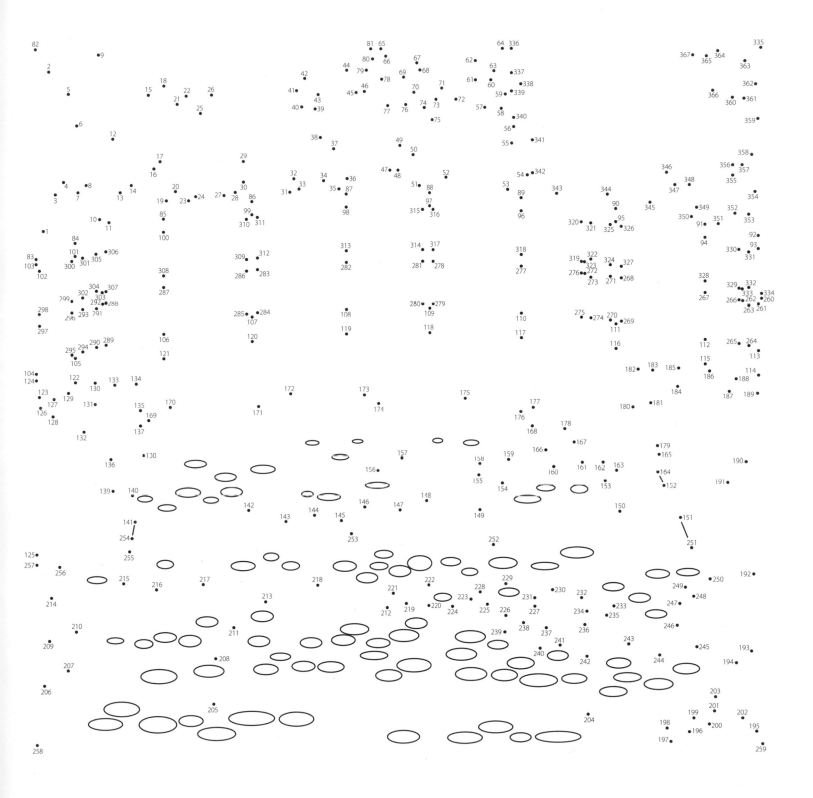

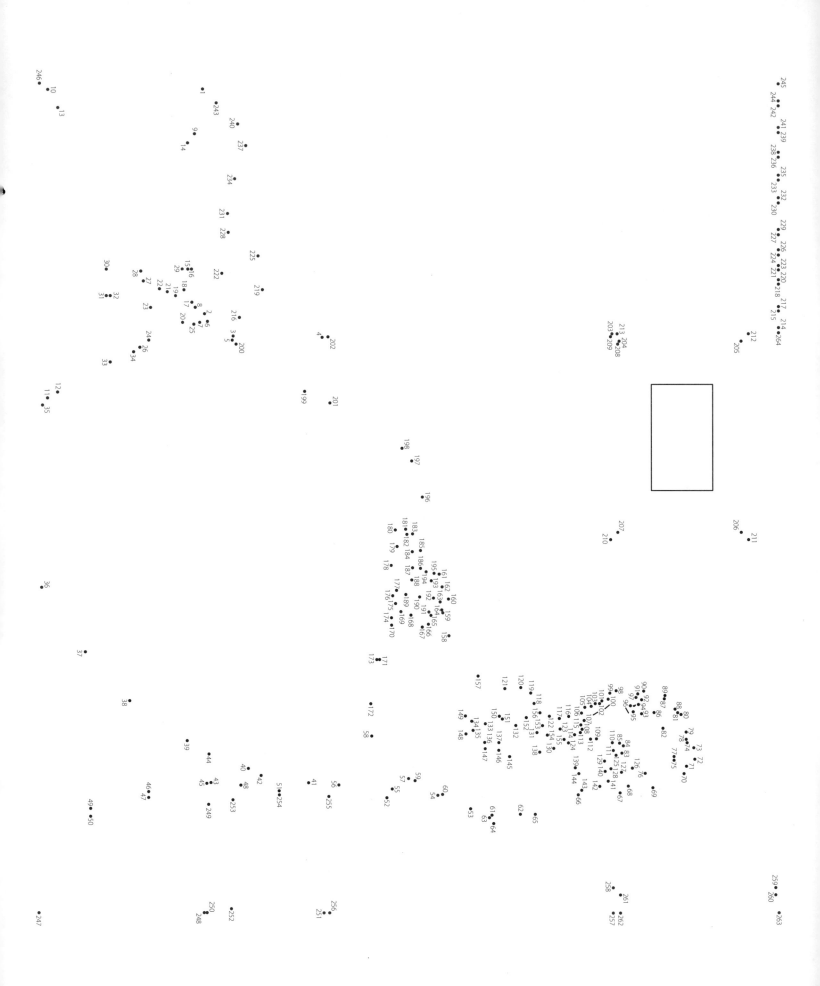

The Royal Family

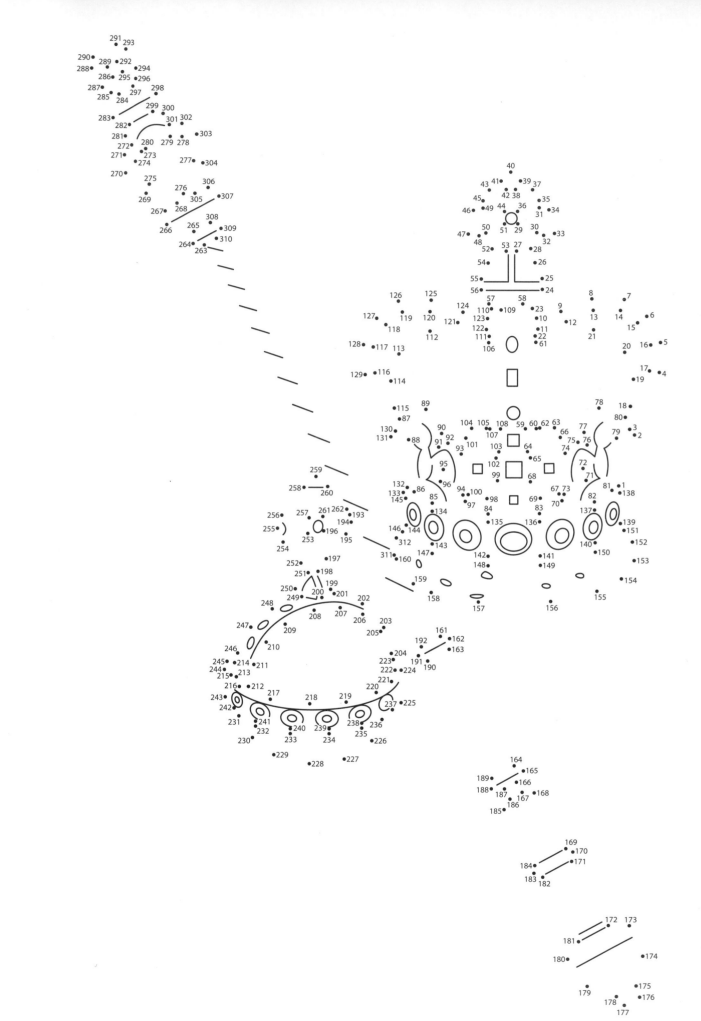

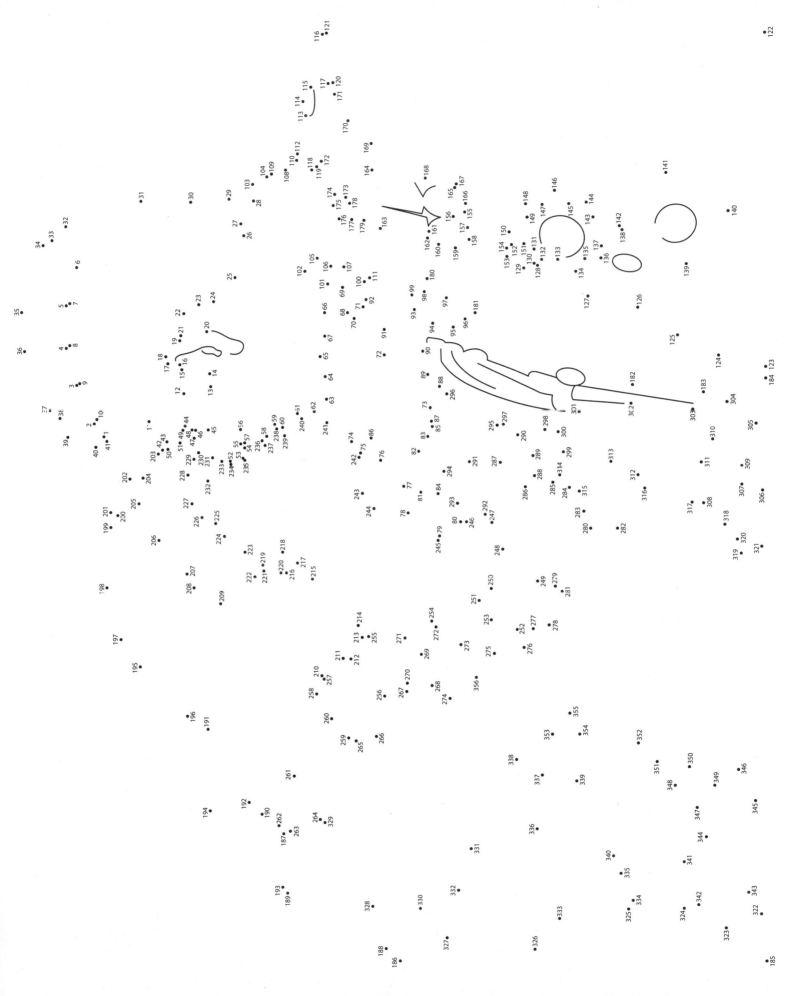

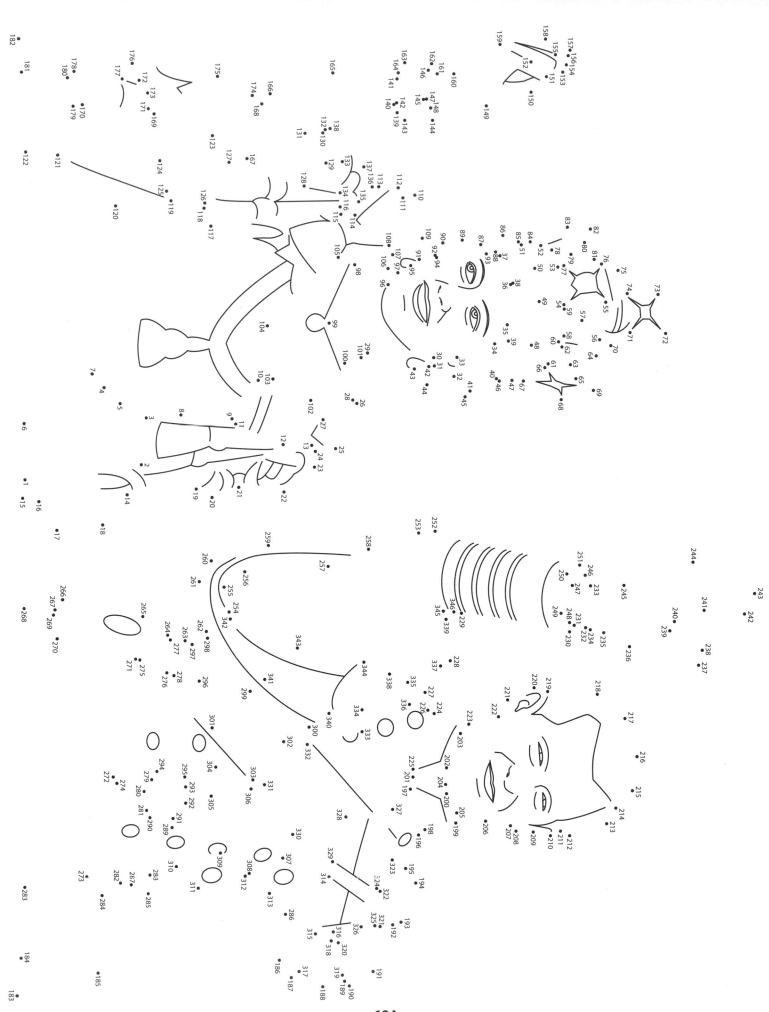

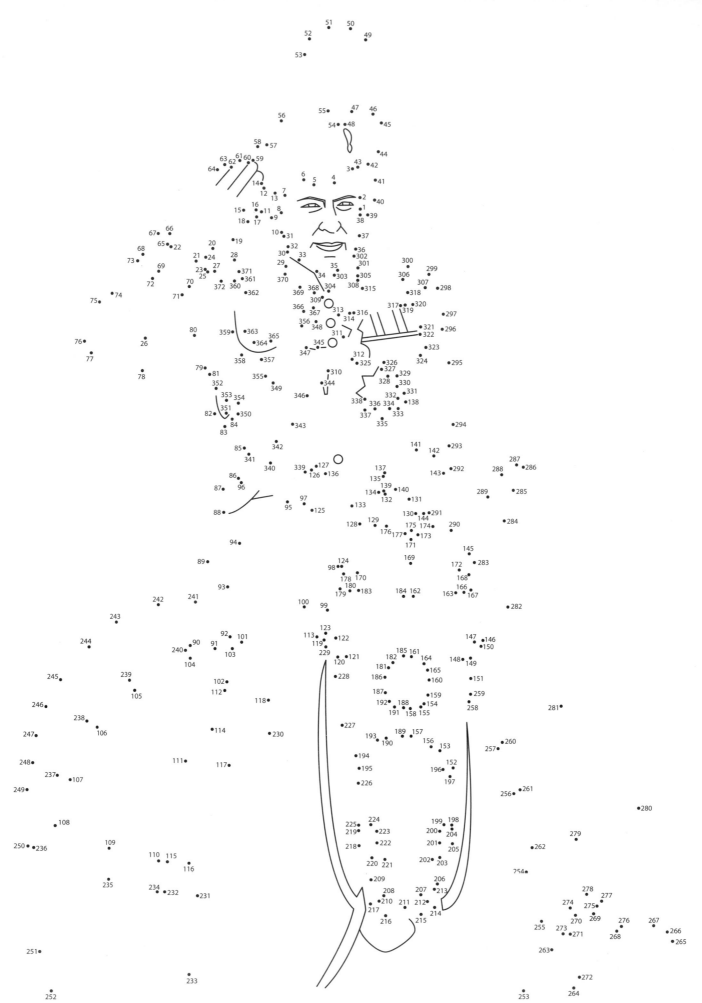

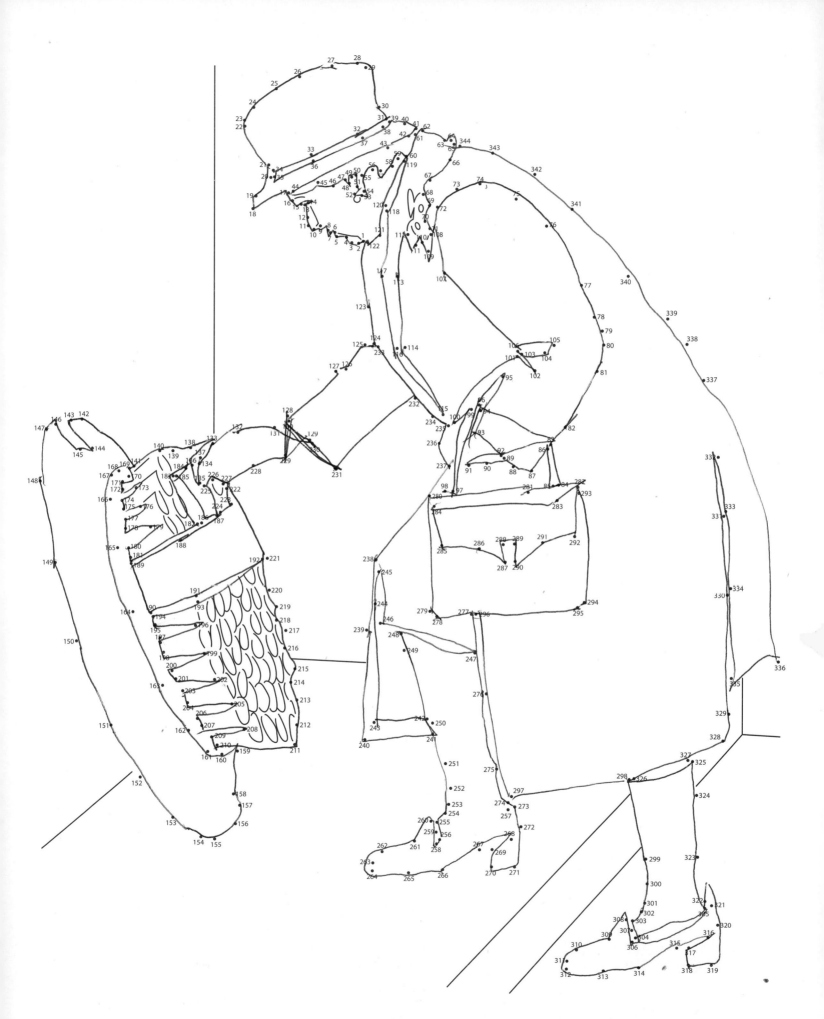

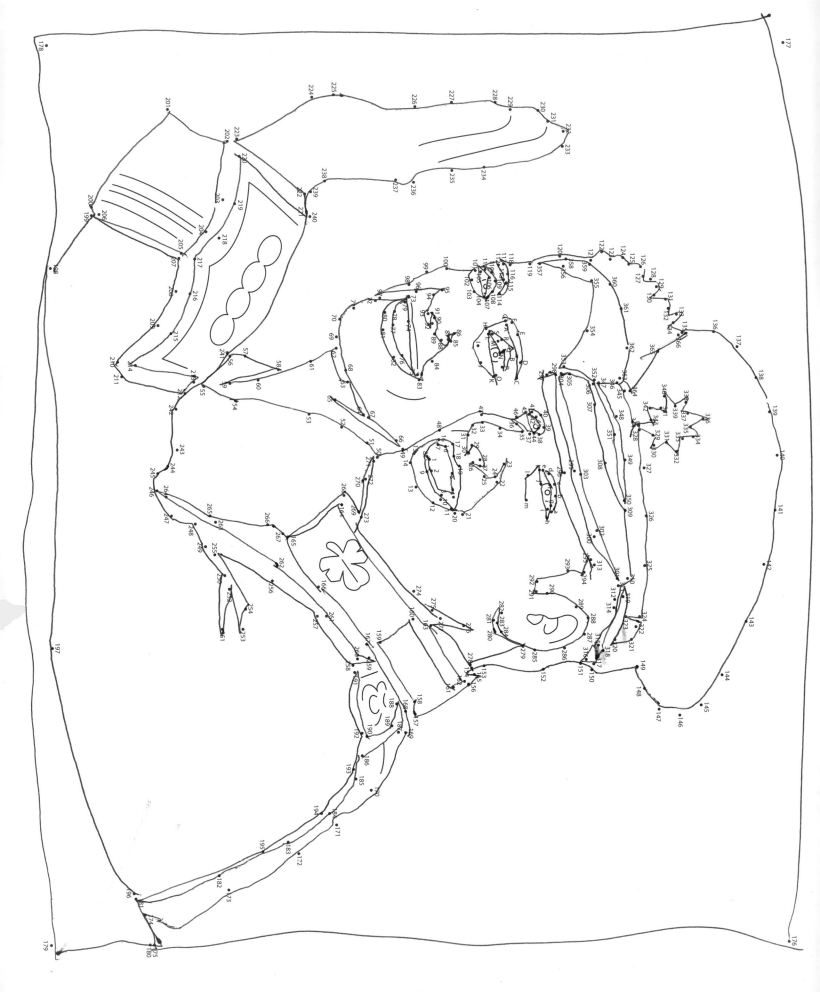

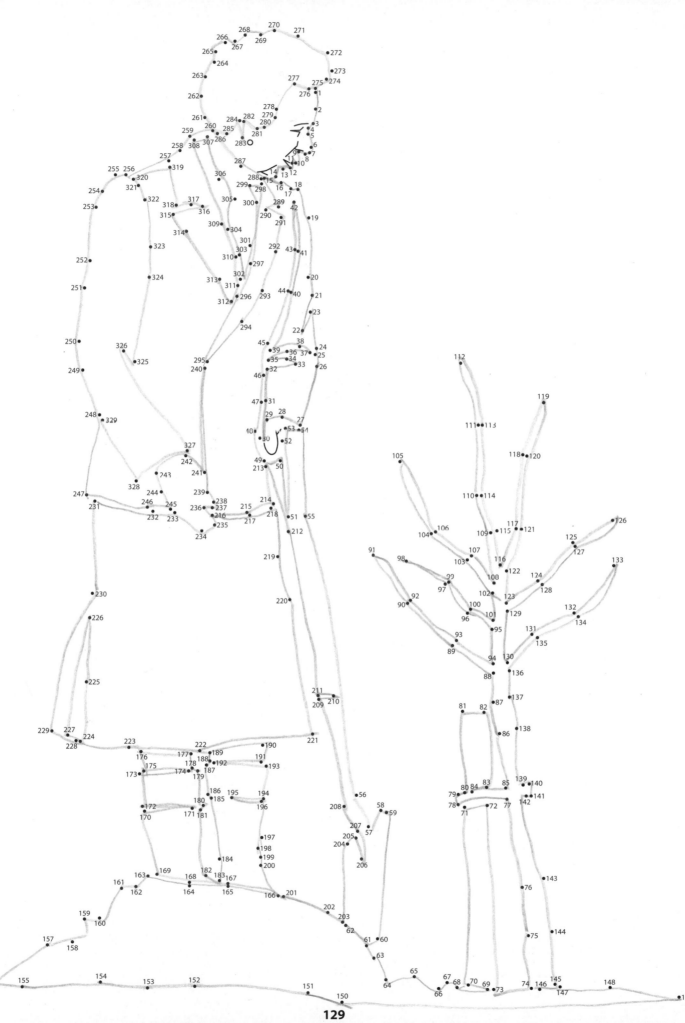

129

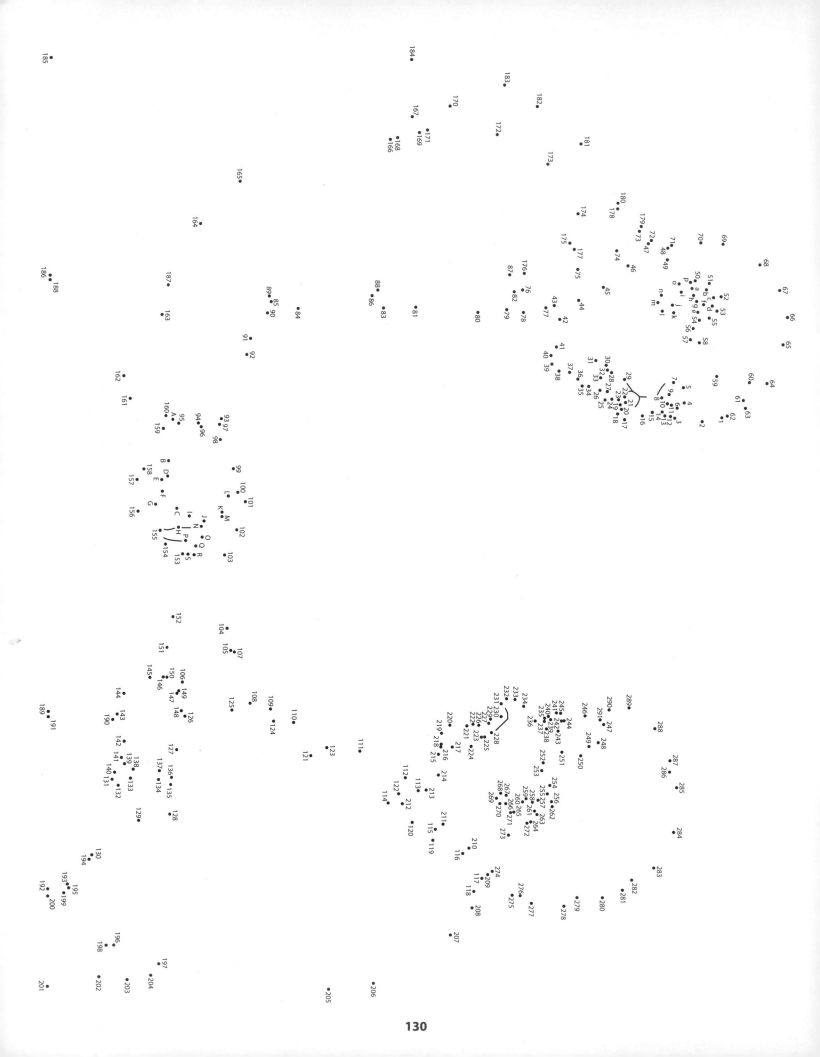

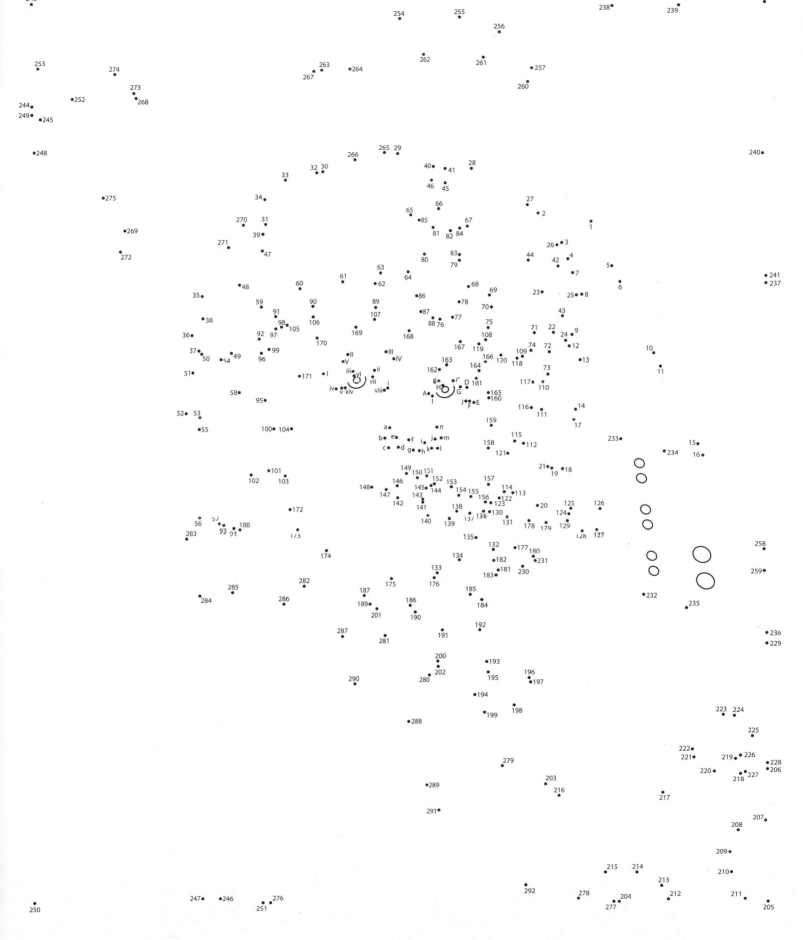

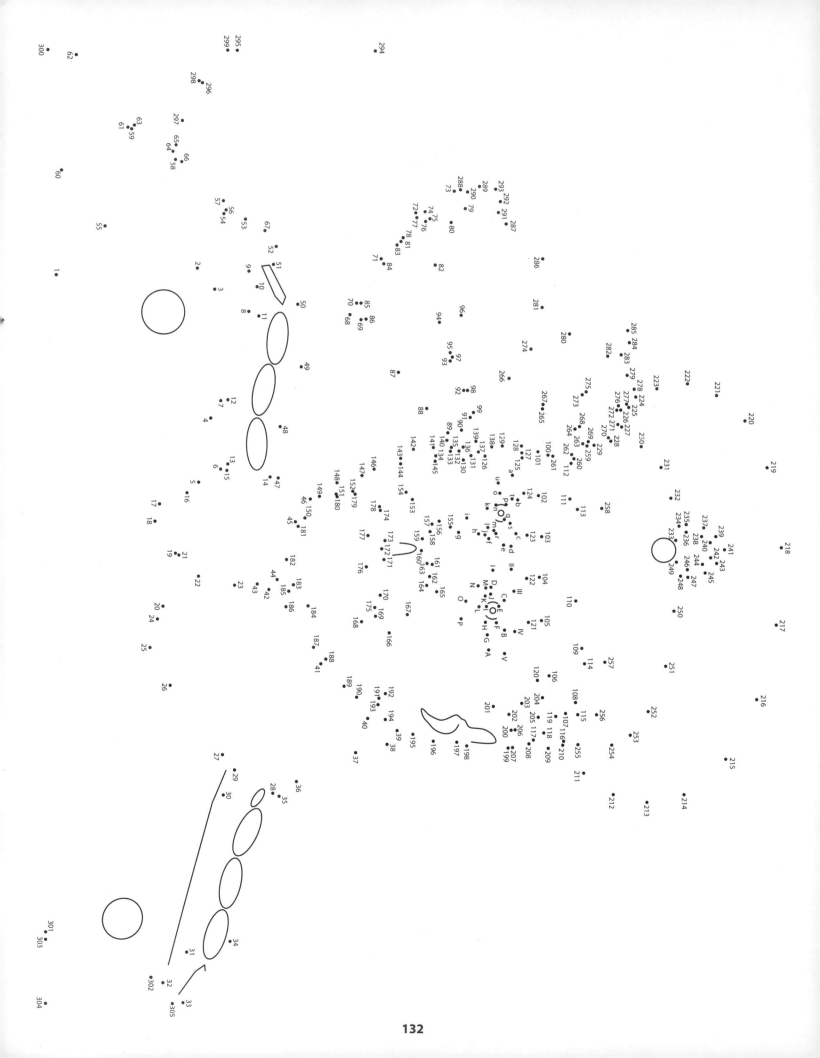

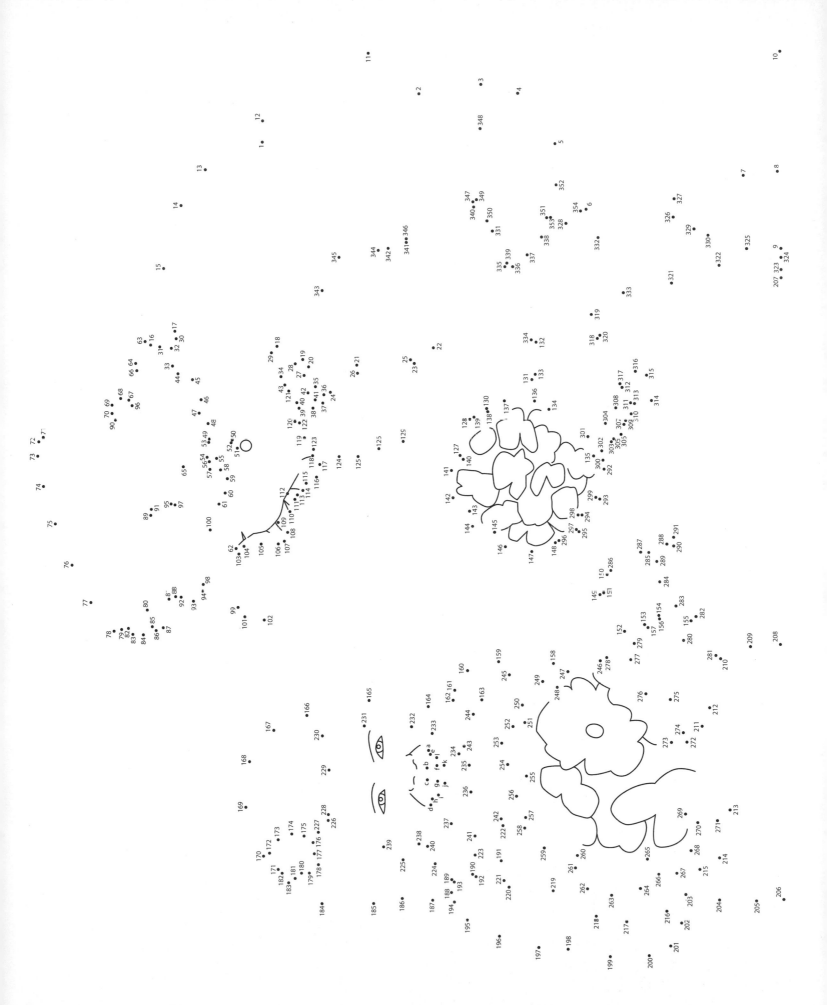

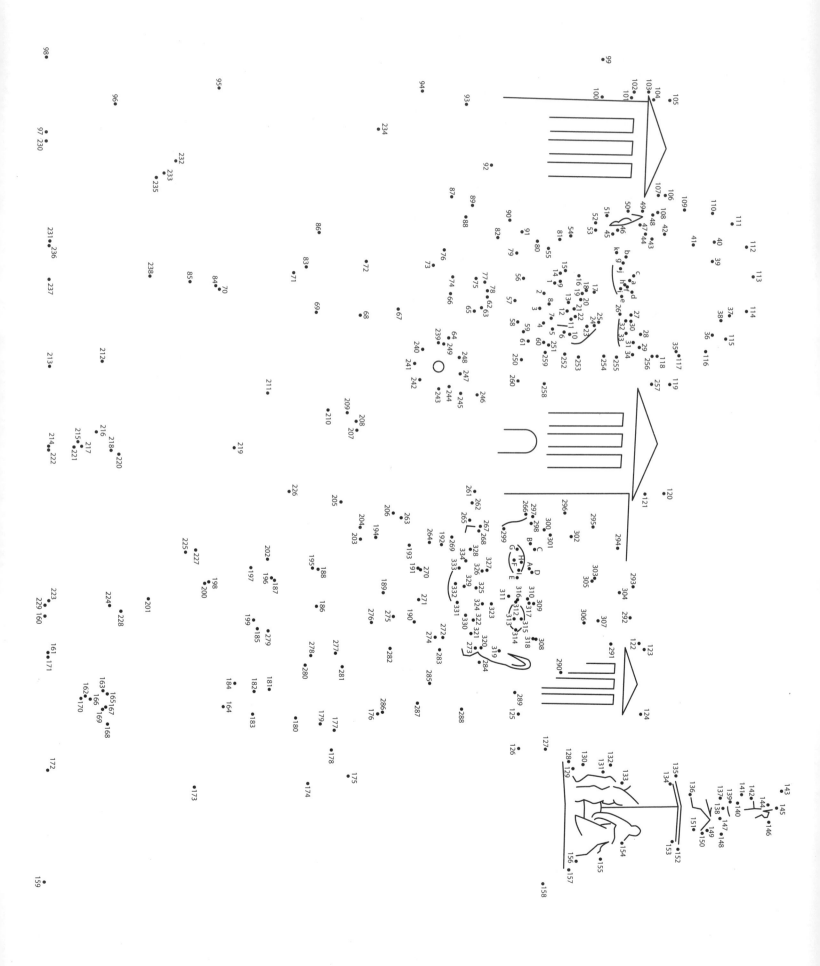

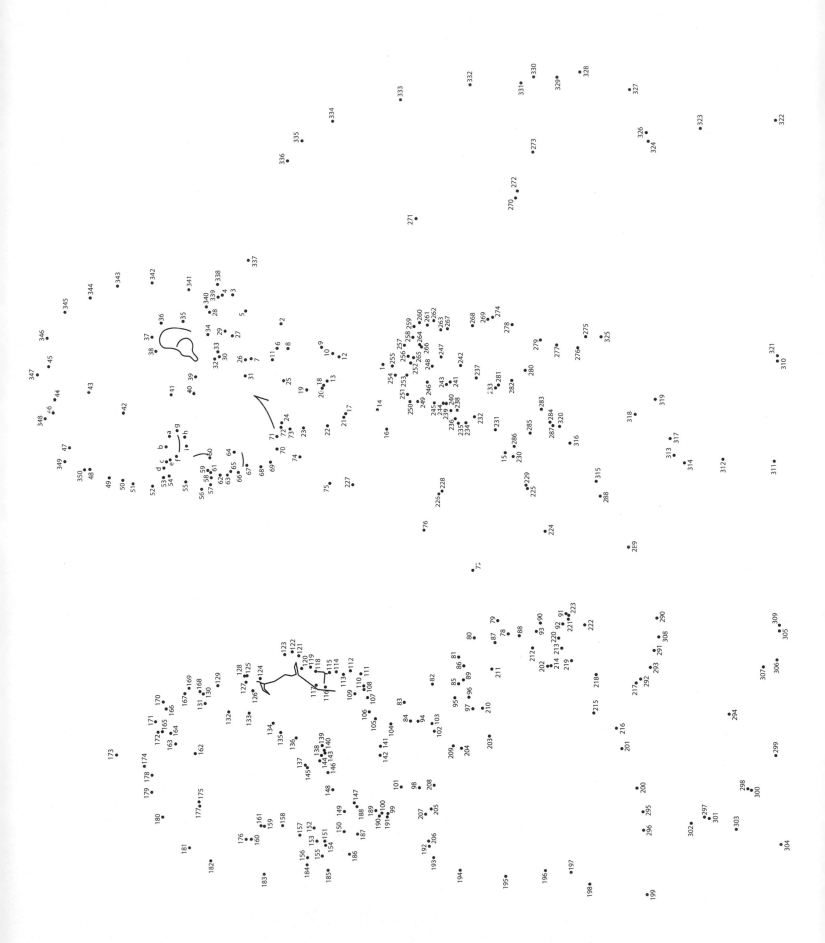

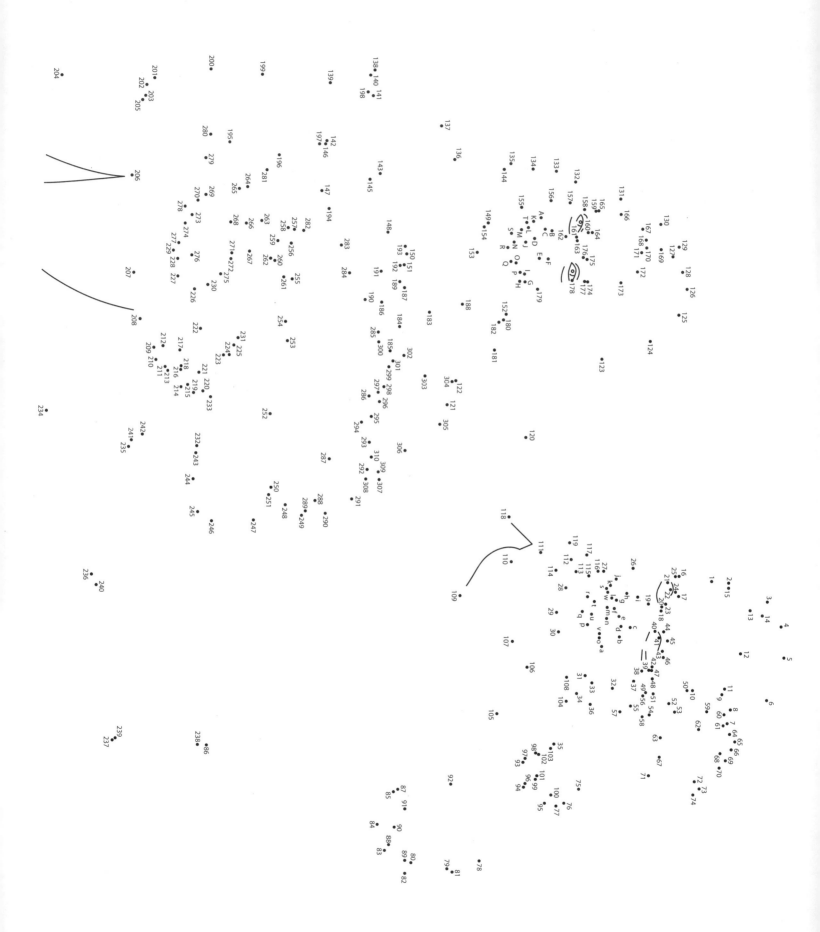

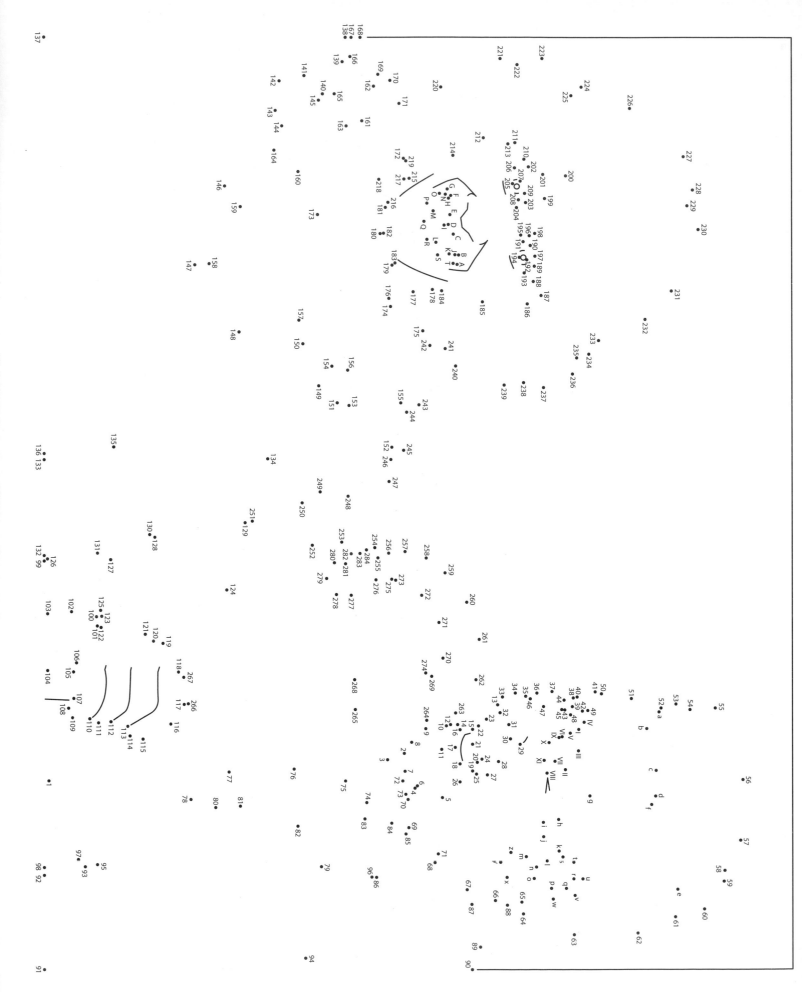

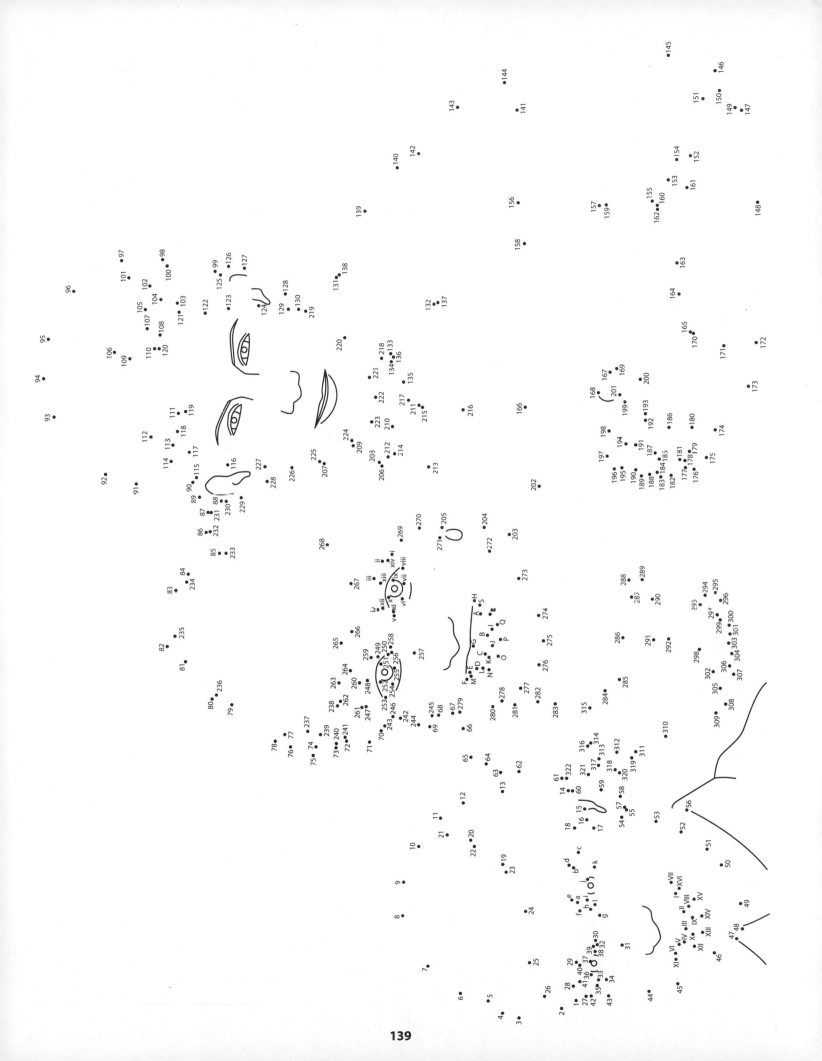

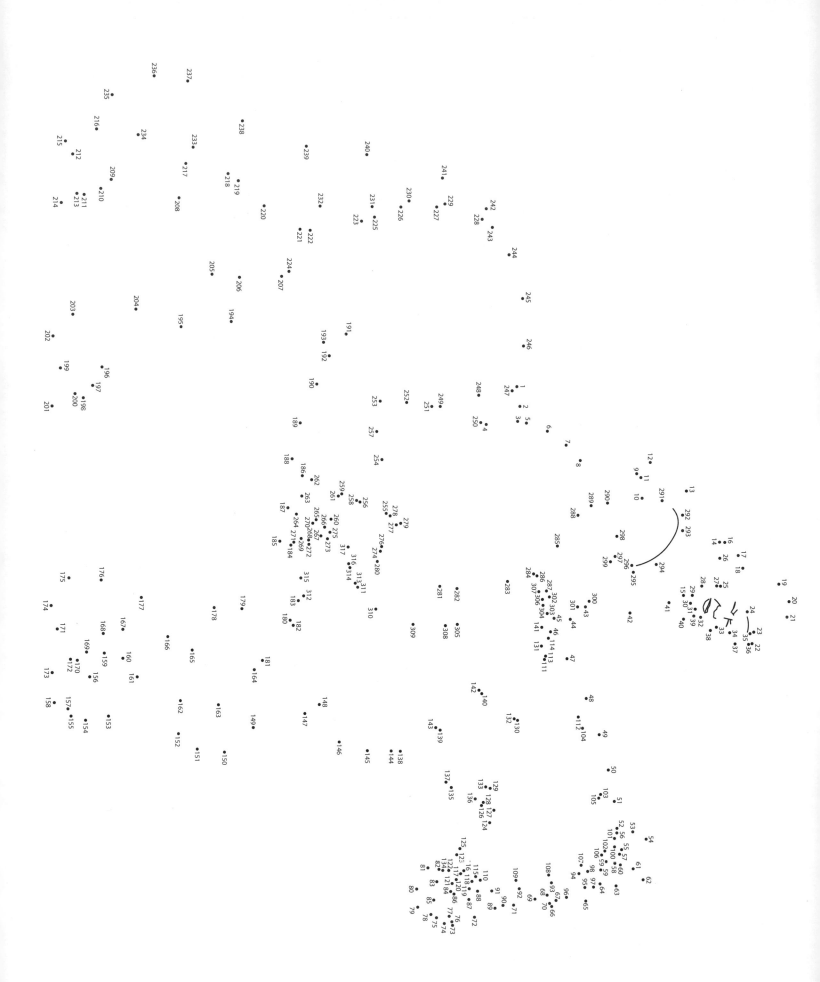

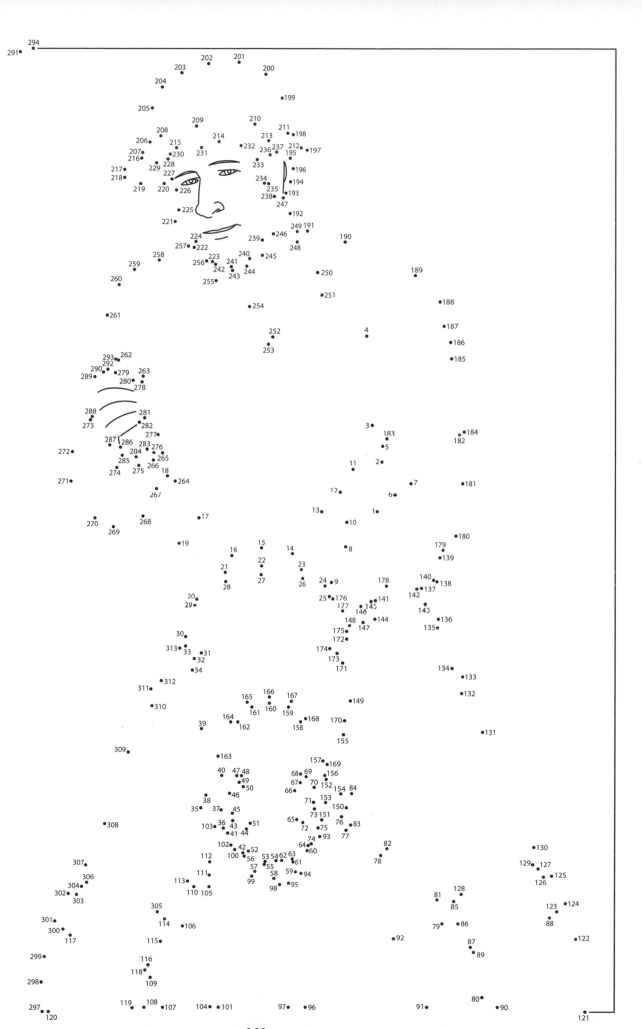

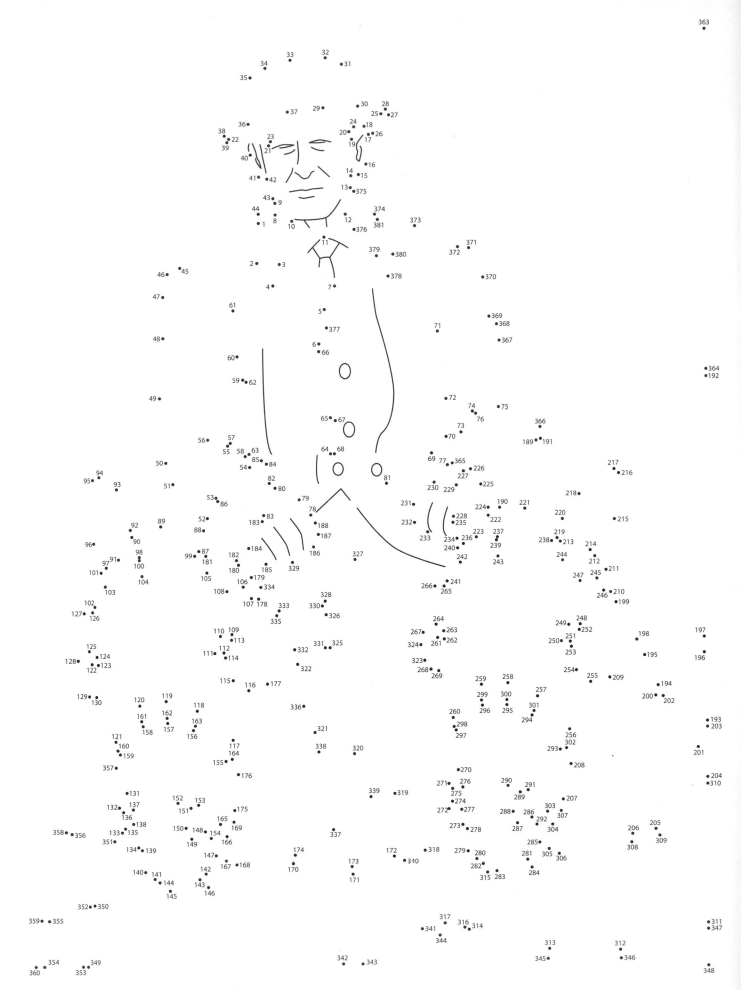

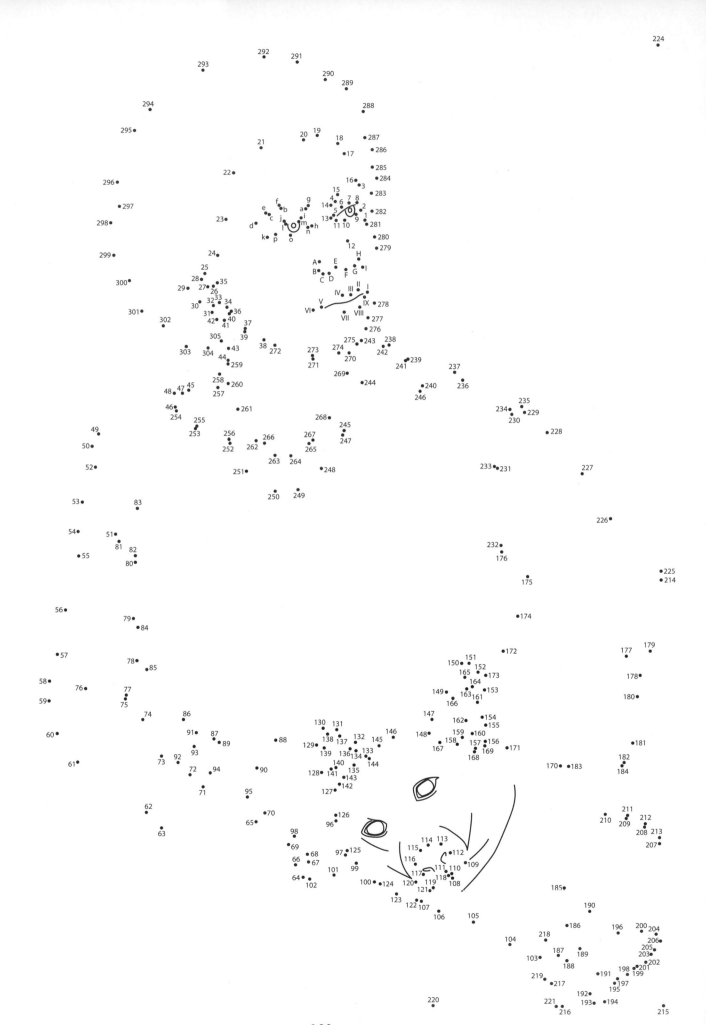

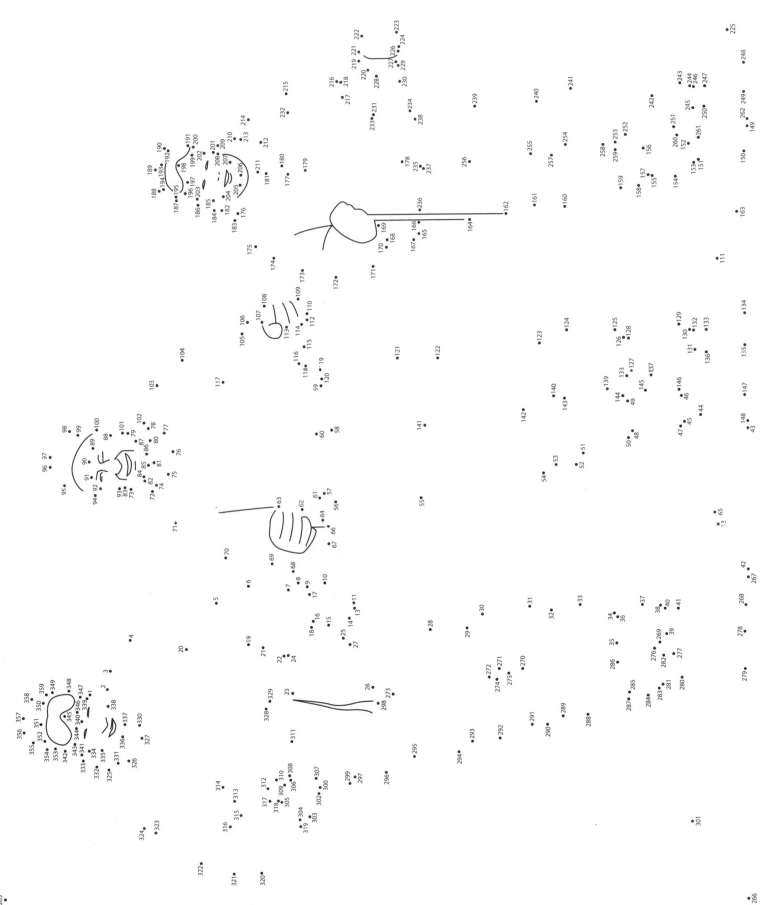

145

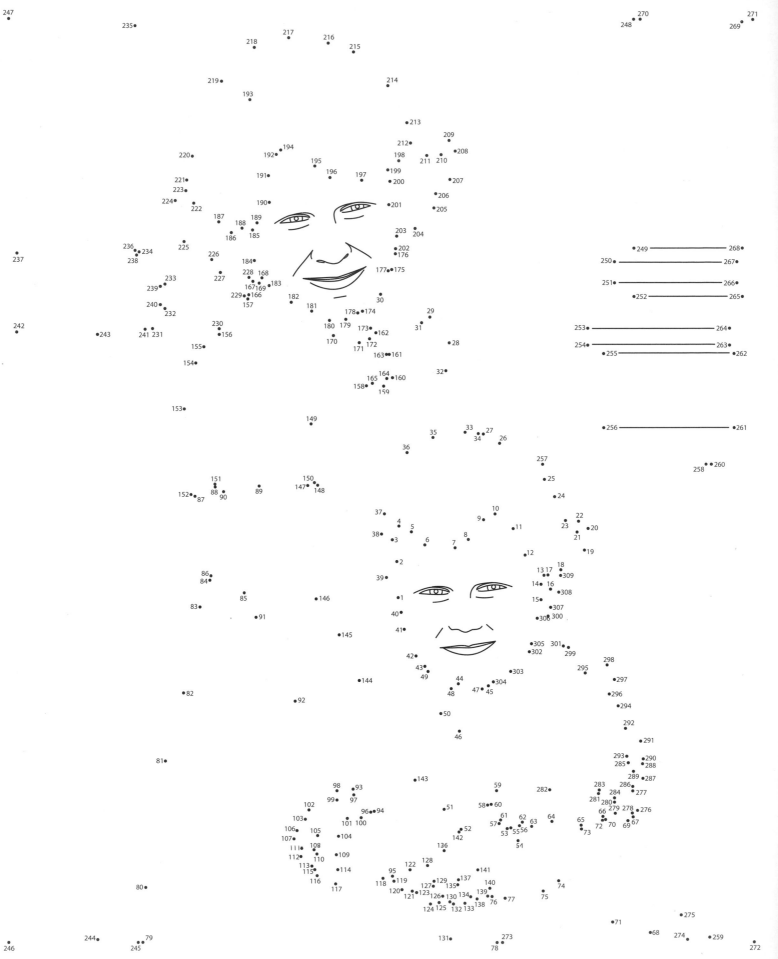

Entertainment

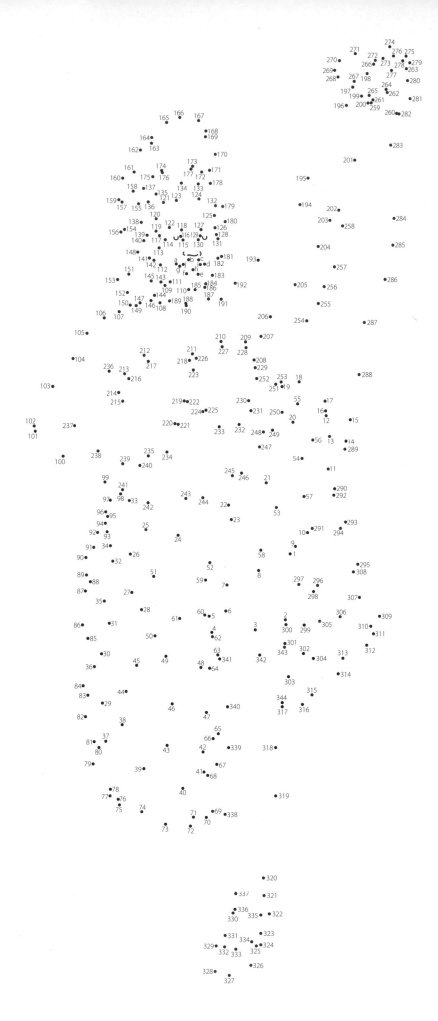

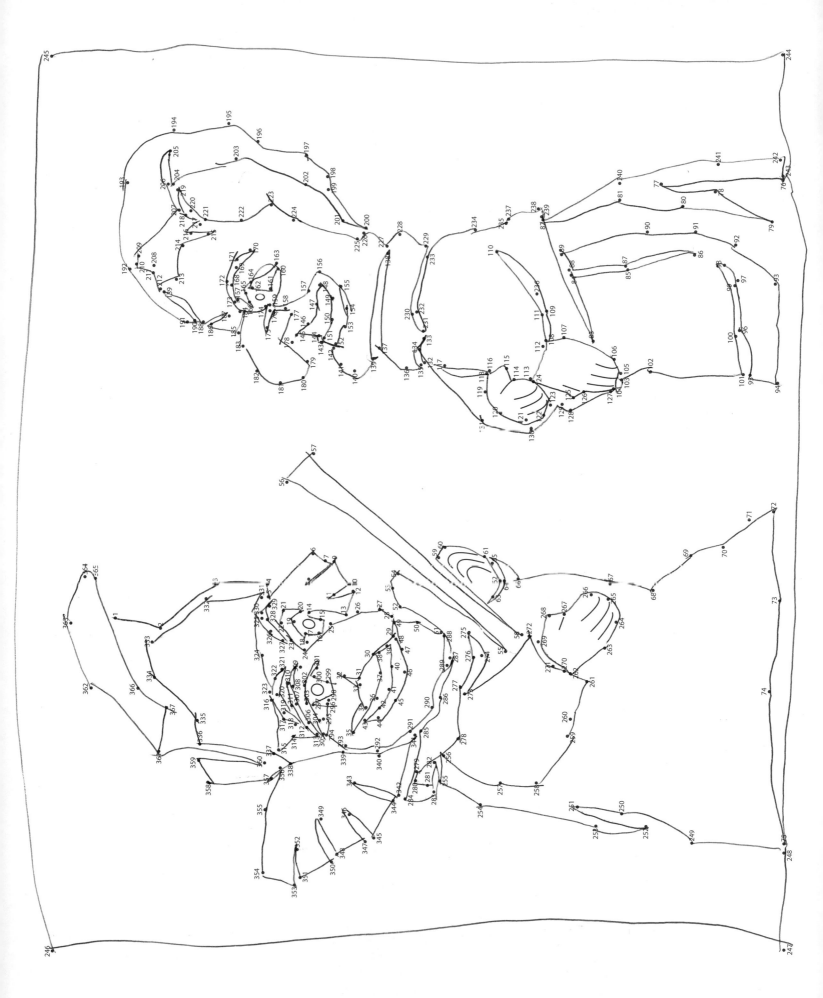

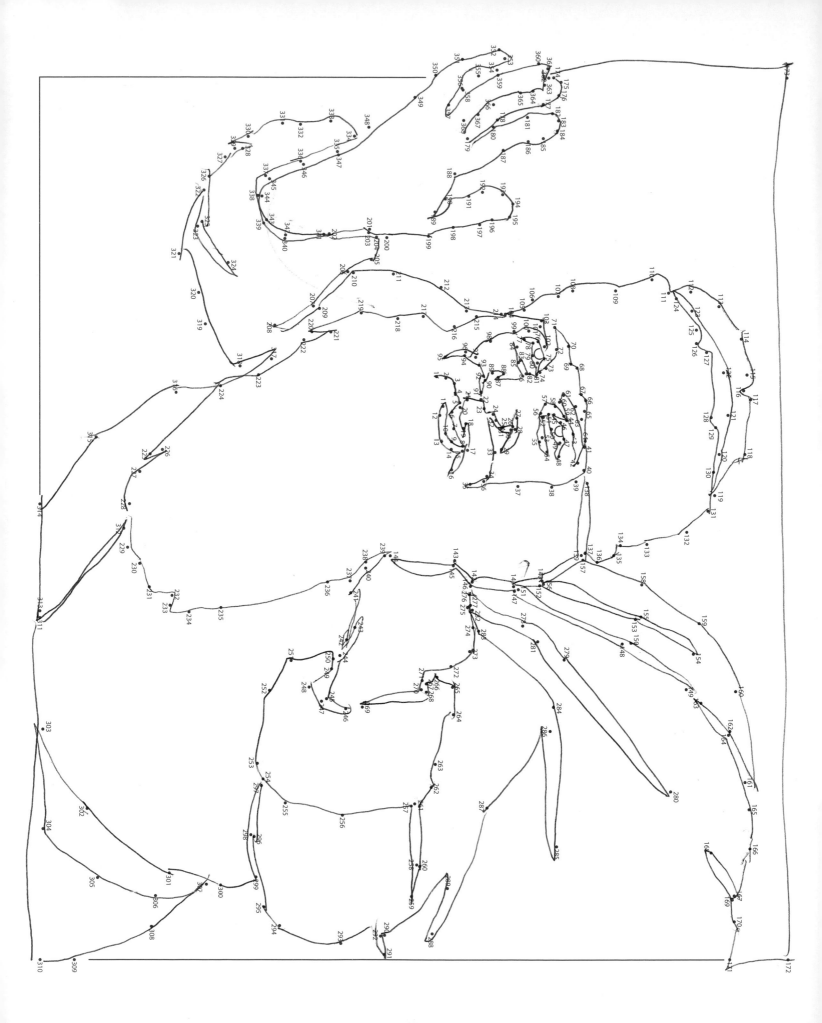

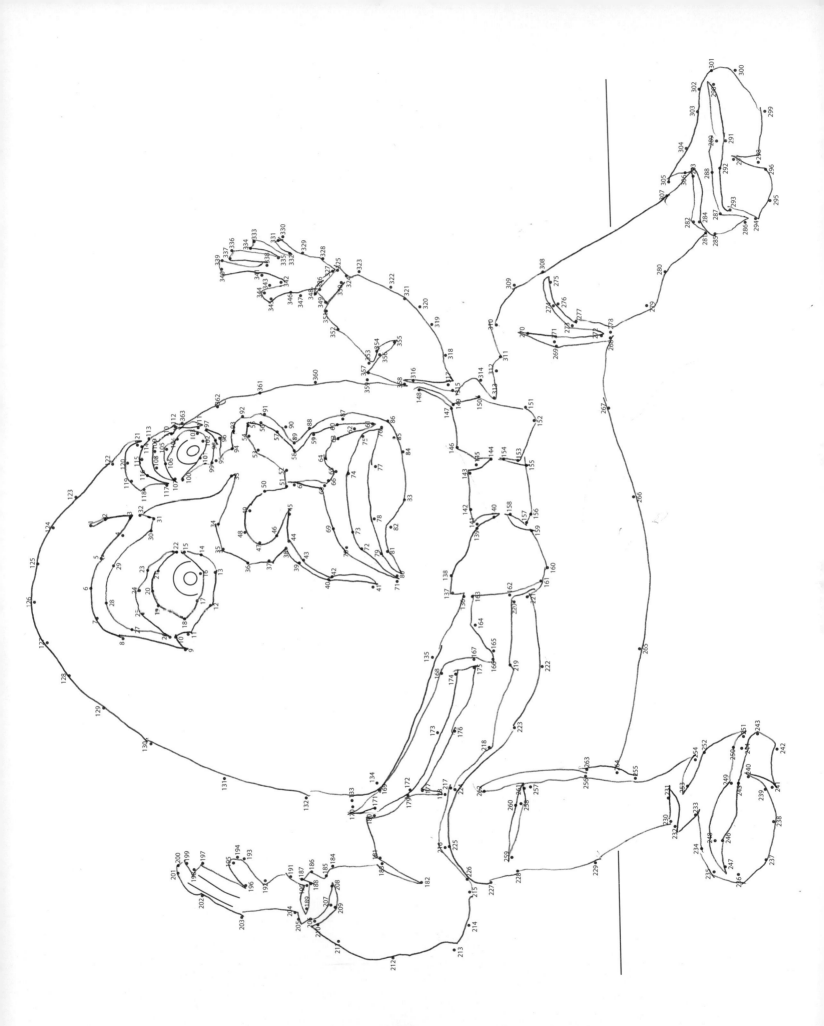

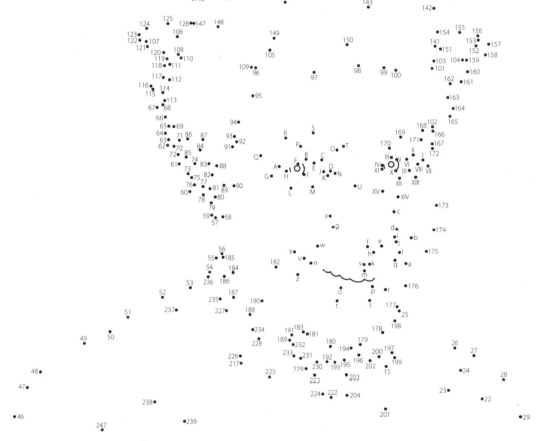

153

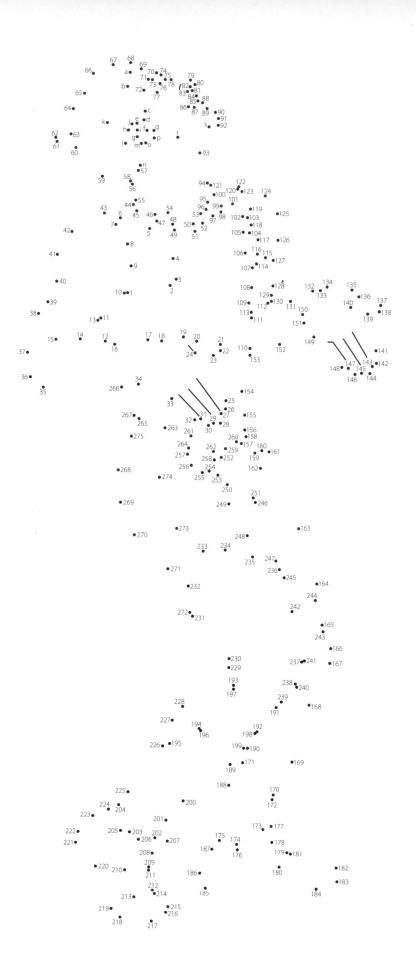

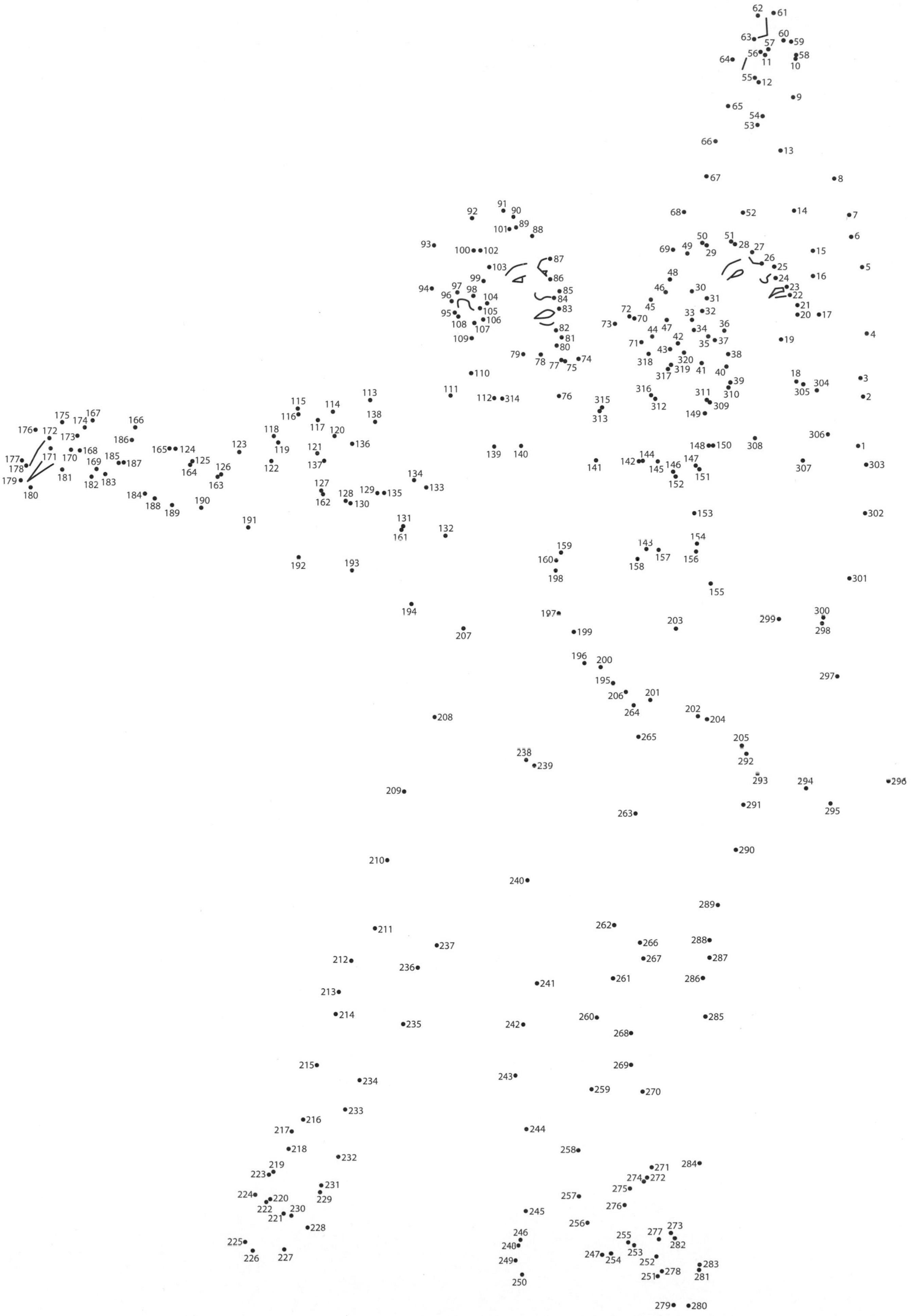

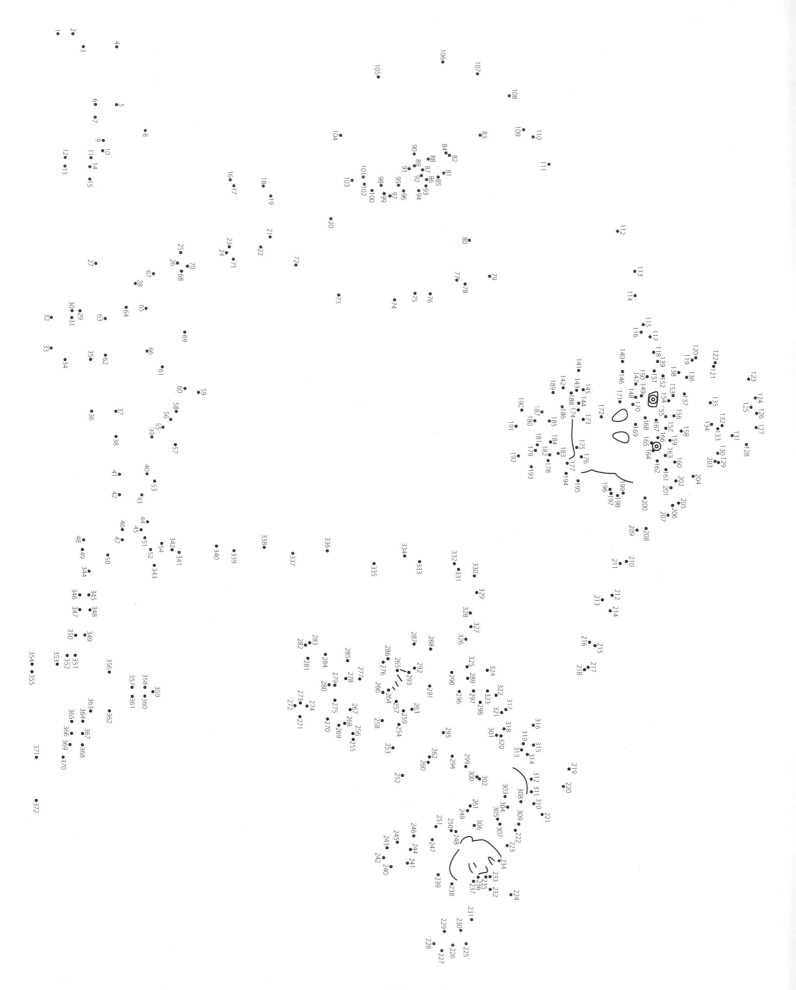

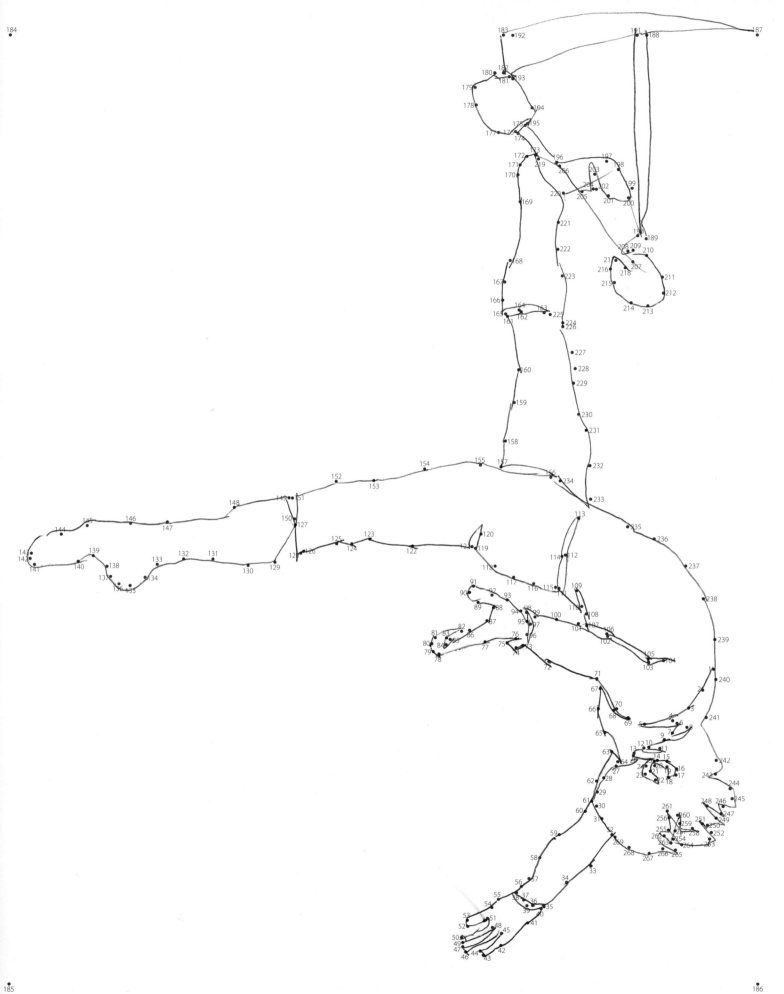

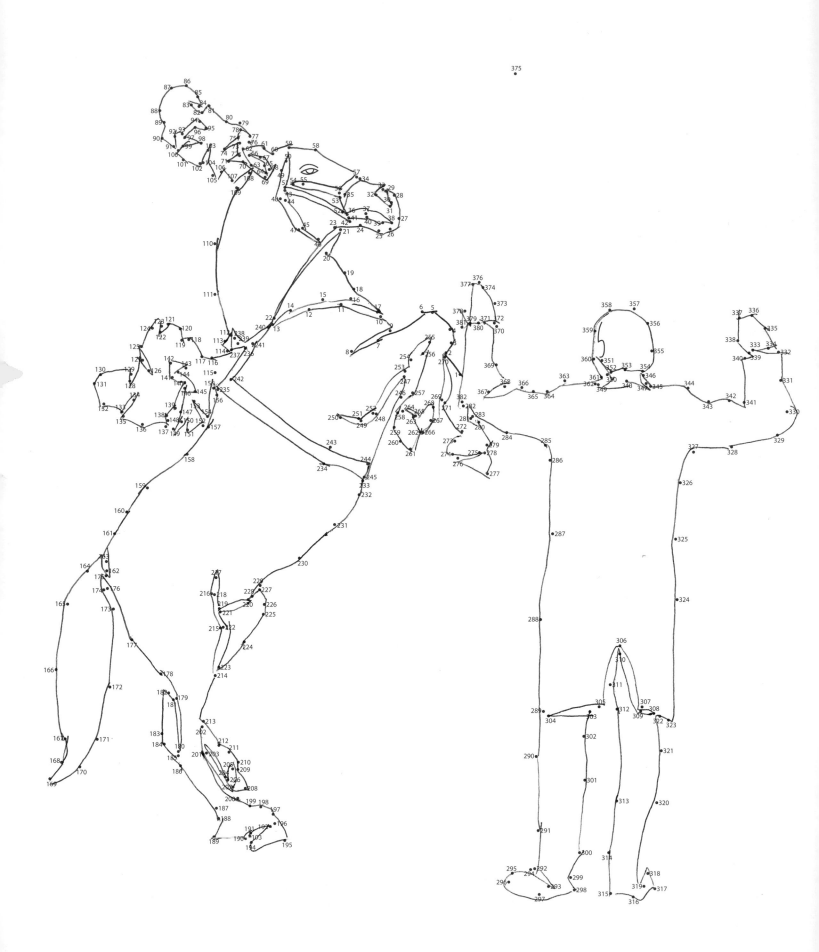

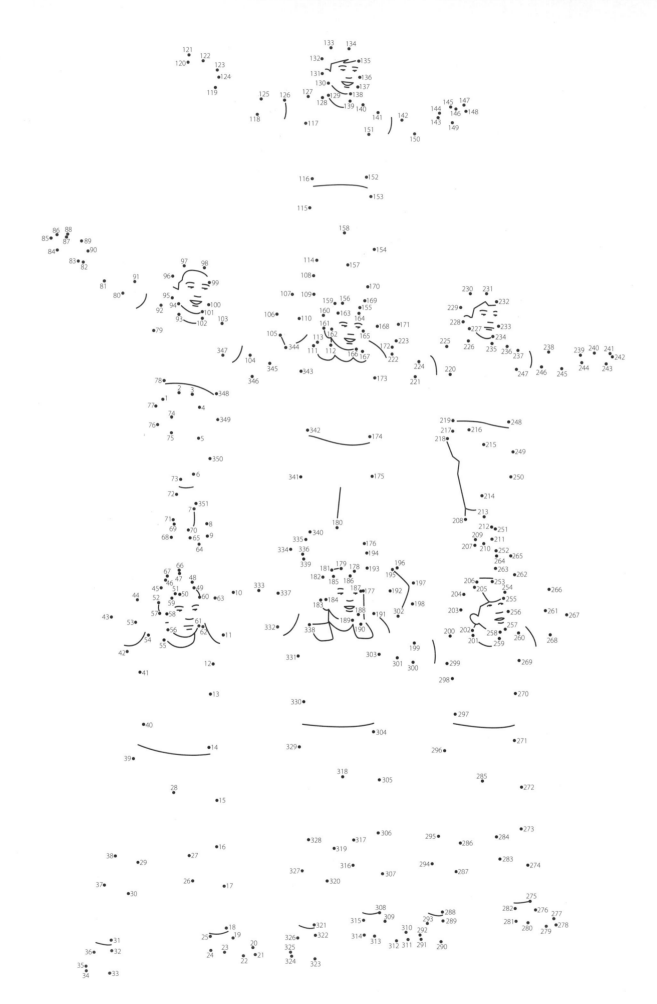

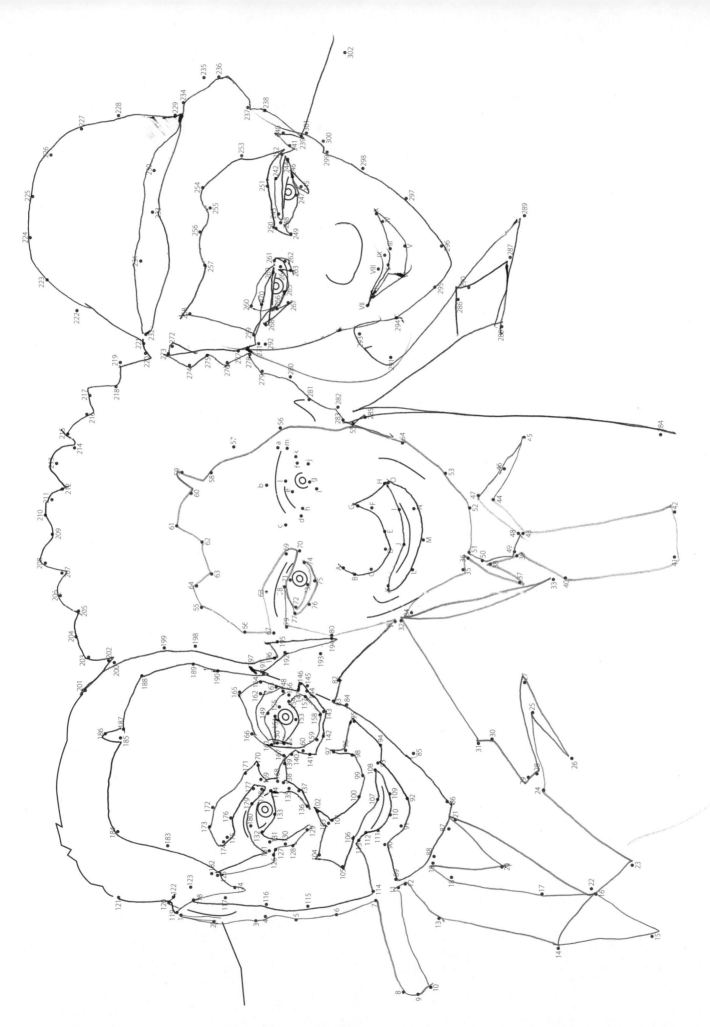

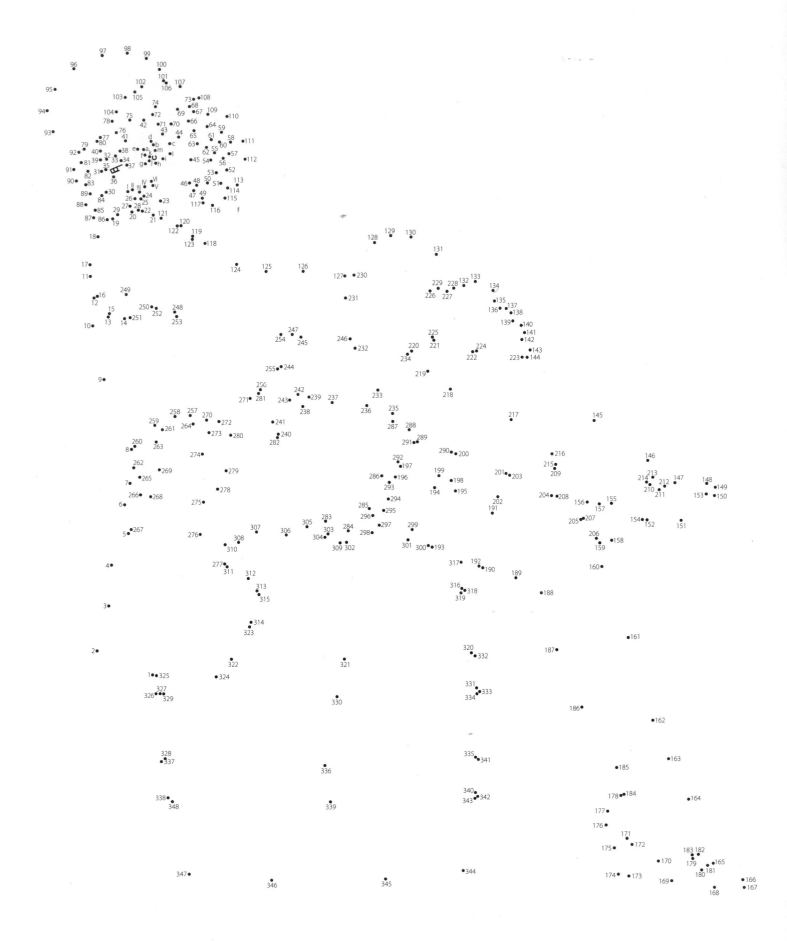

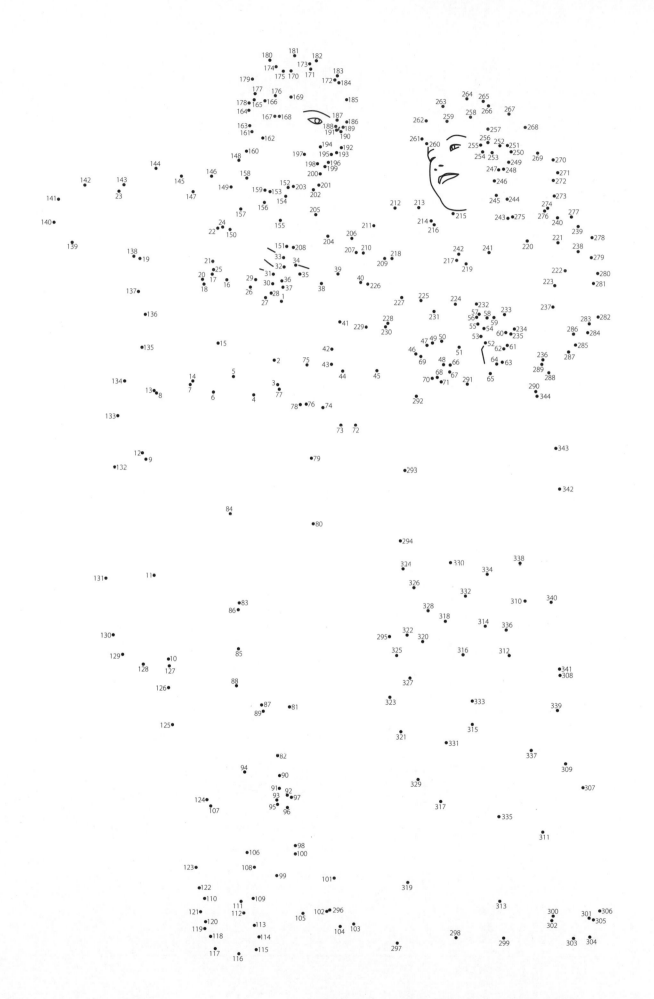

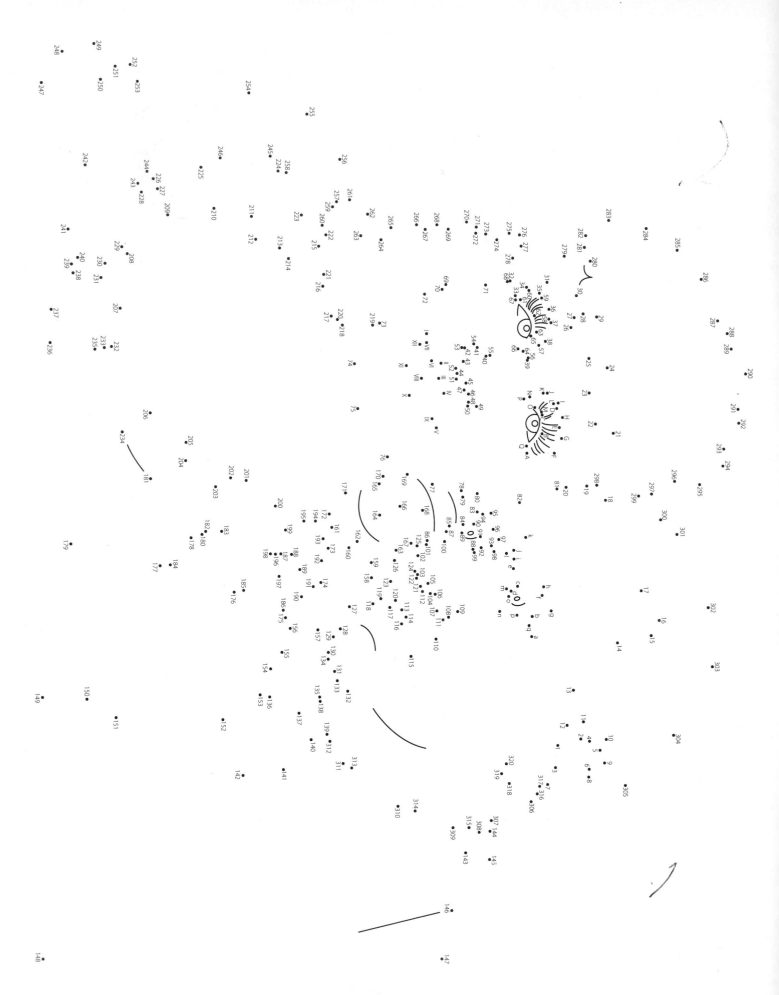

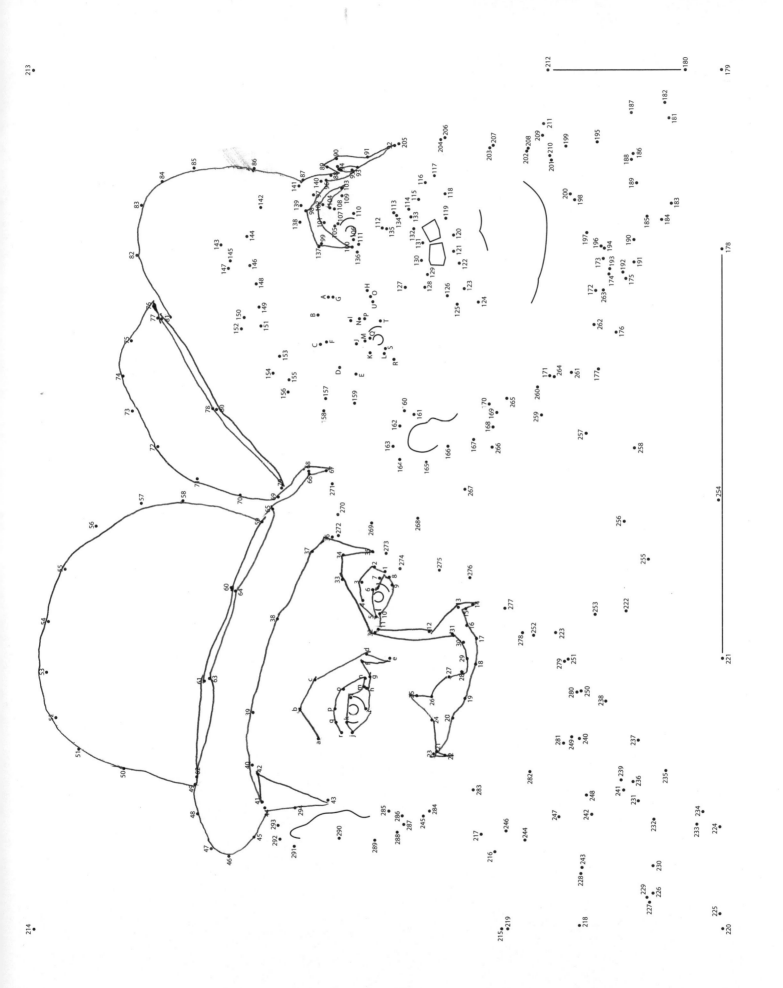

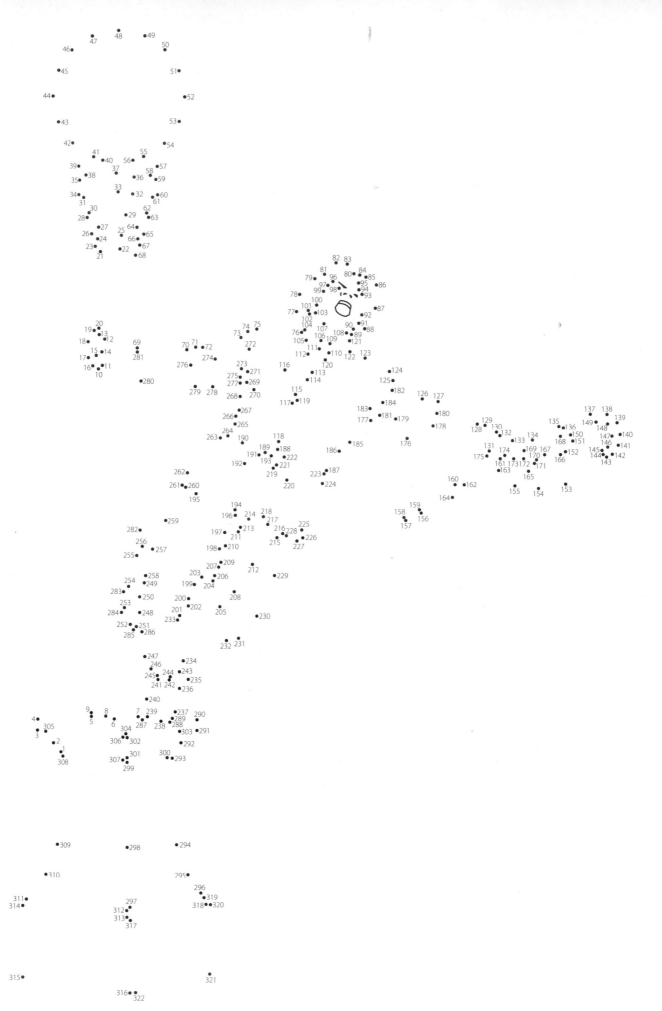

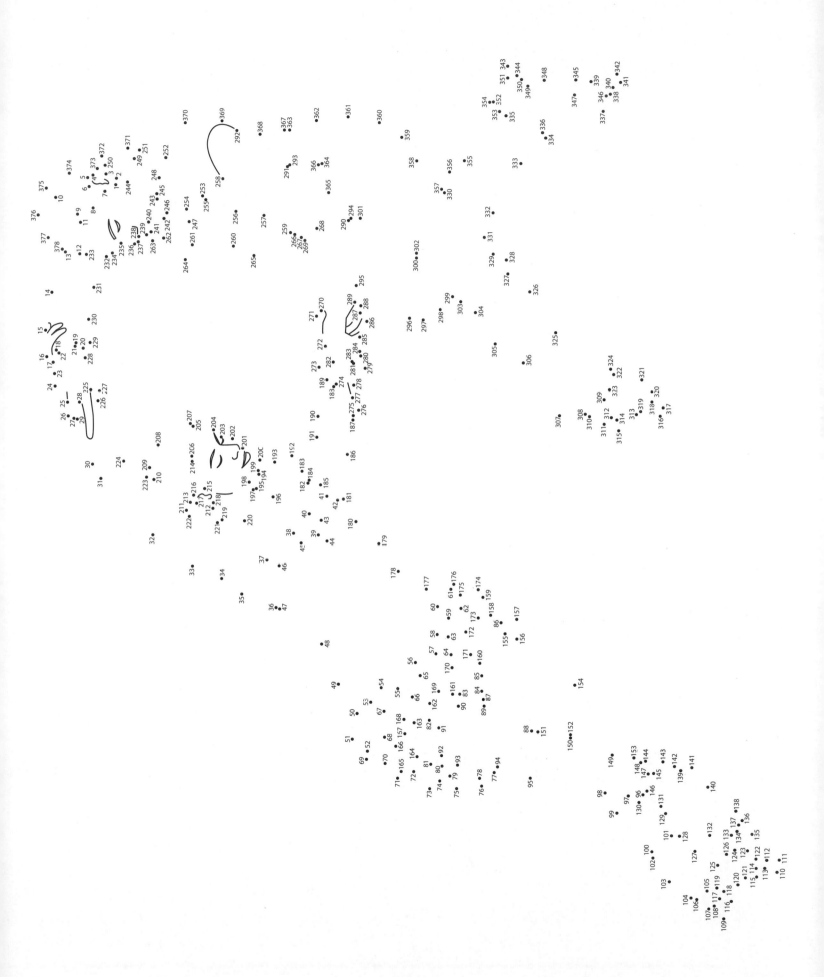

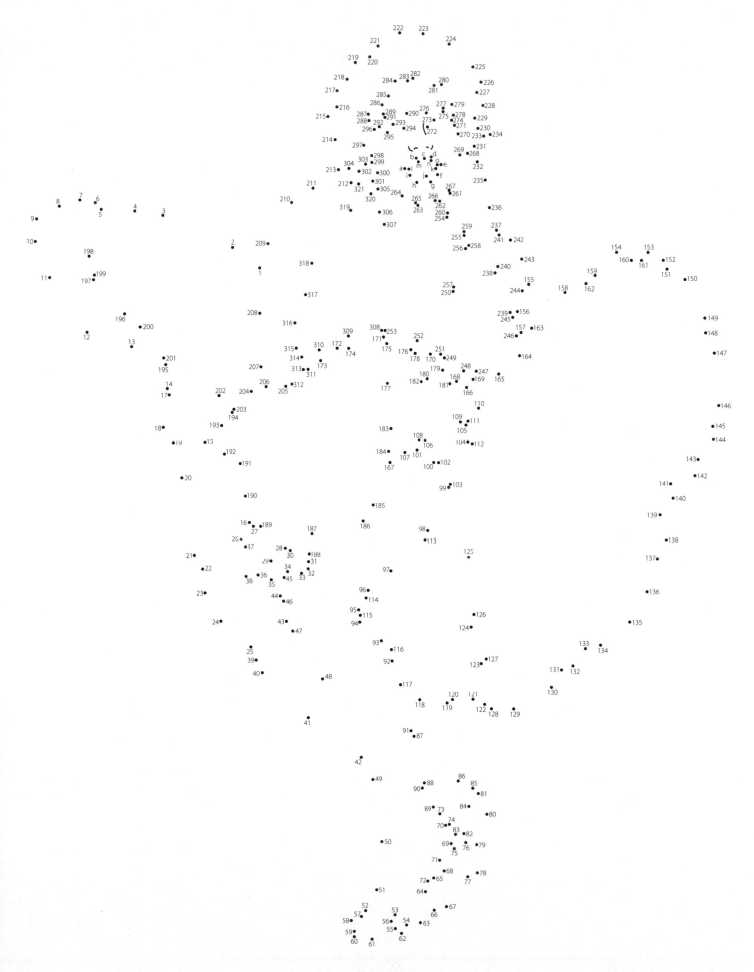

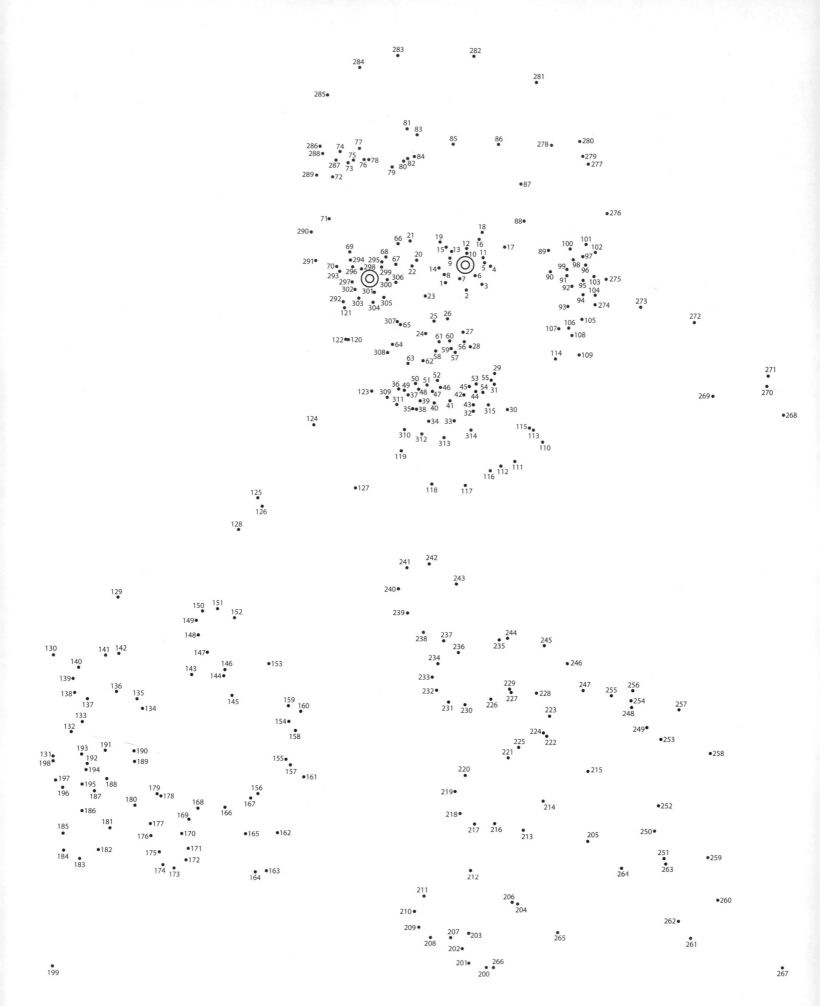

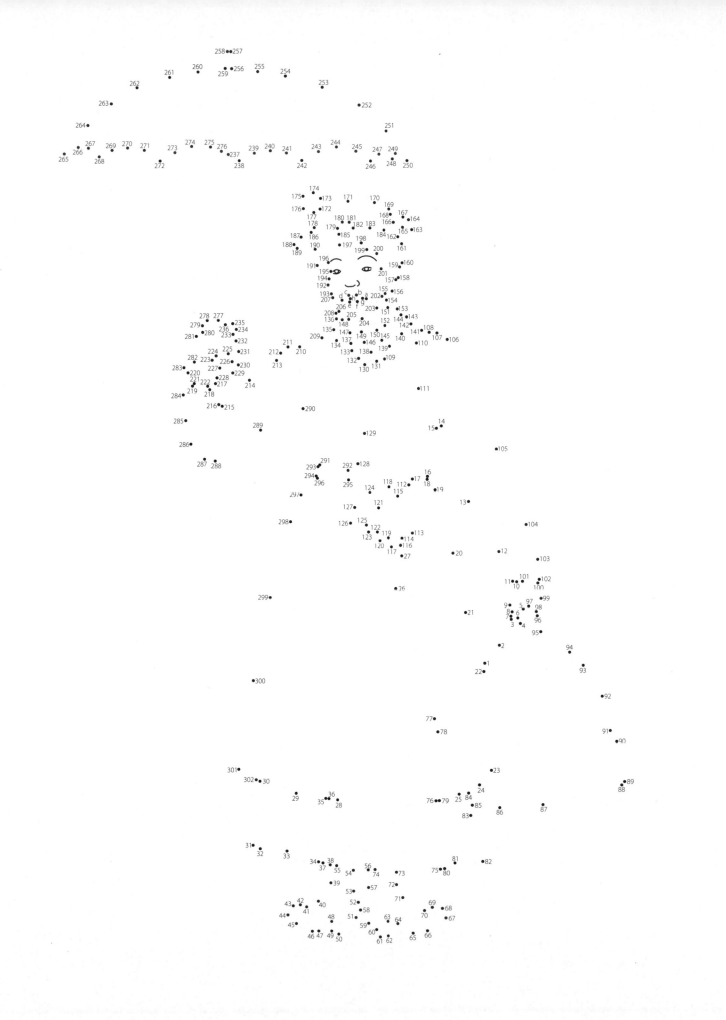

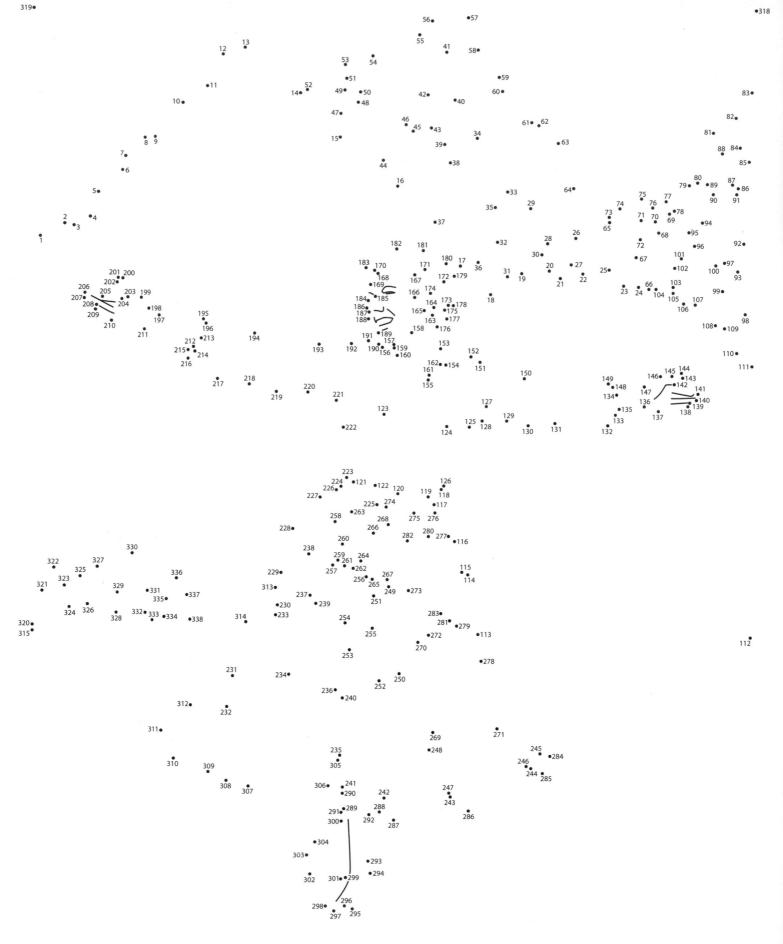

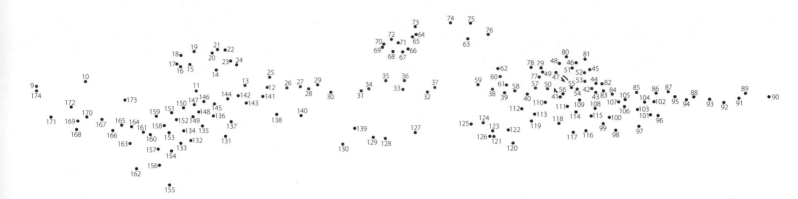

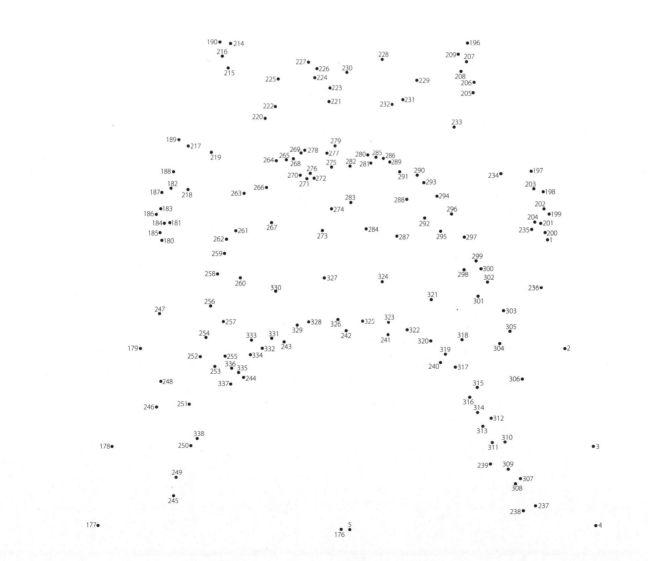

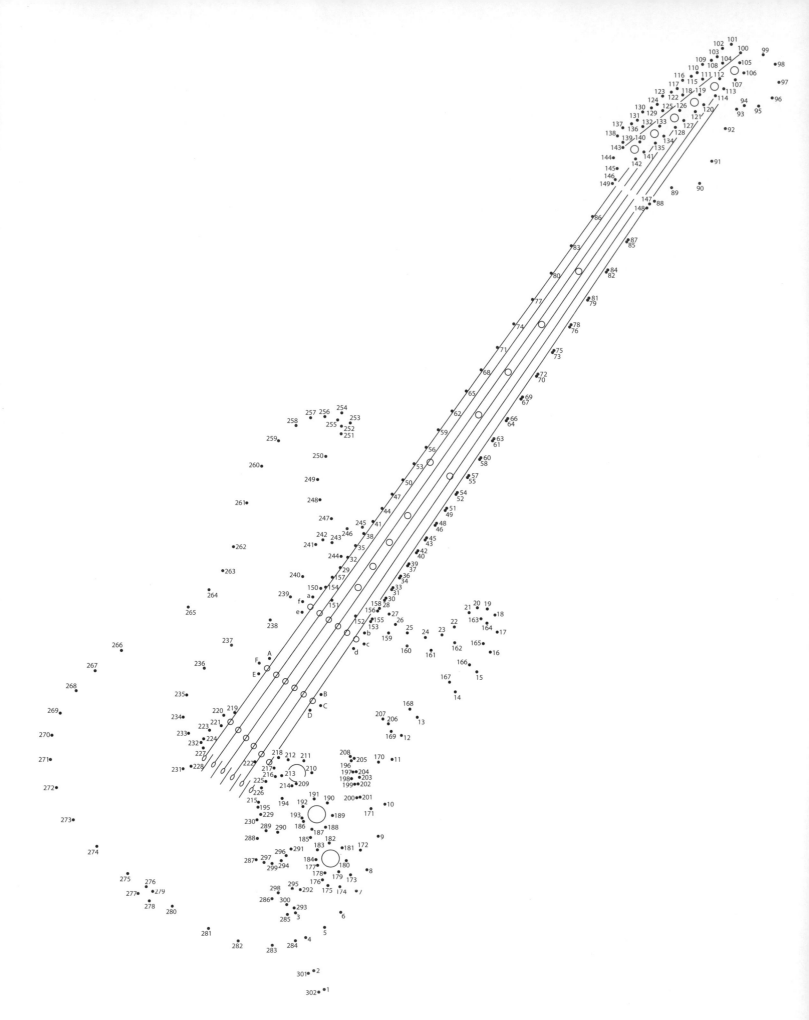

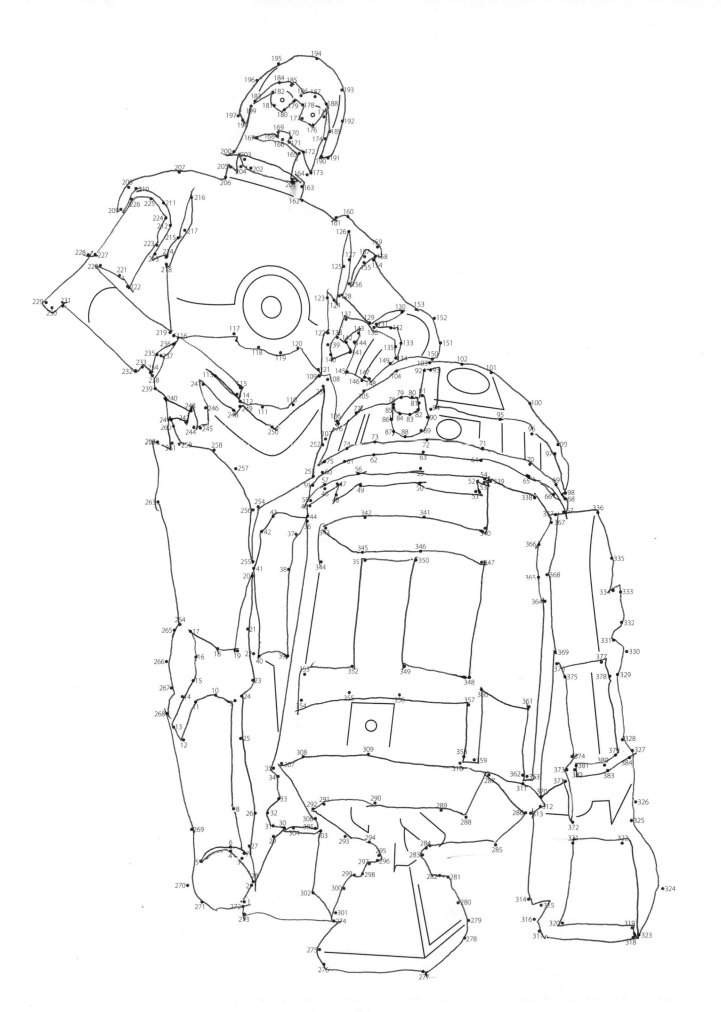

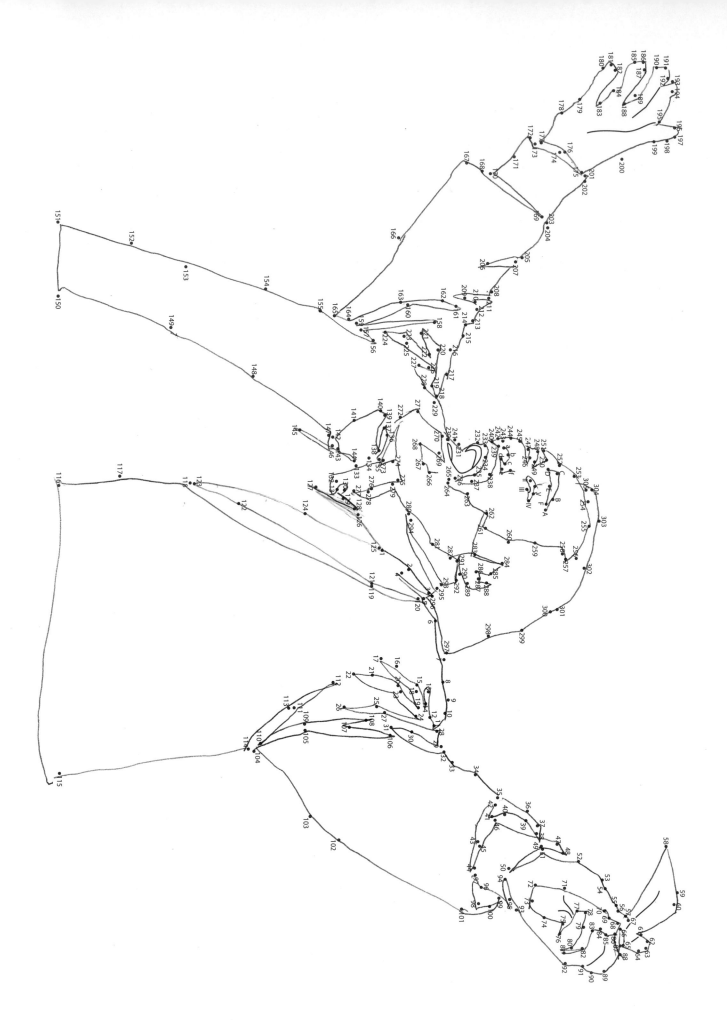

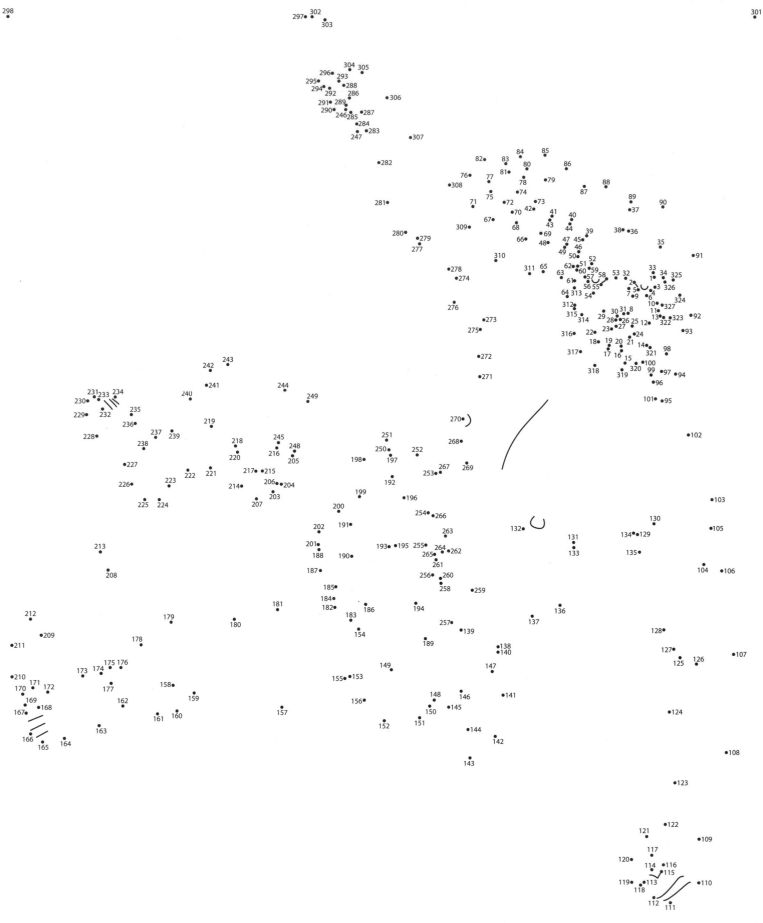

Sport

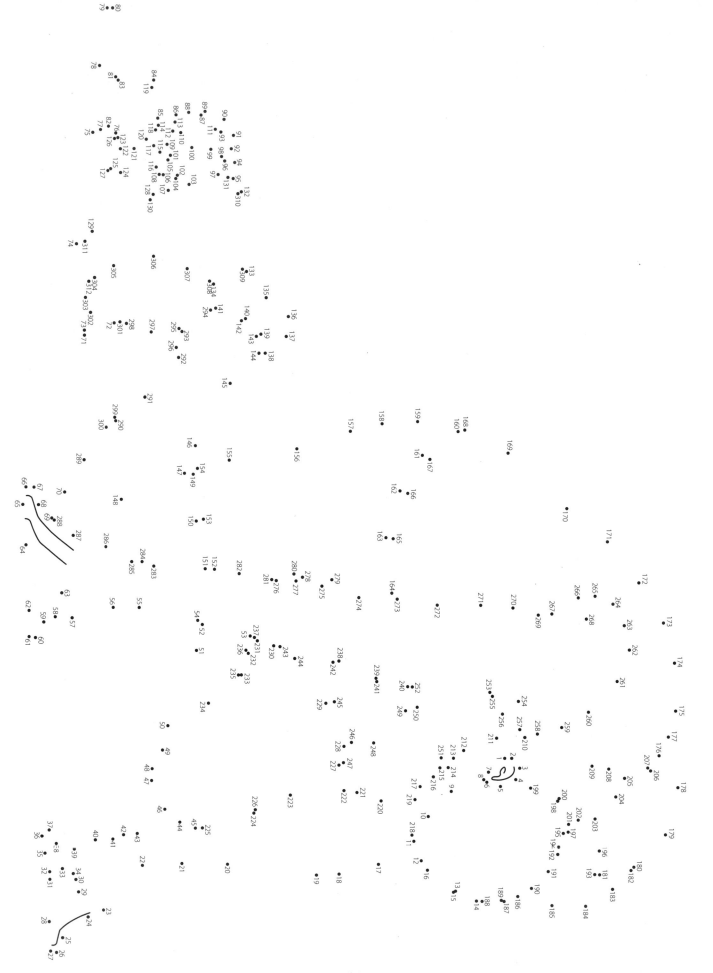

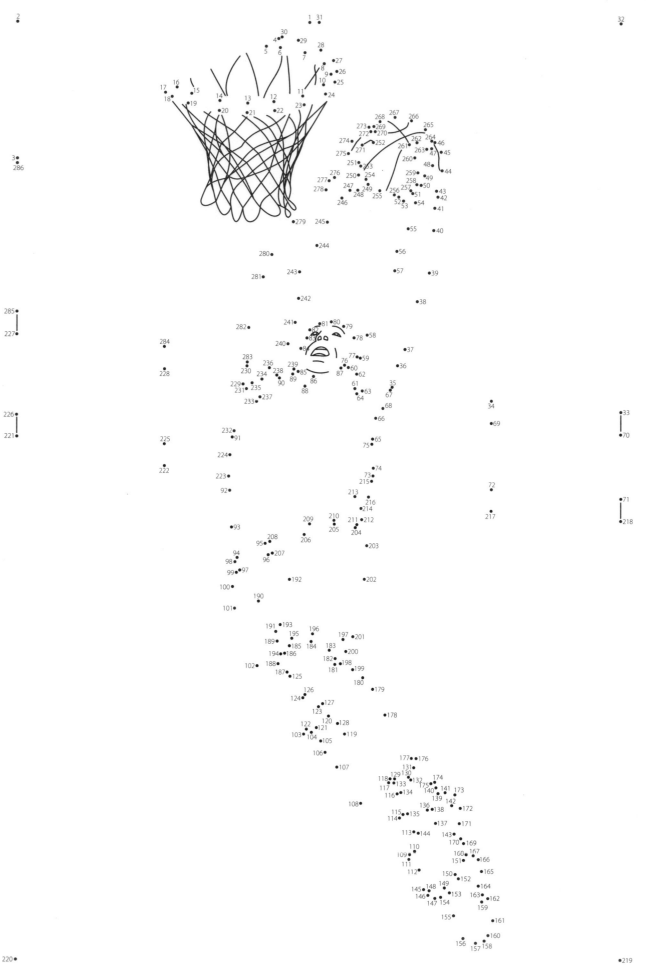

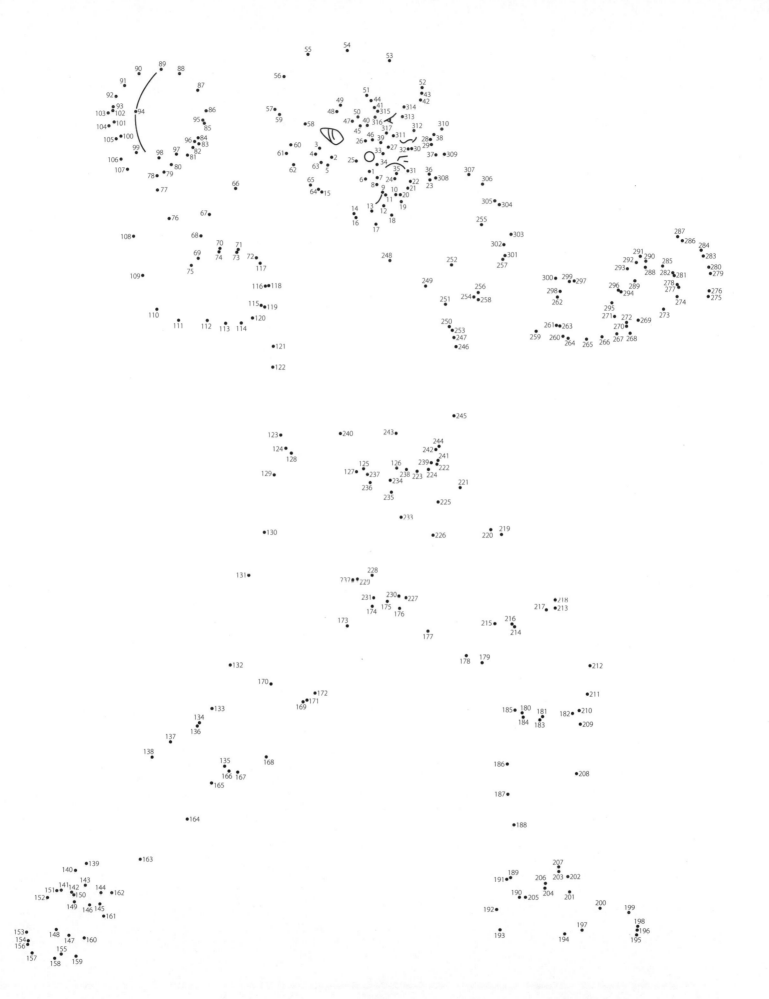

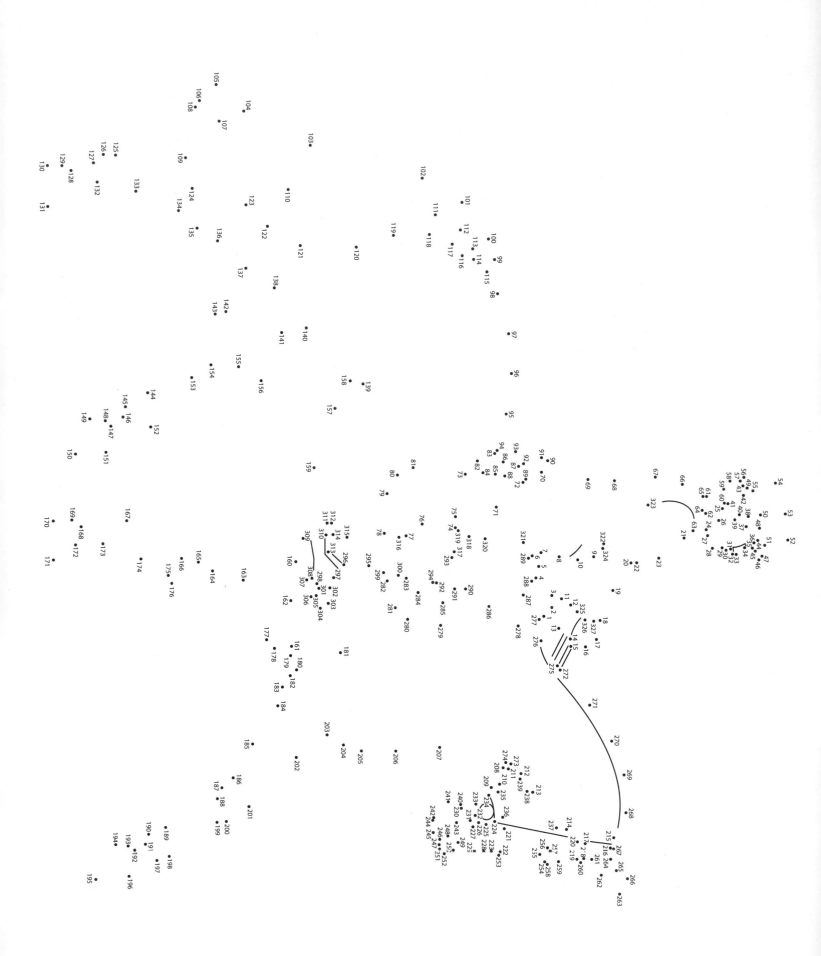

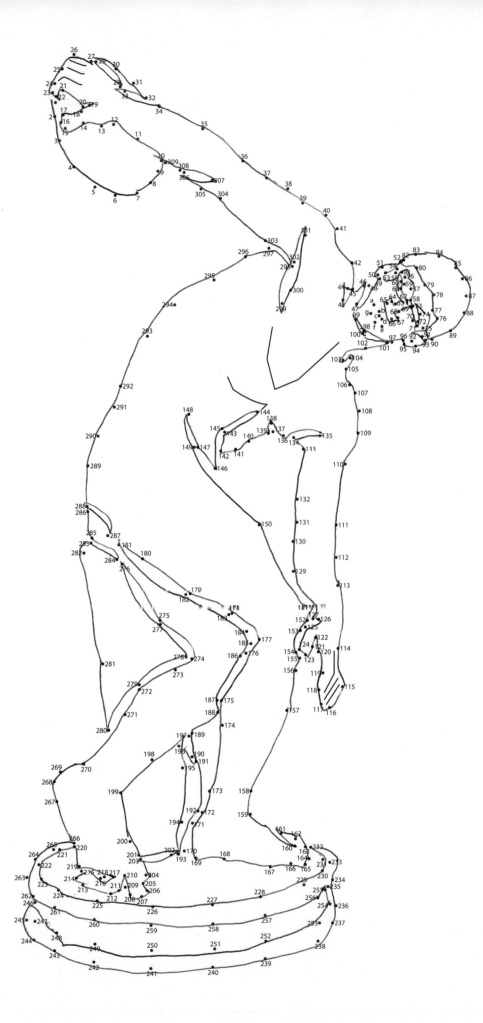

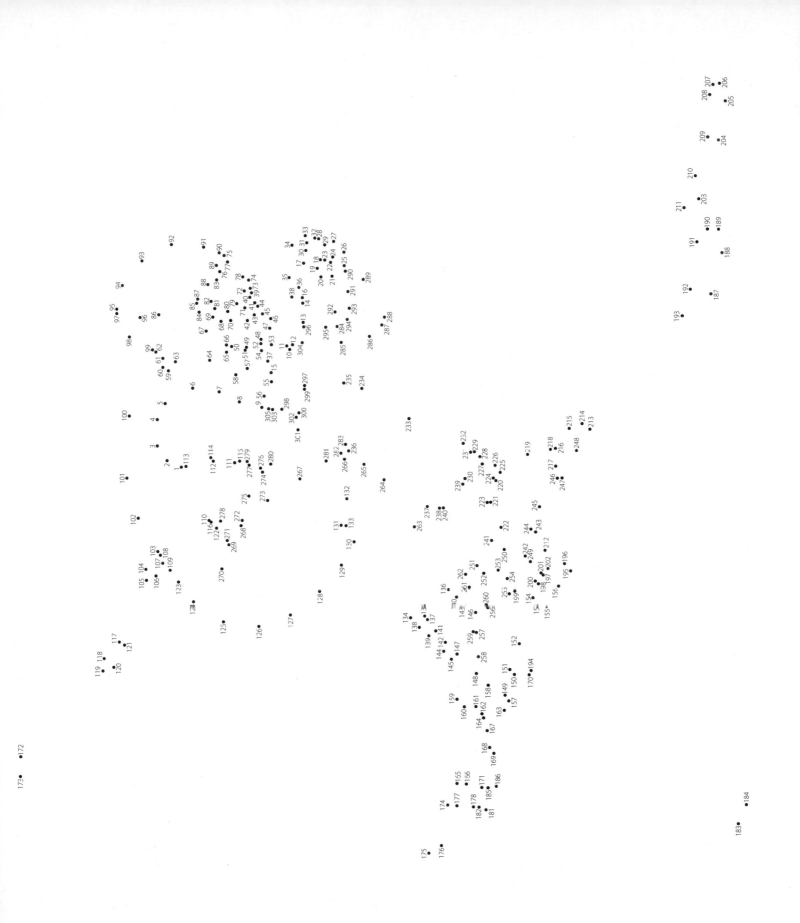

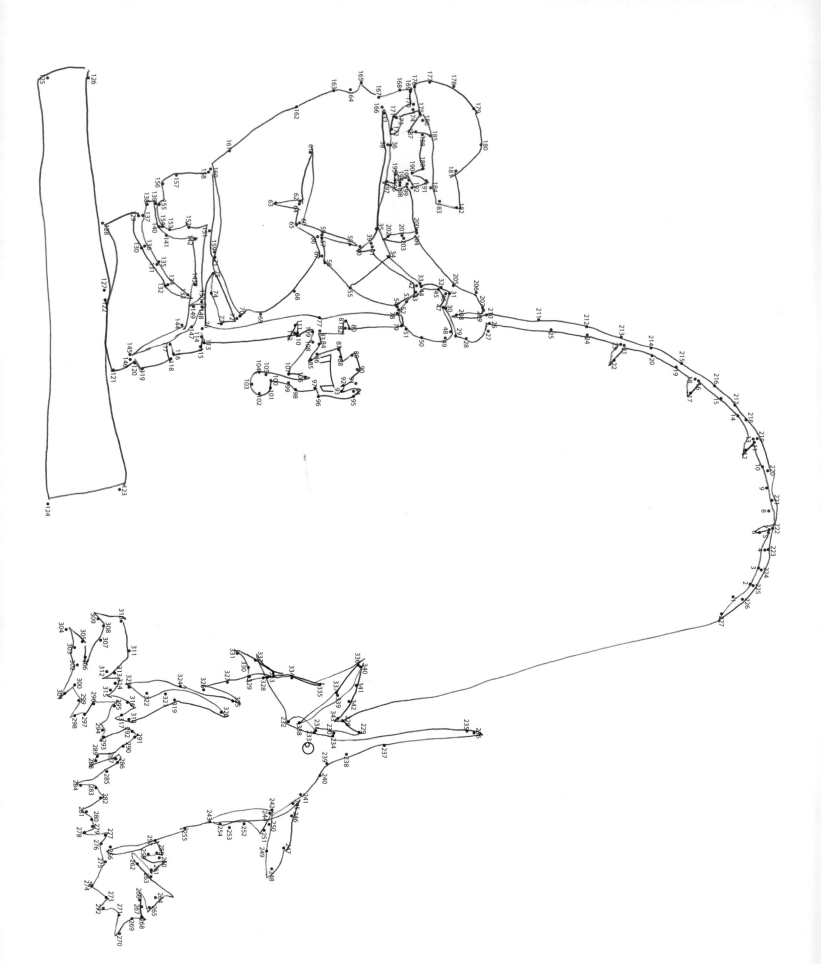

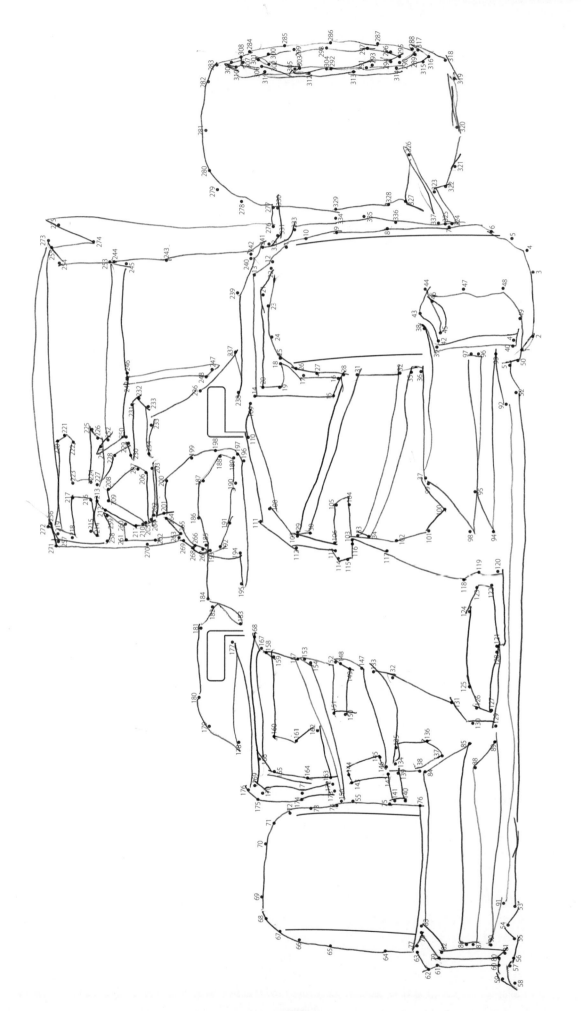

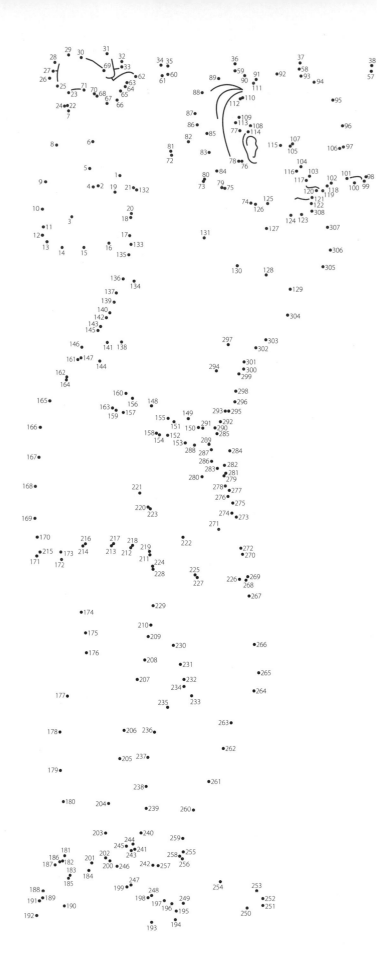

194

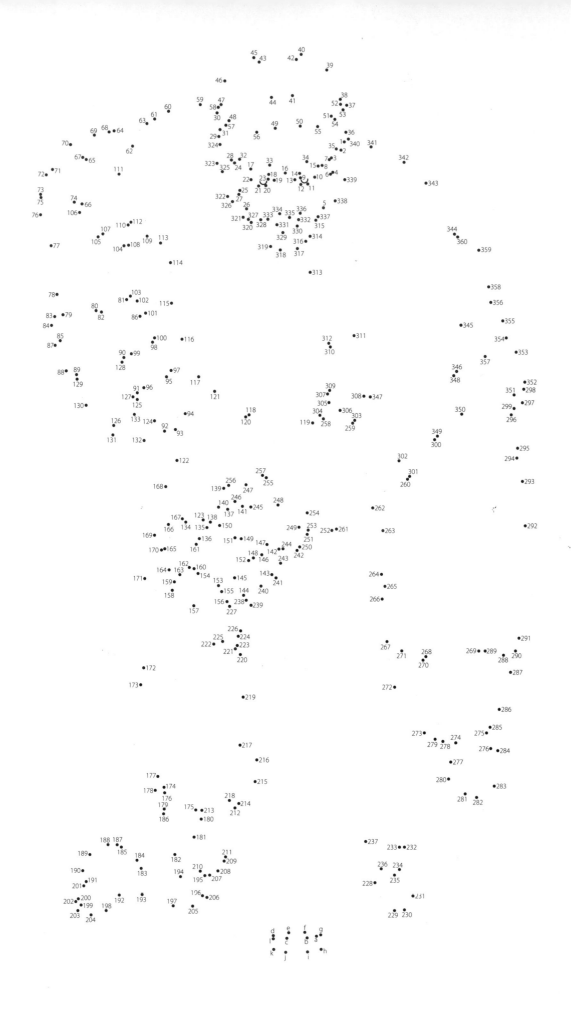

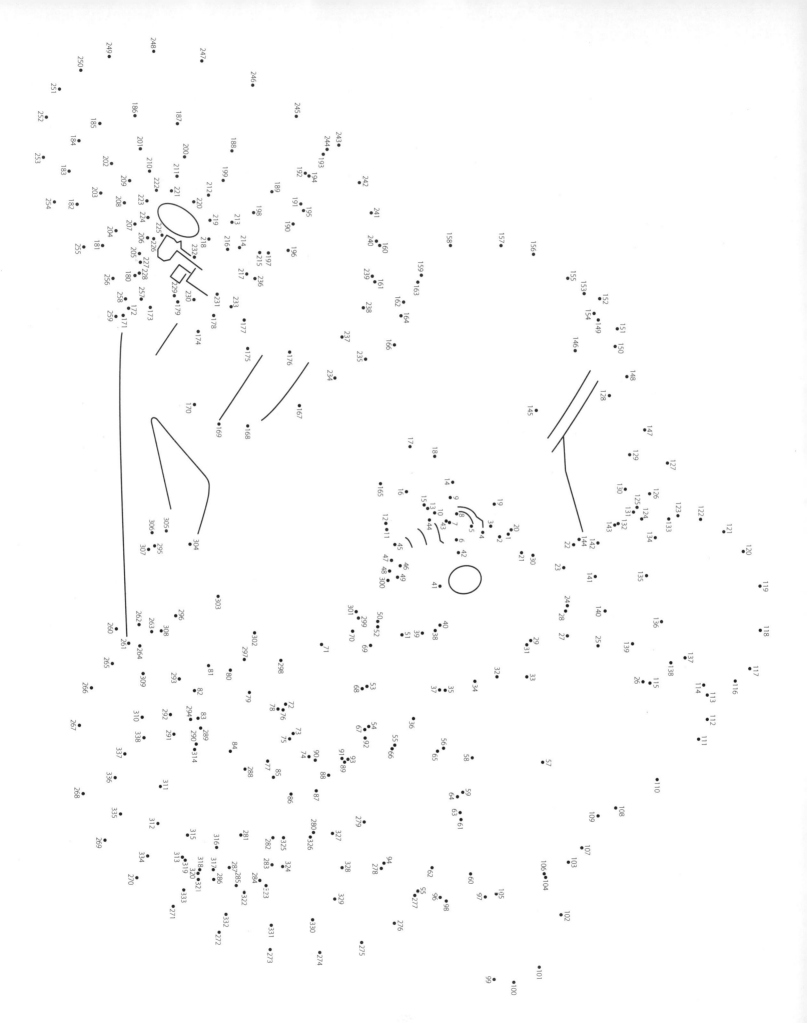

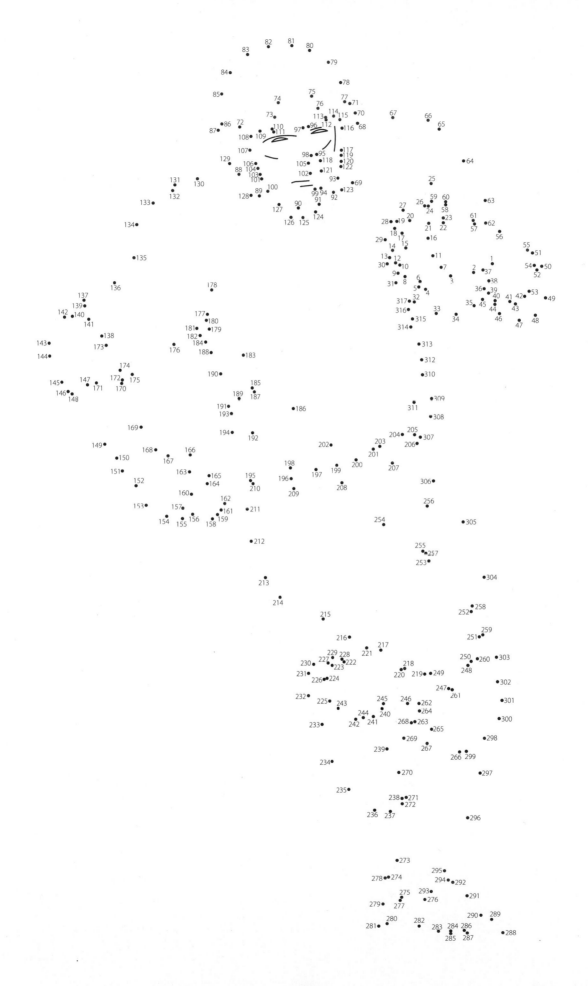

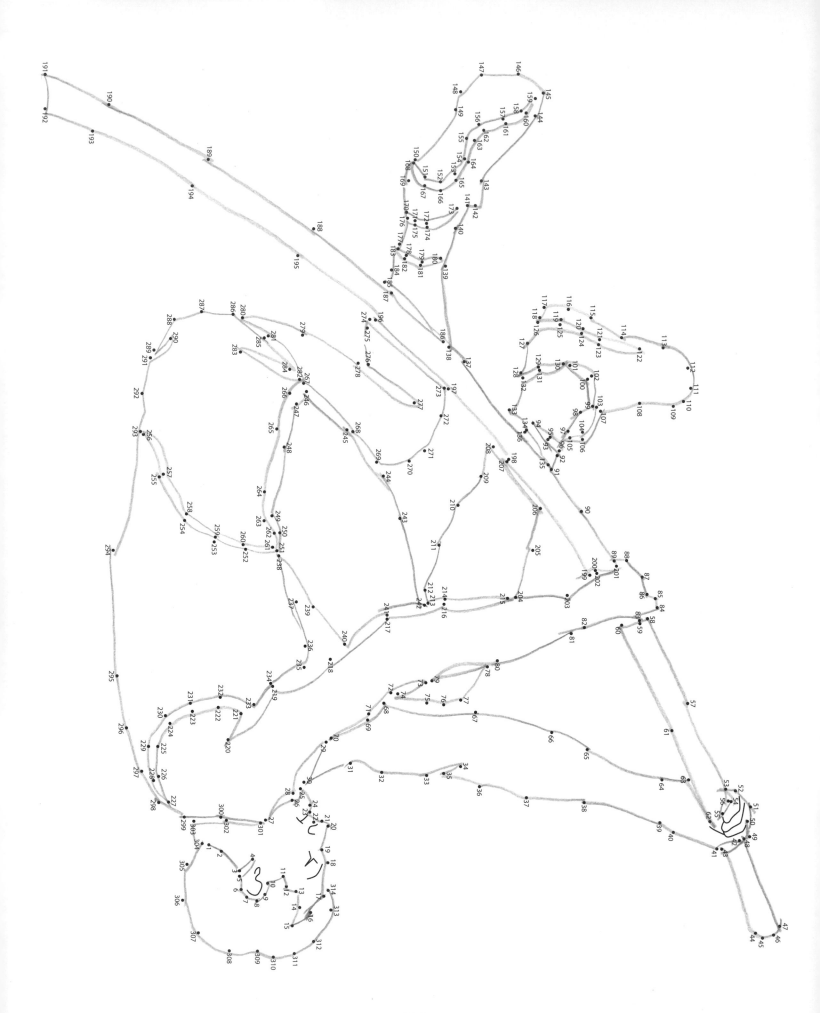

201

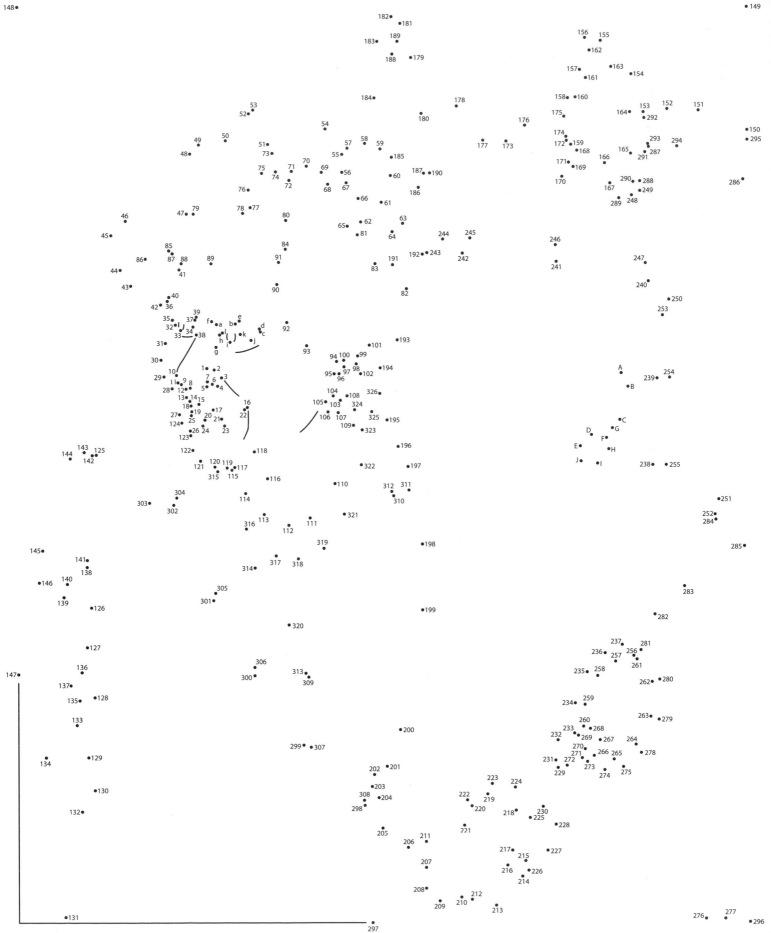

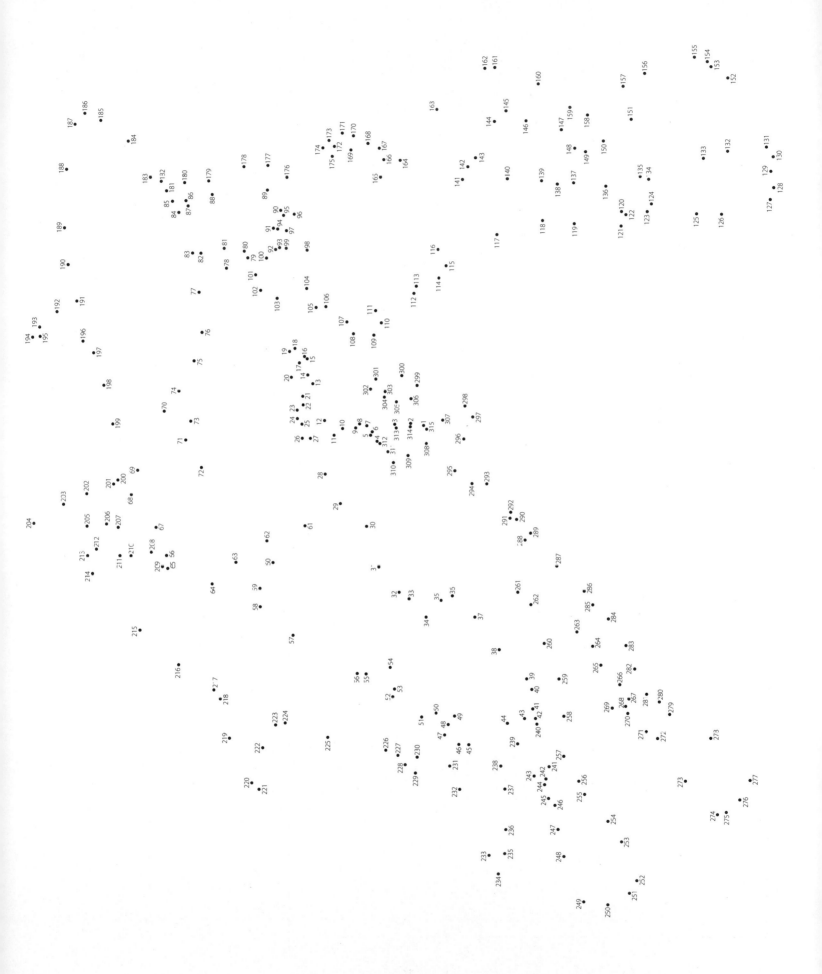

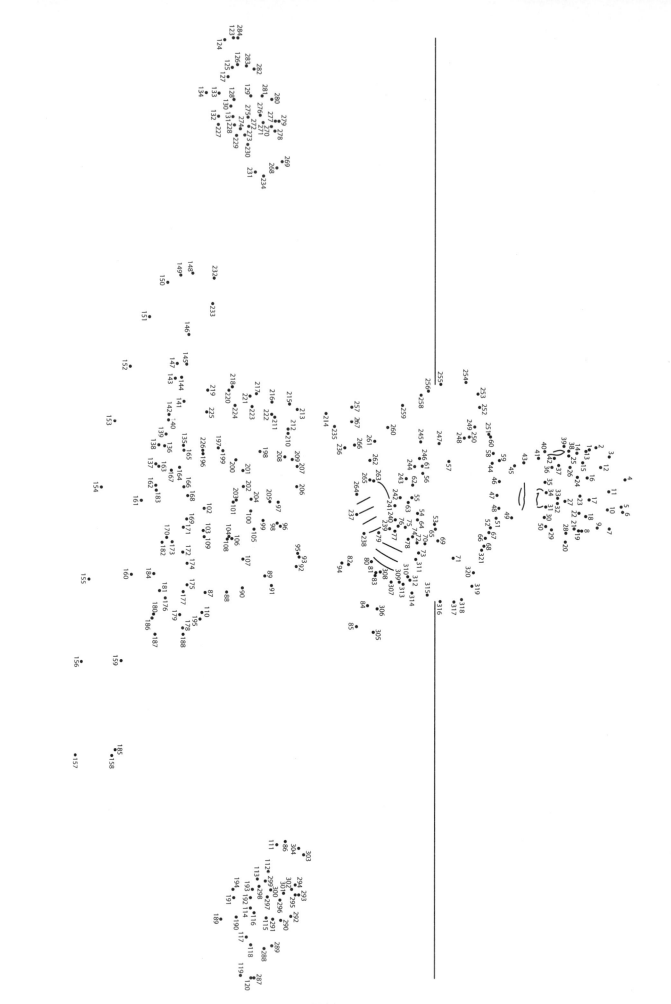

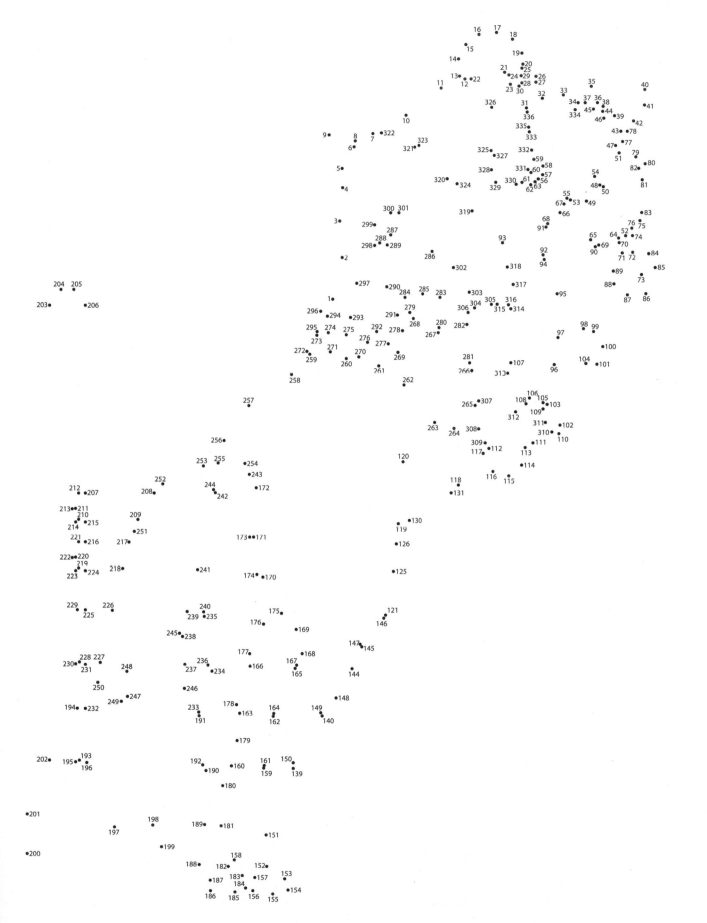

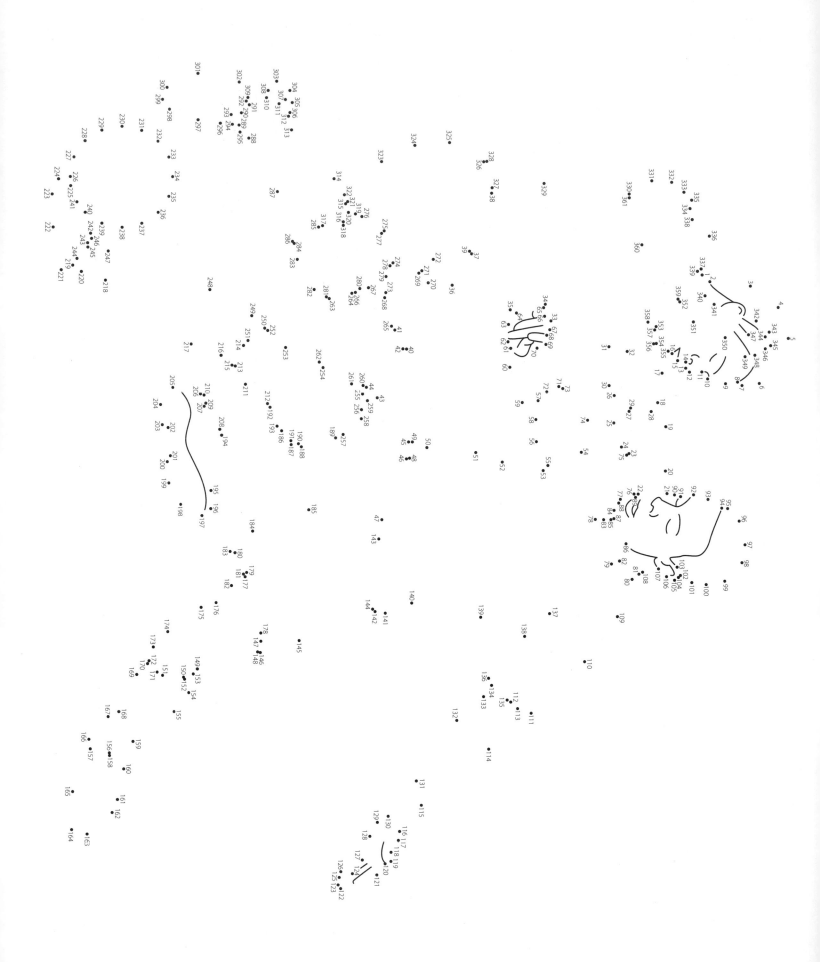

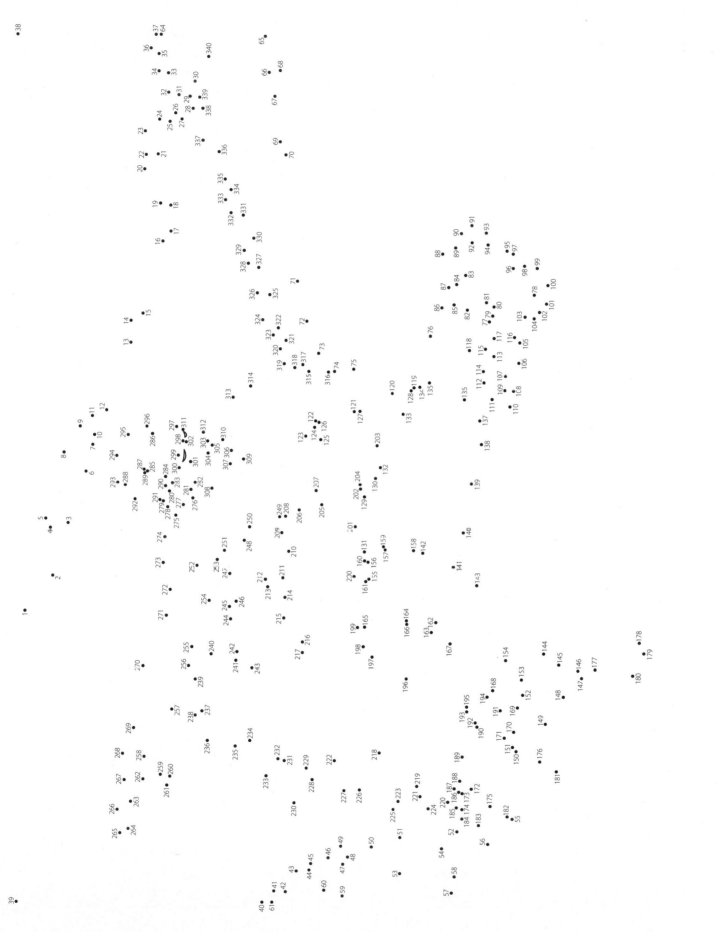

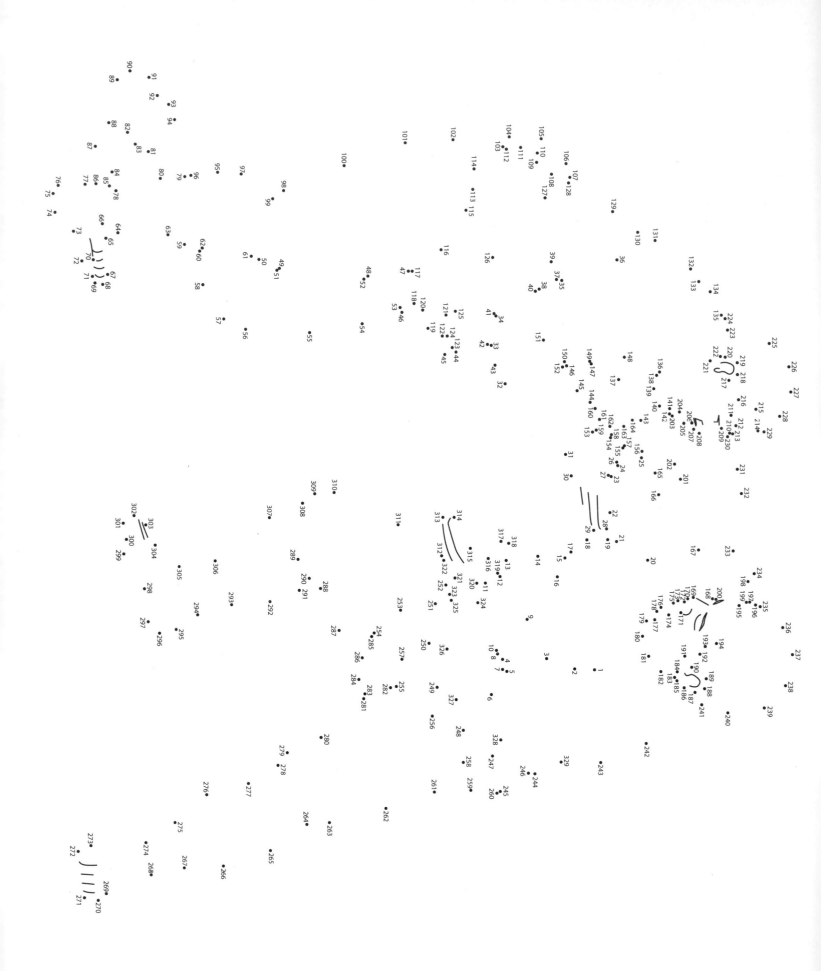

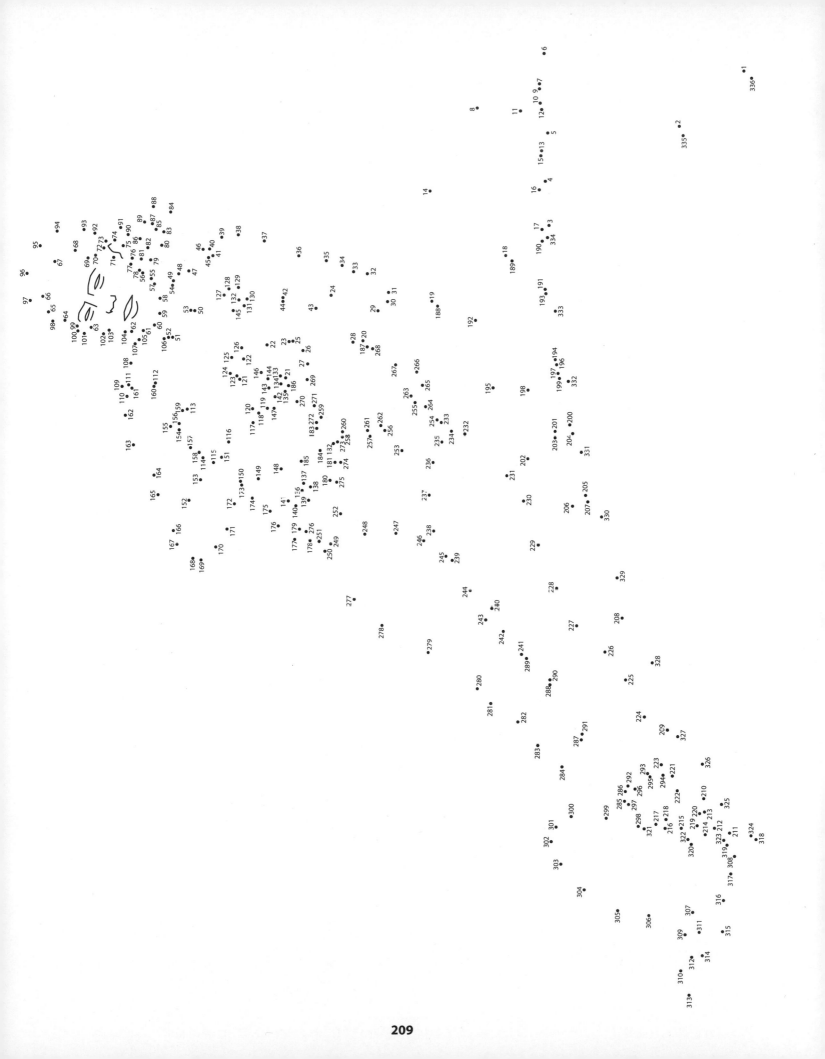

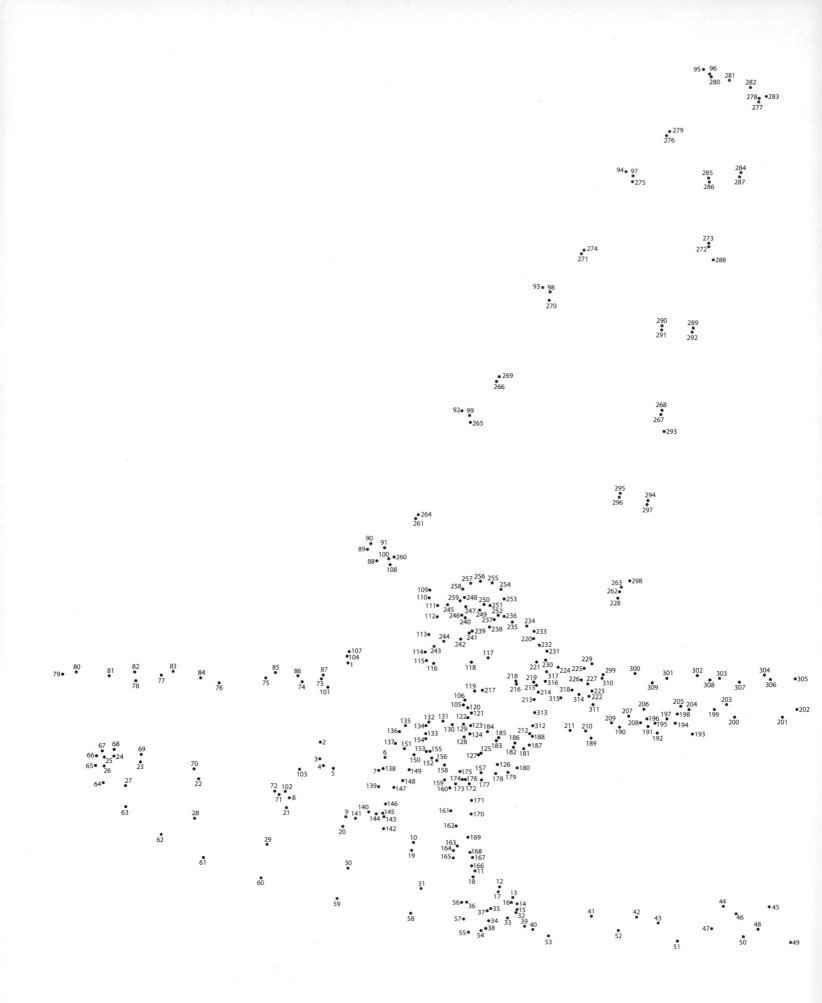

Air, Land & Sea

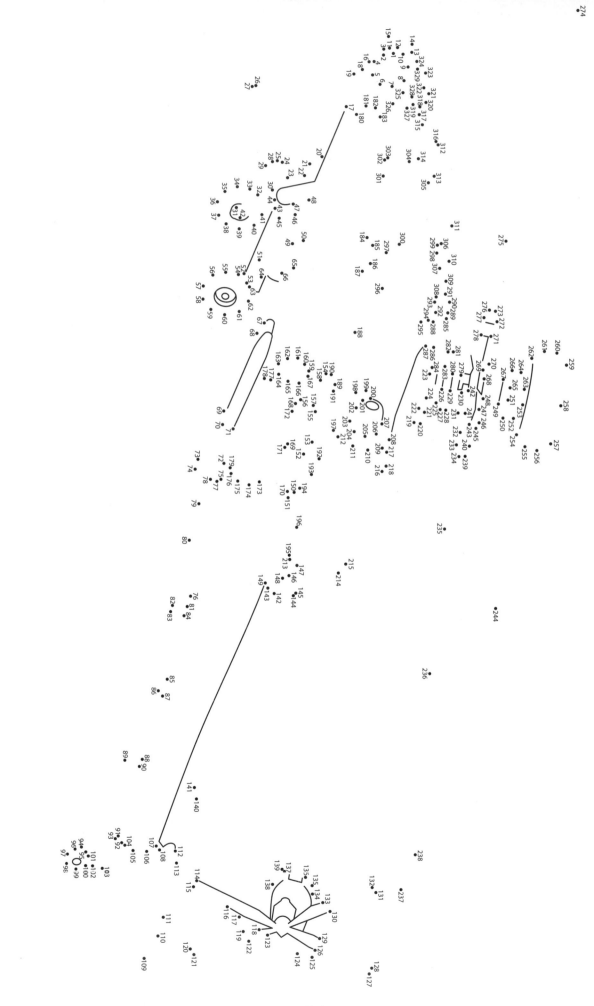

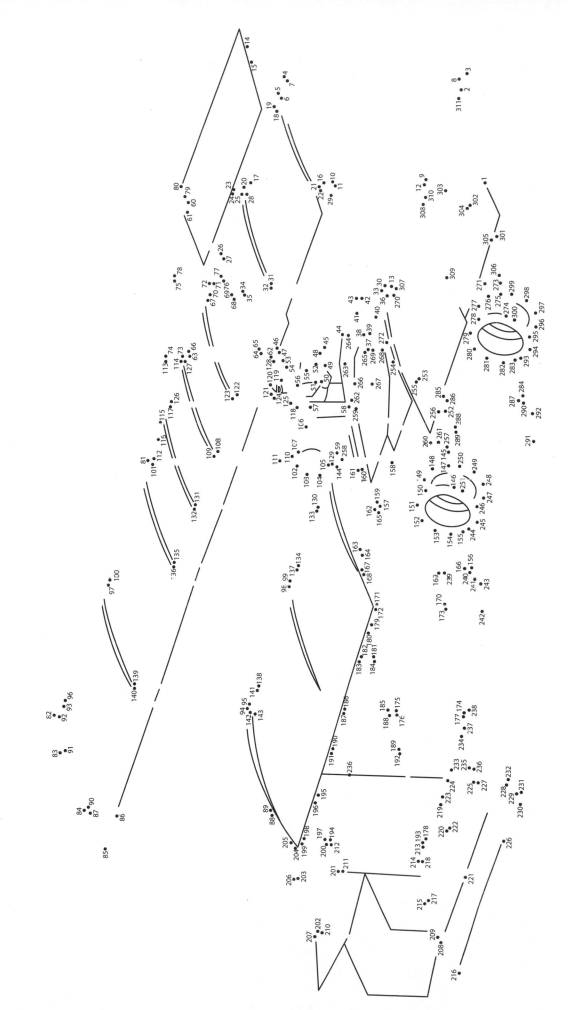

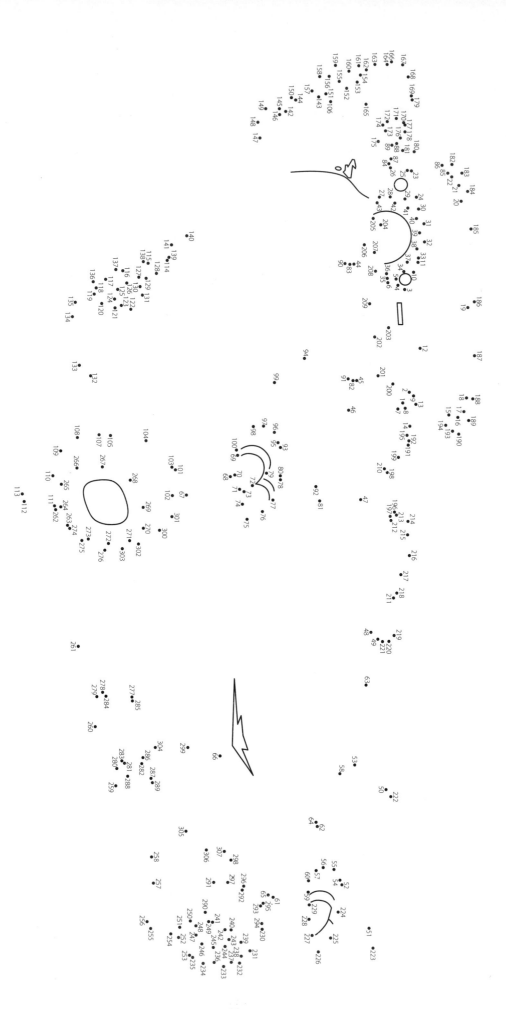

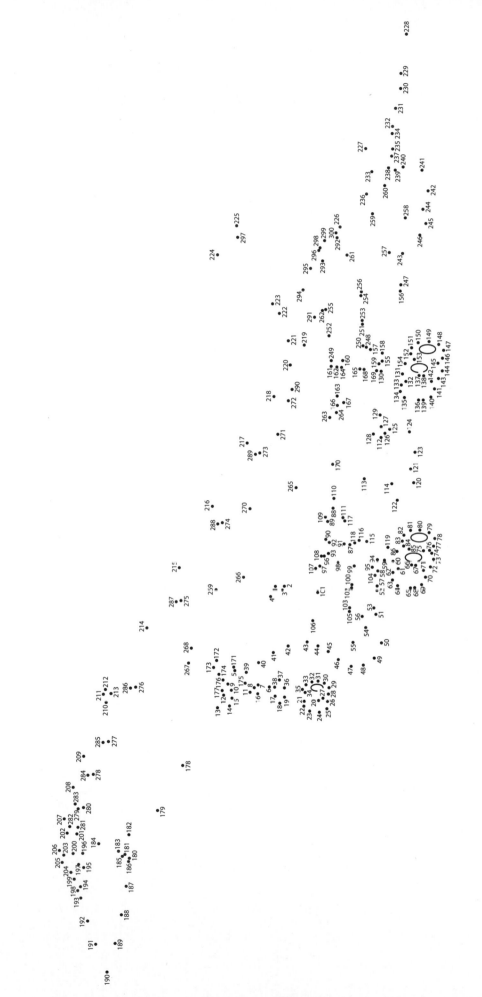

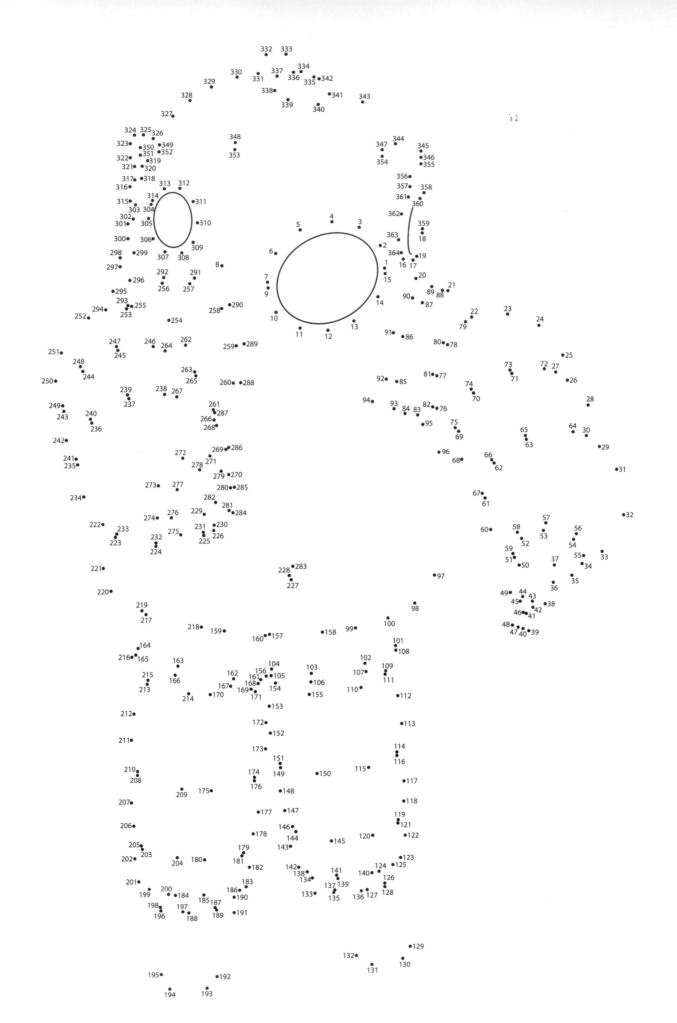

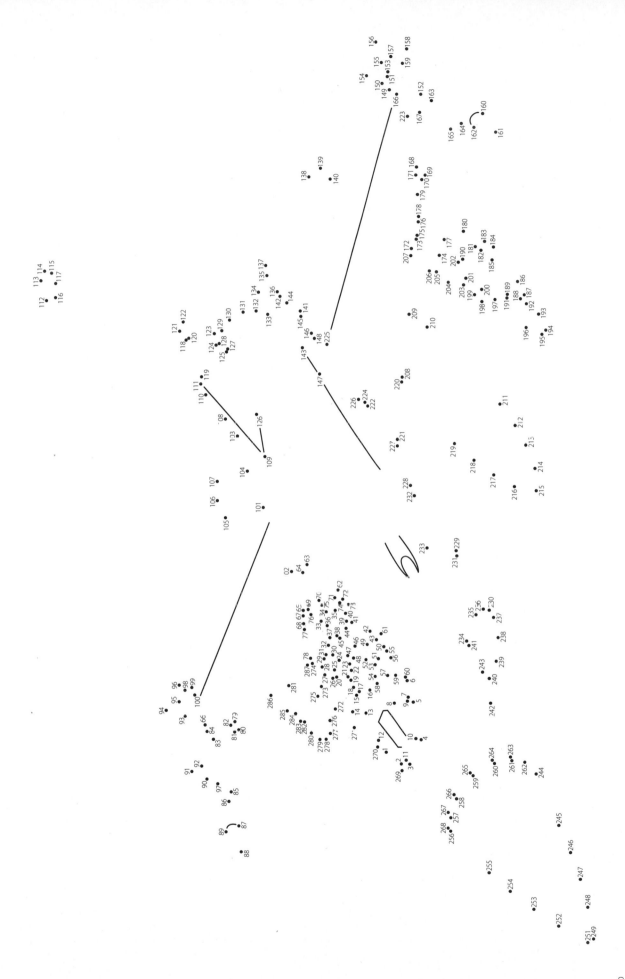

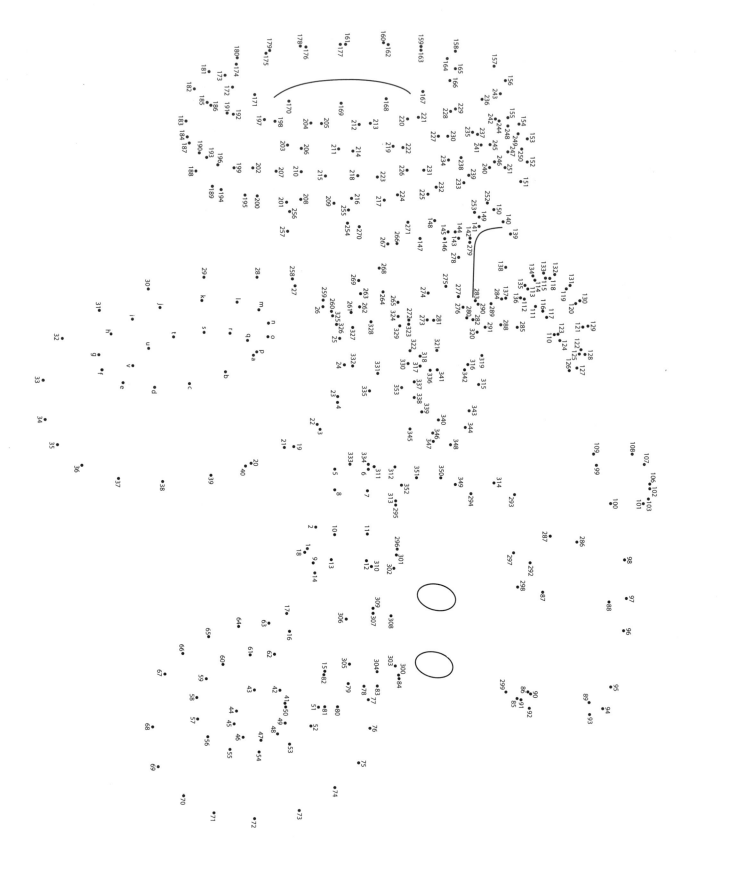

218

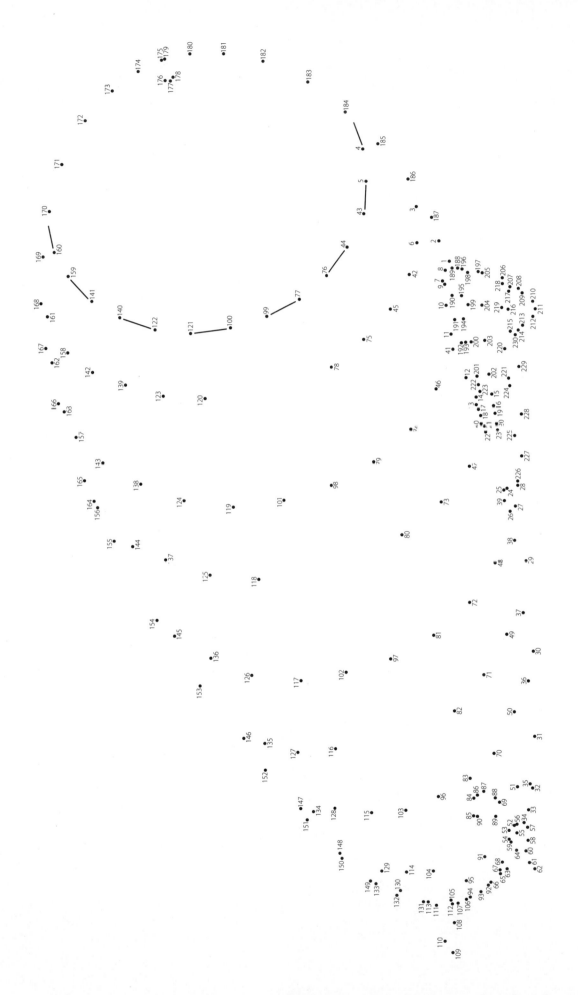

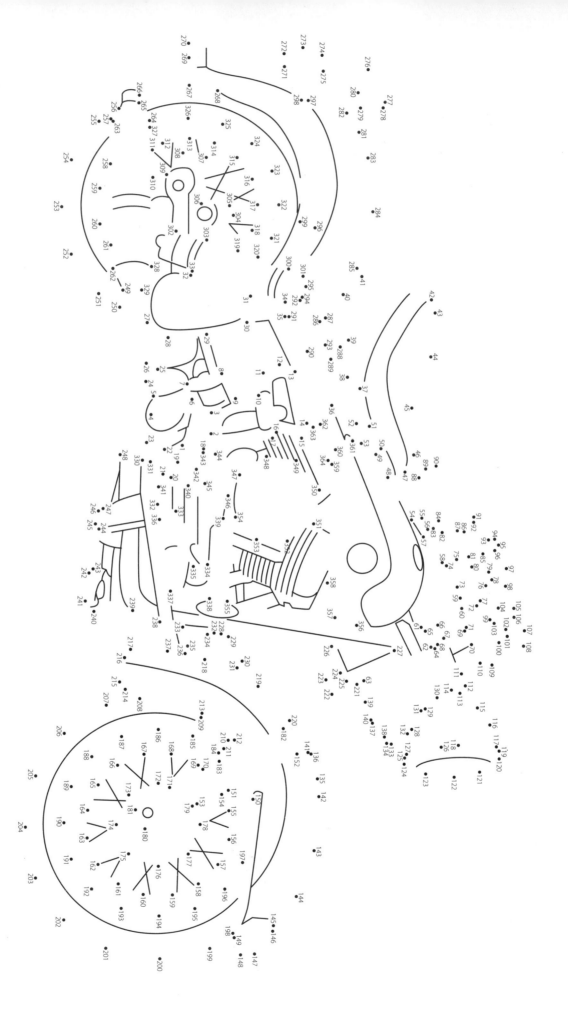

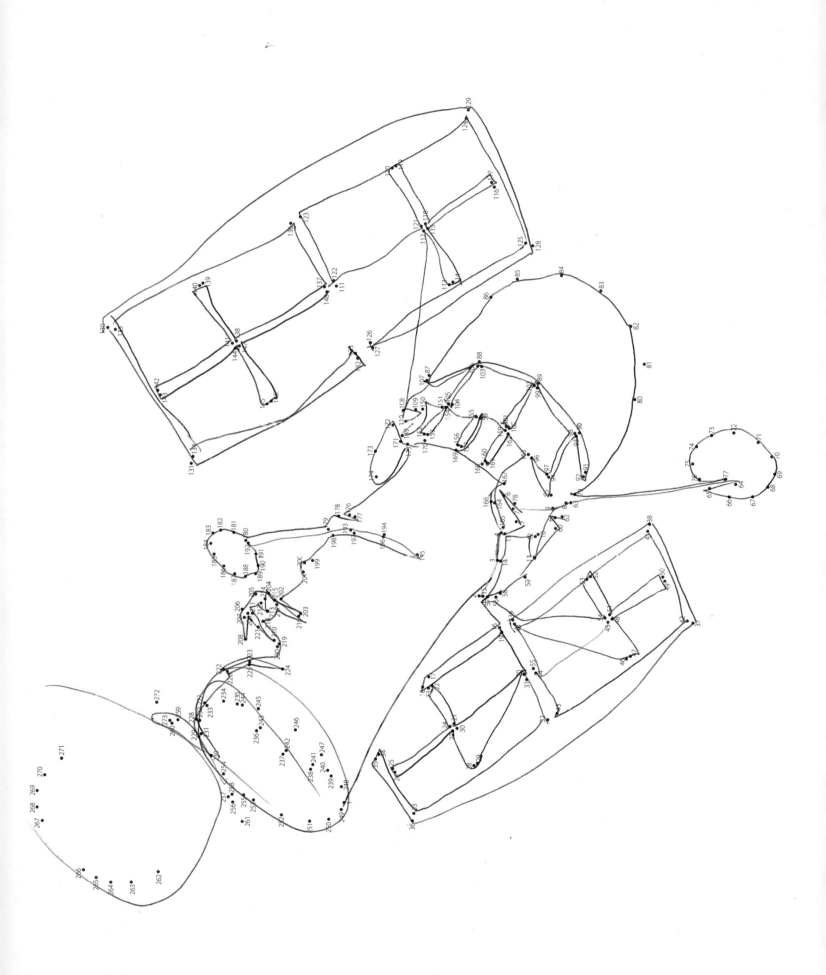

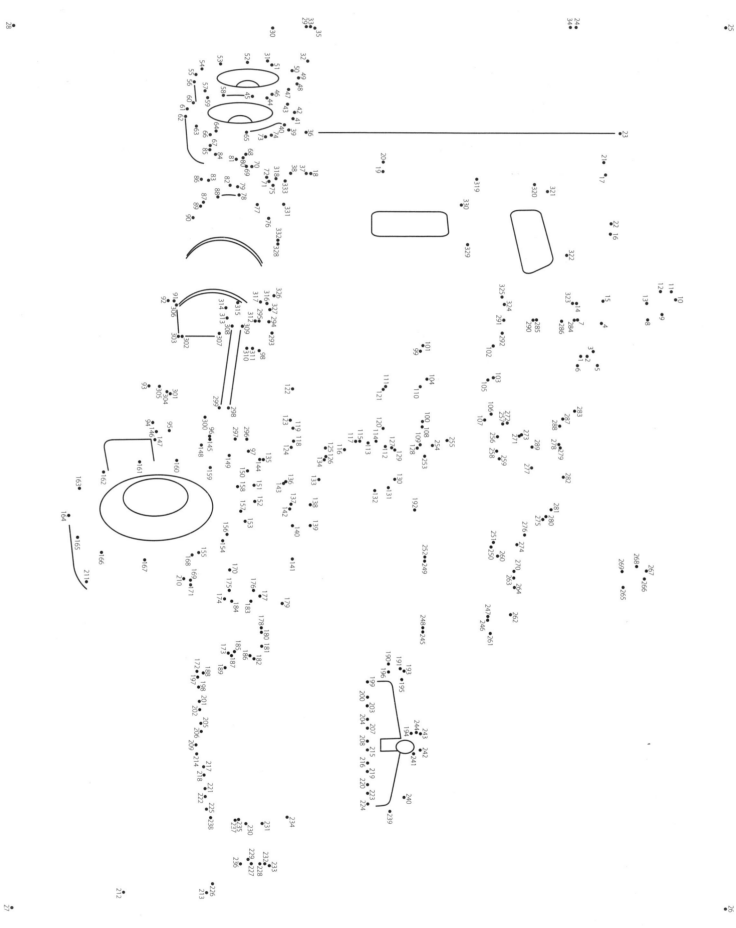

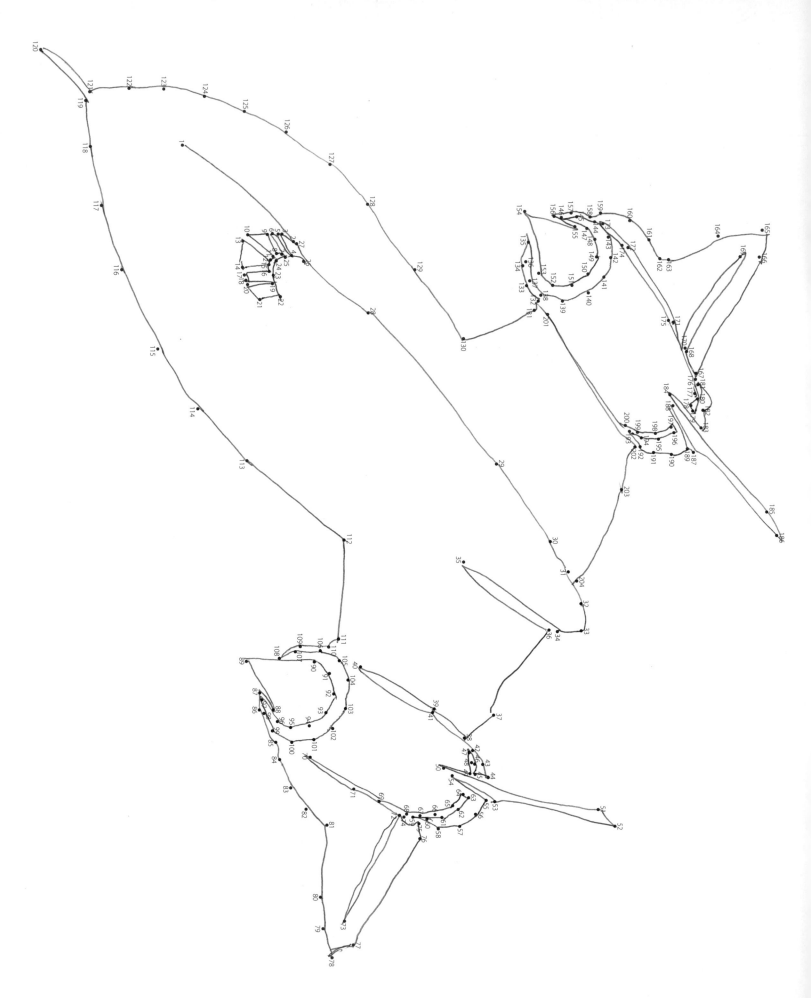

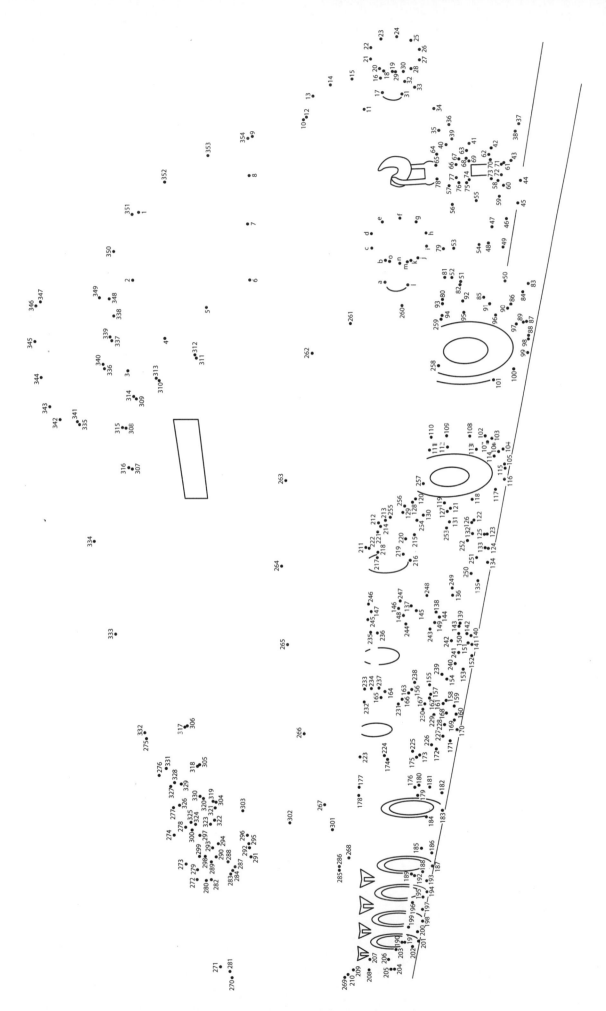

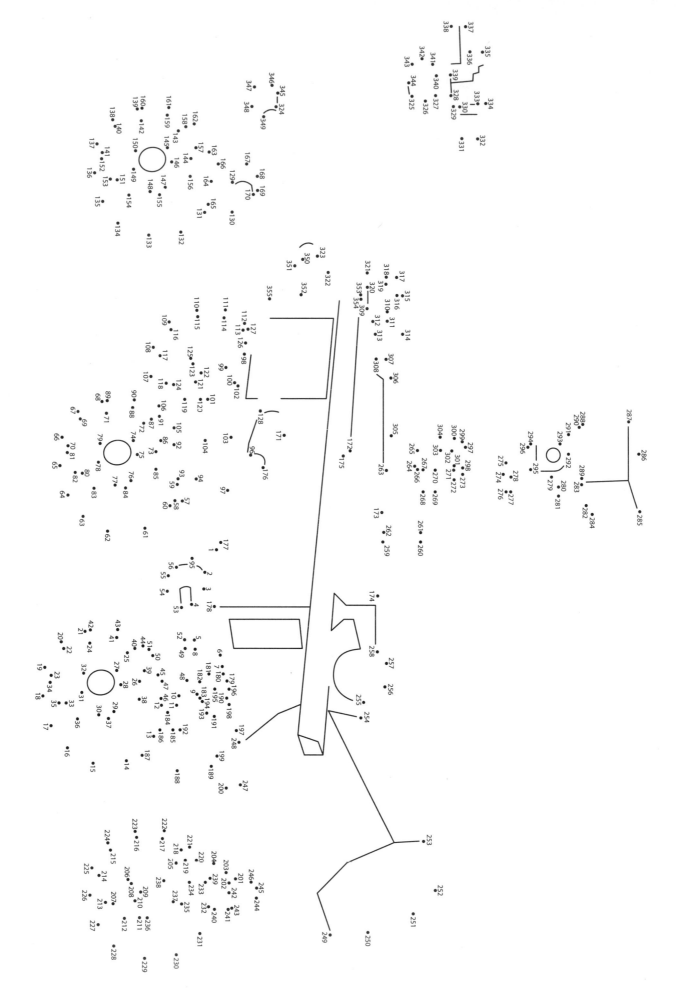

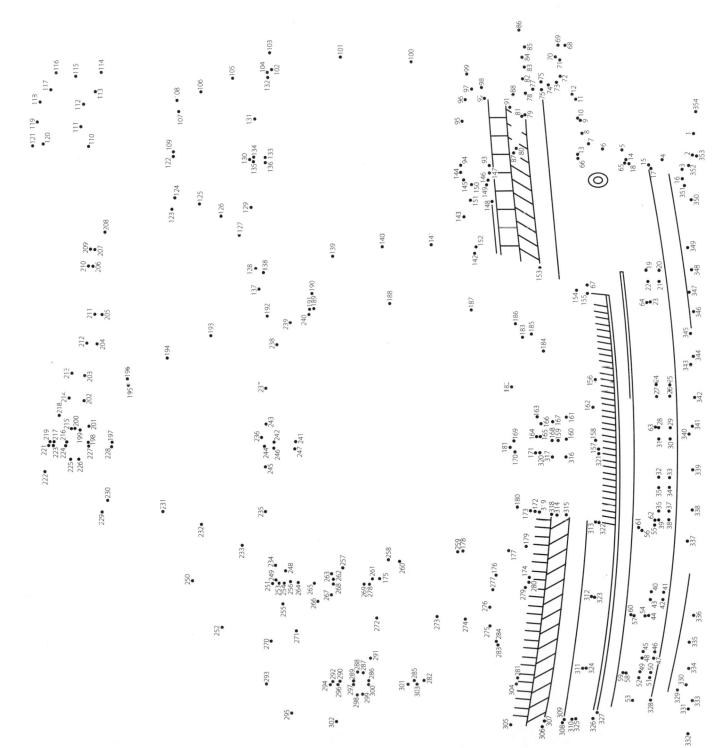

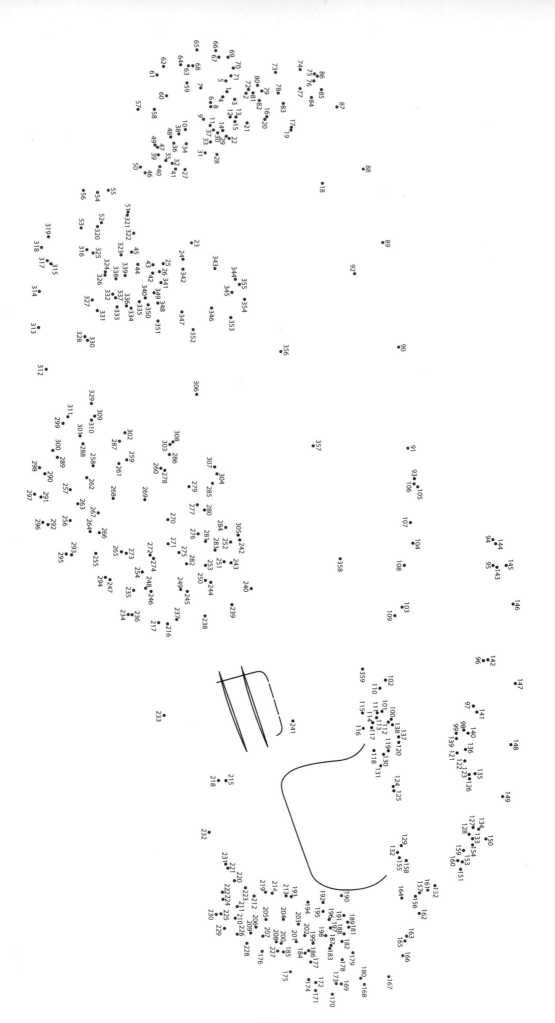

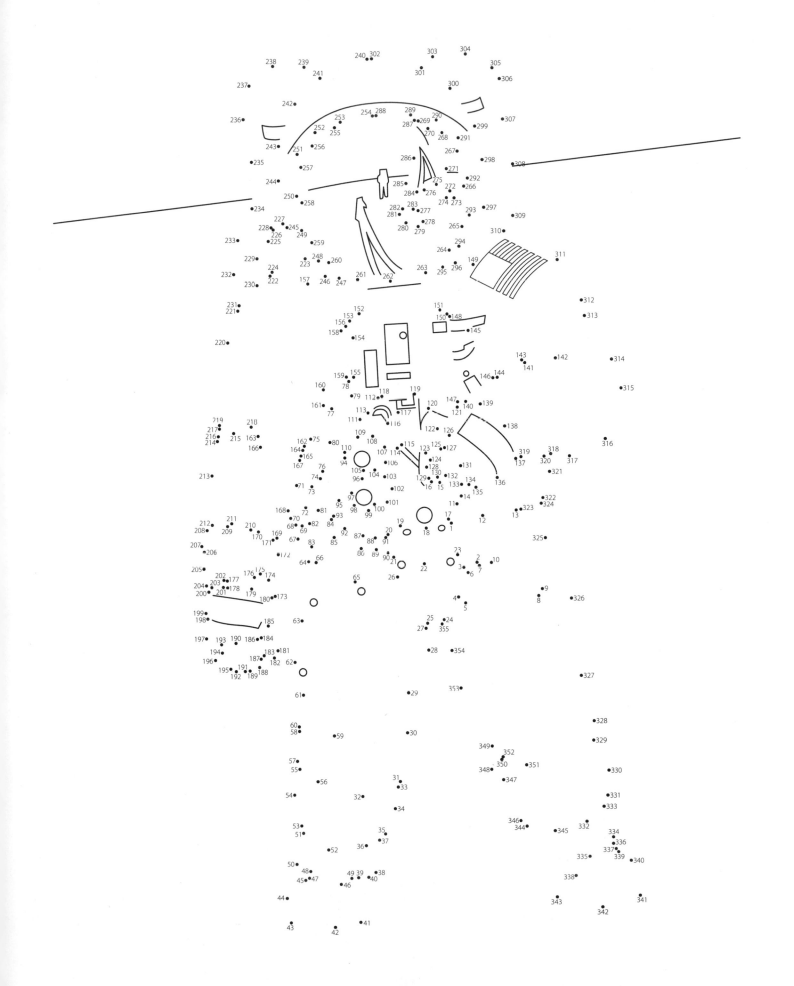

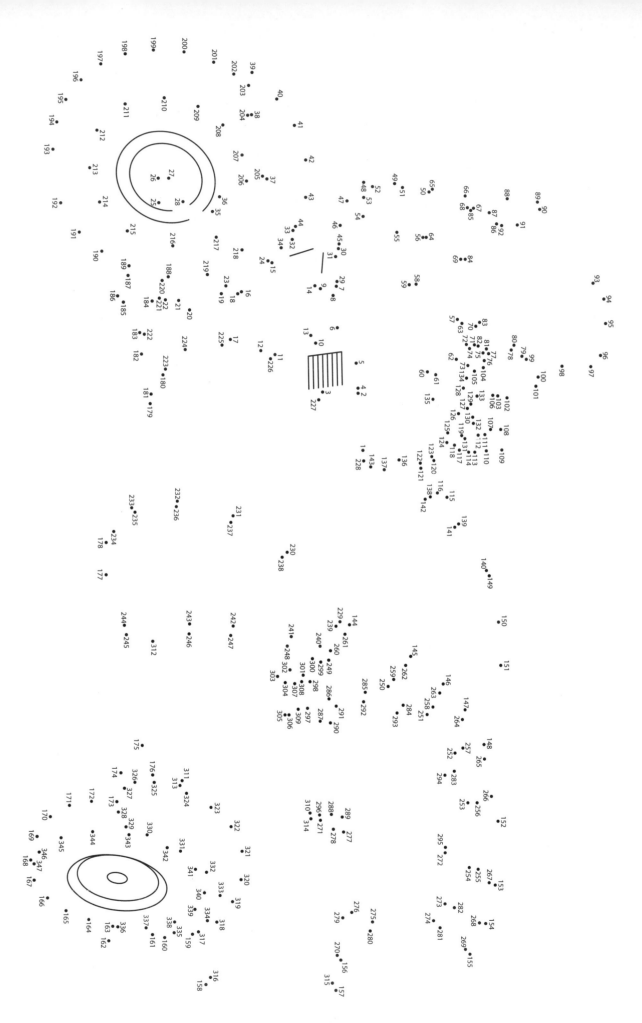

231

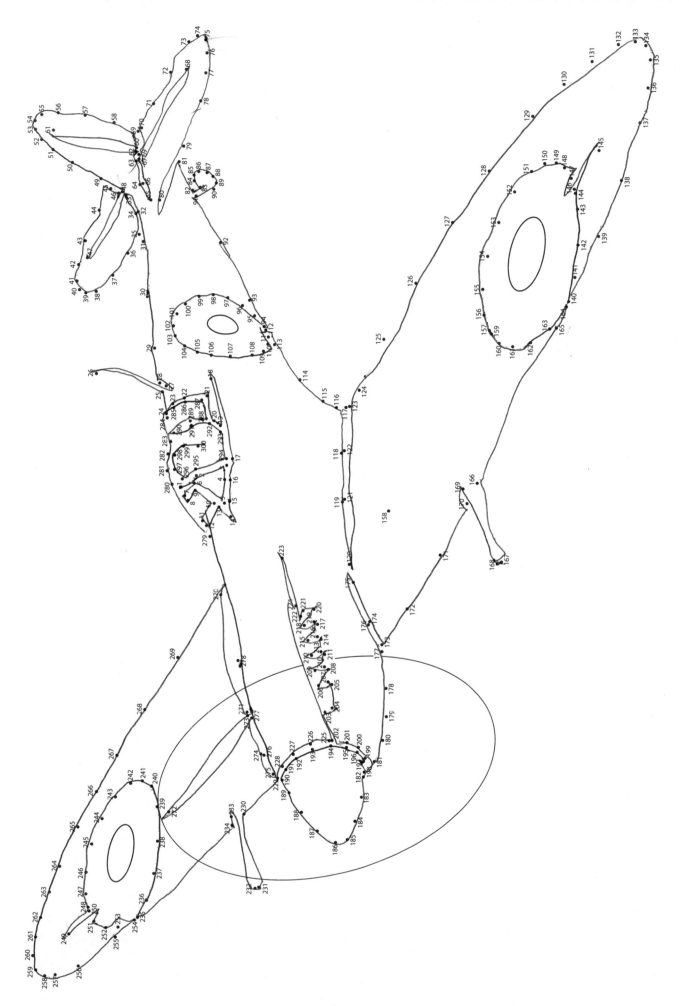

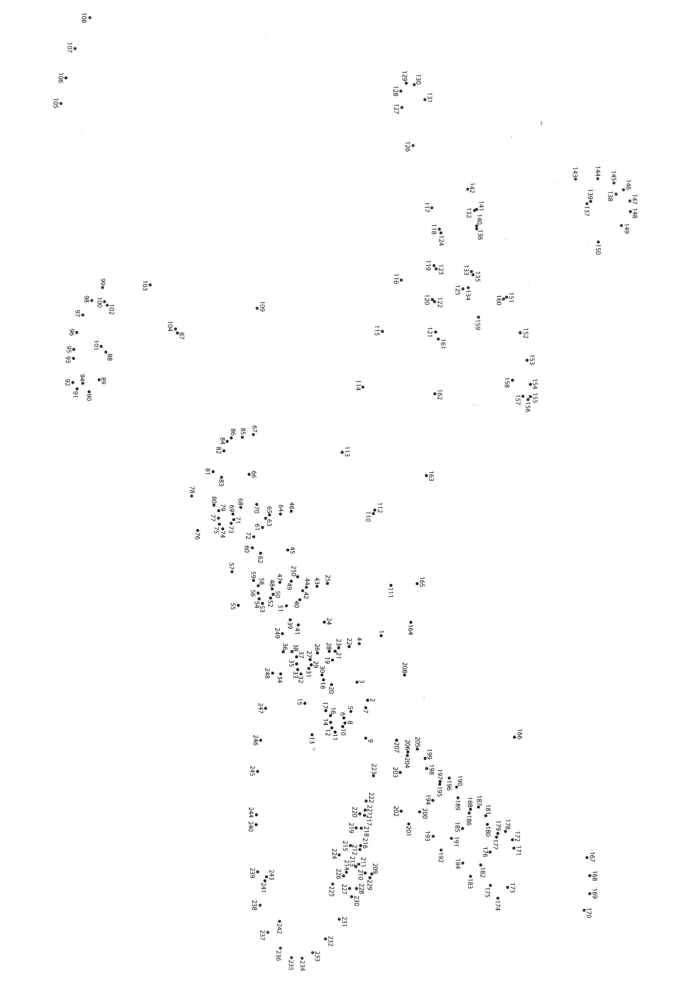

234

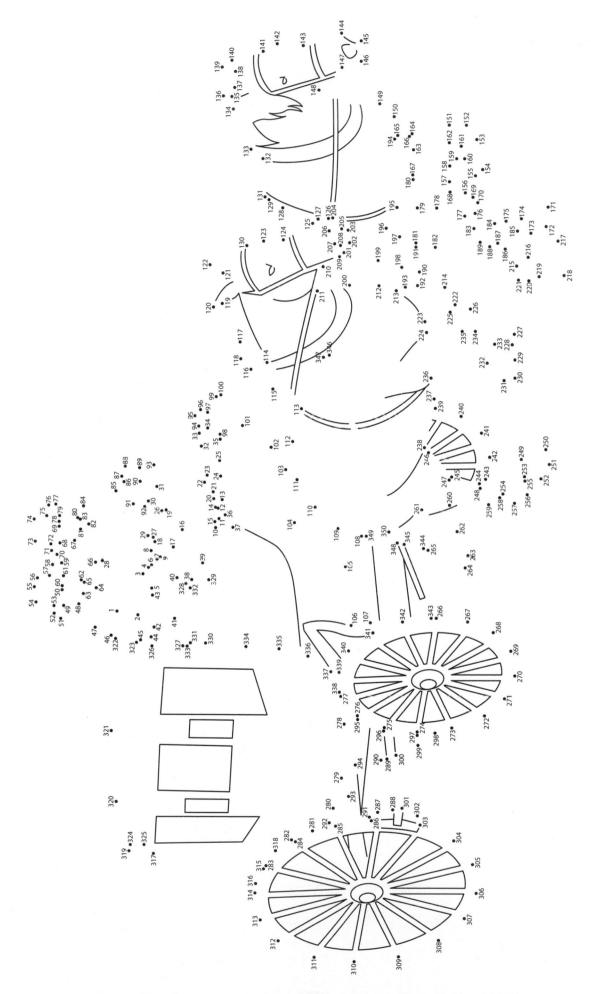

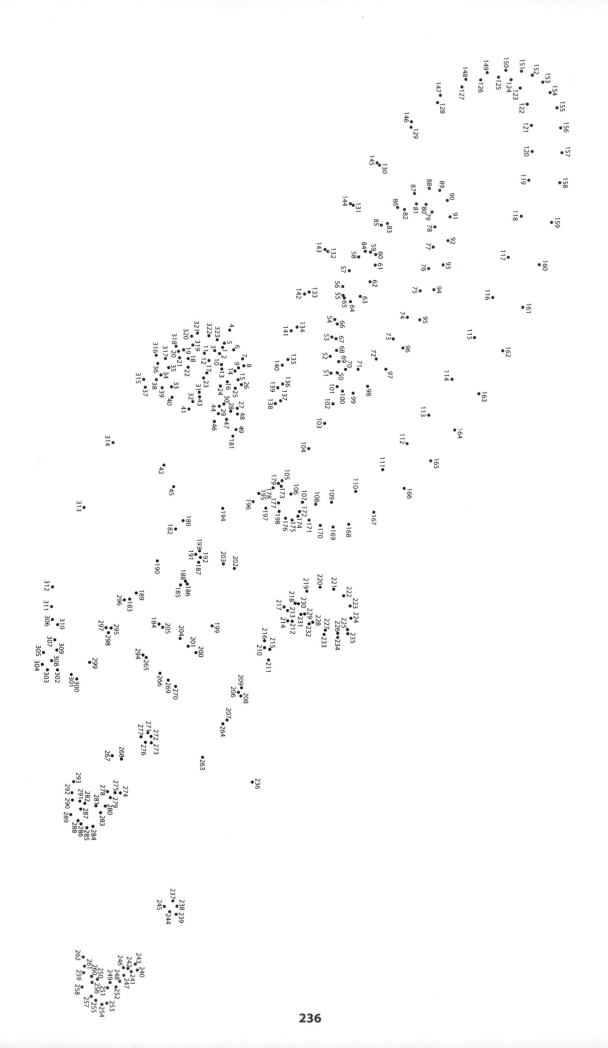

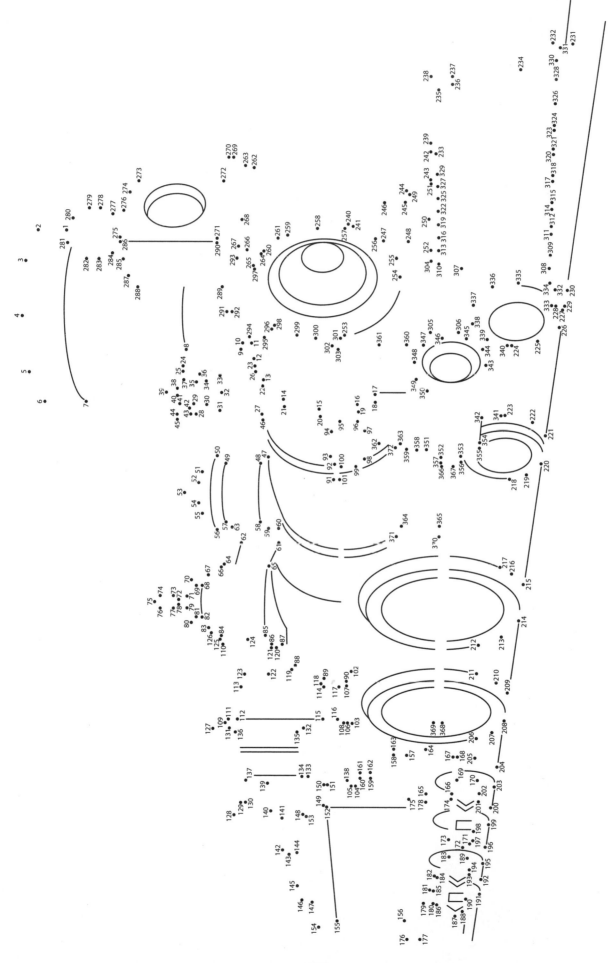

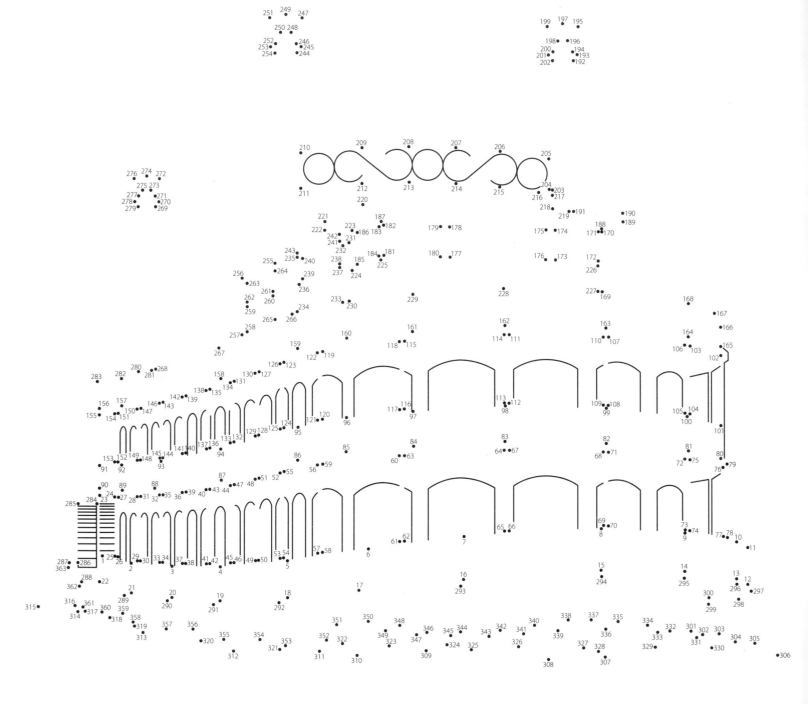

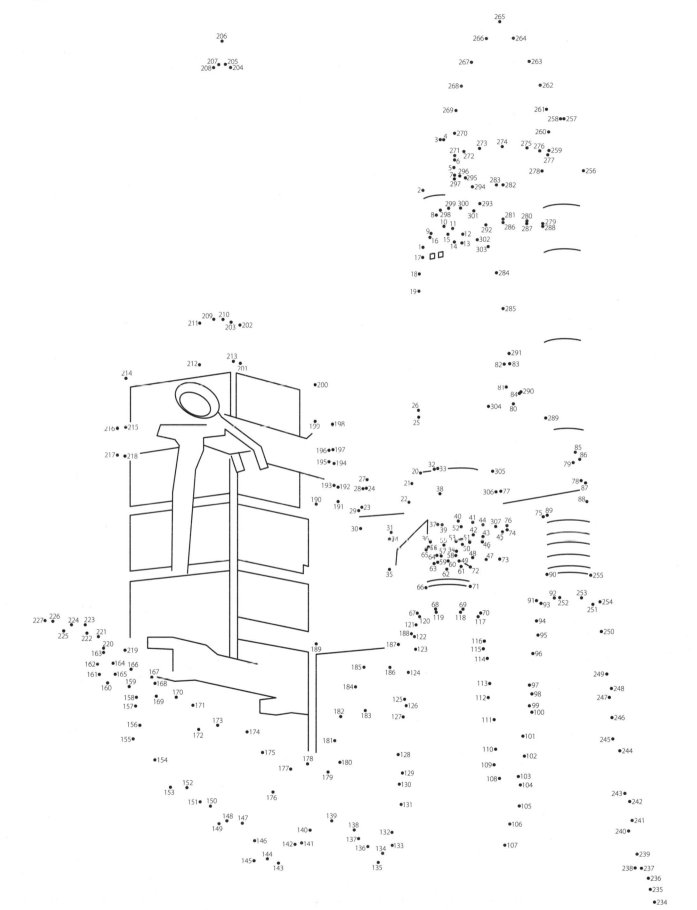

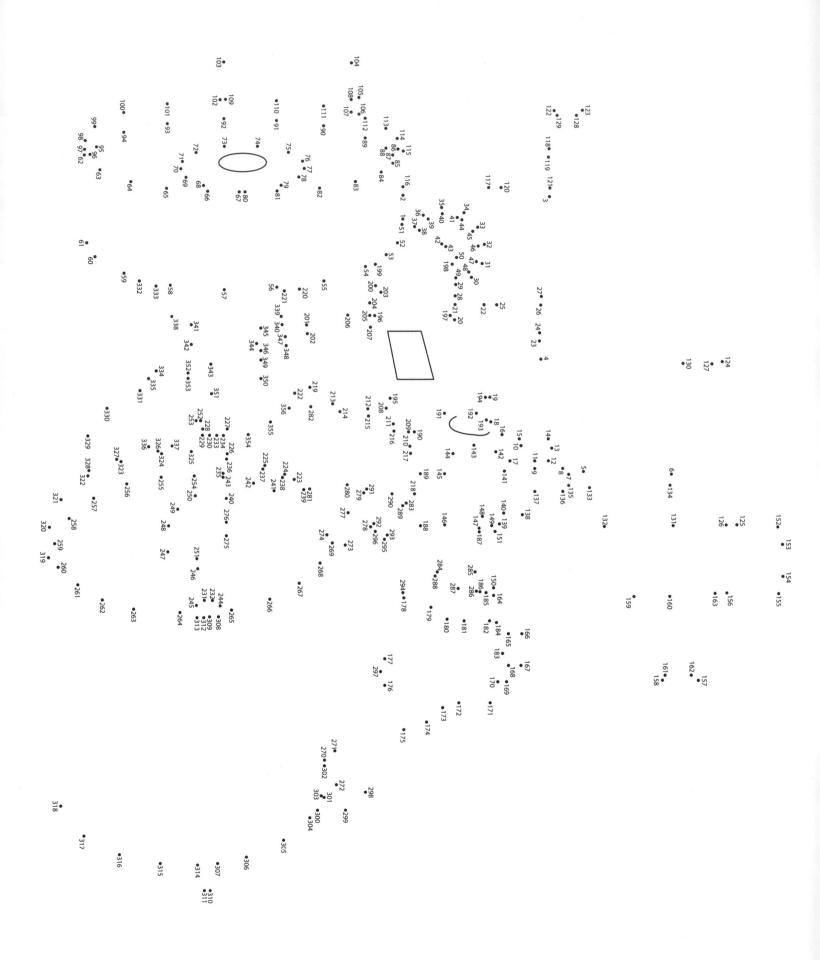

240

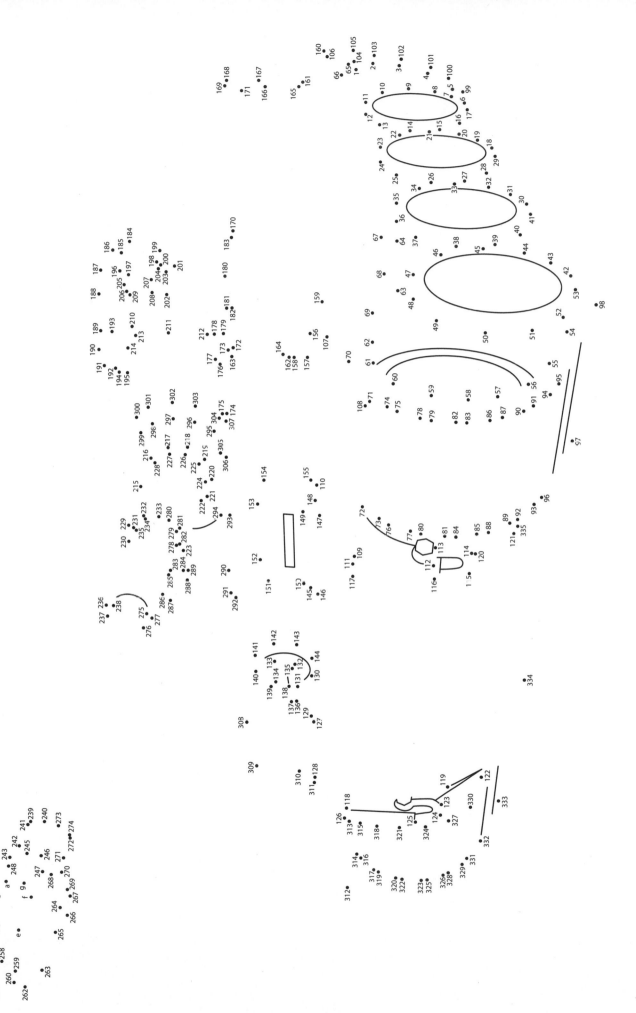

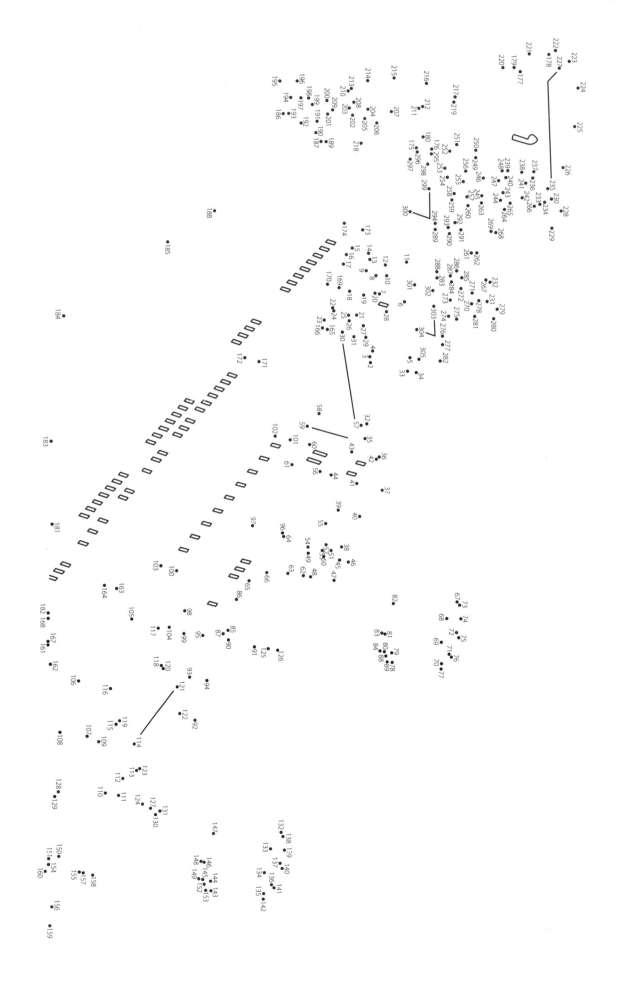

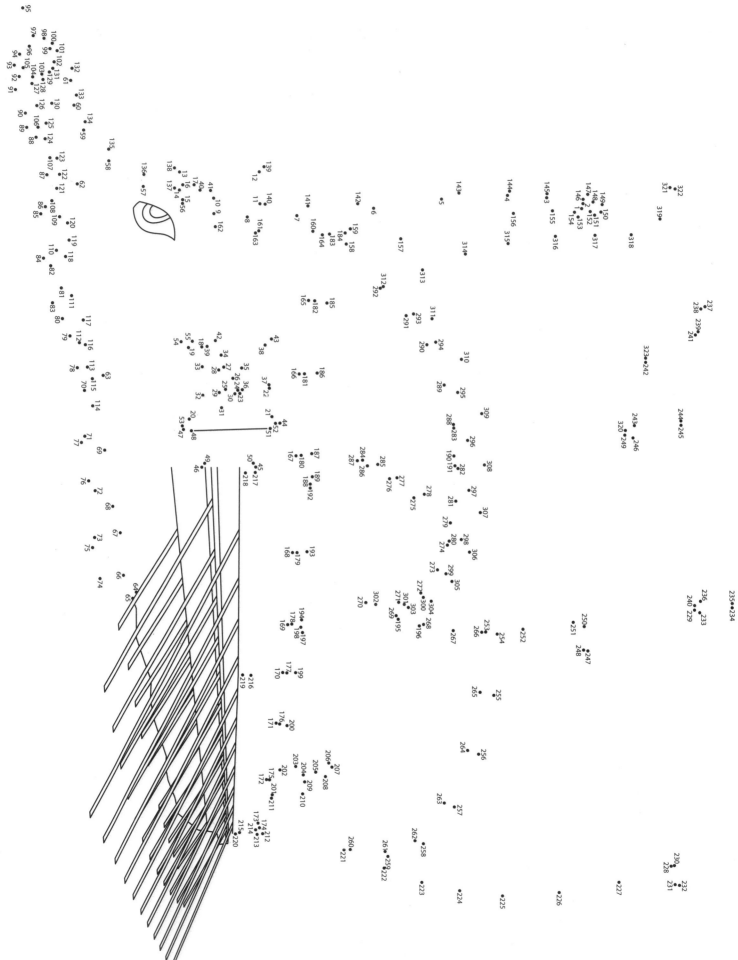

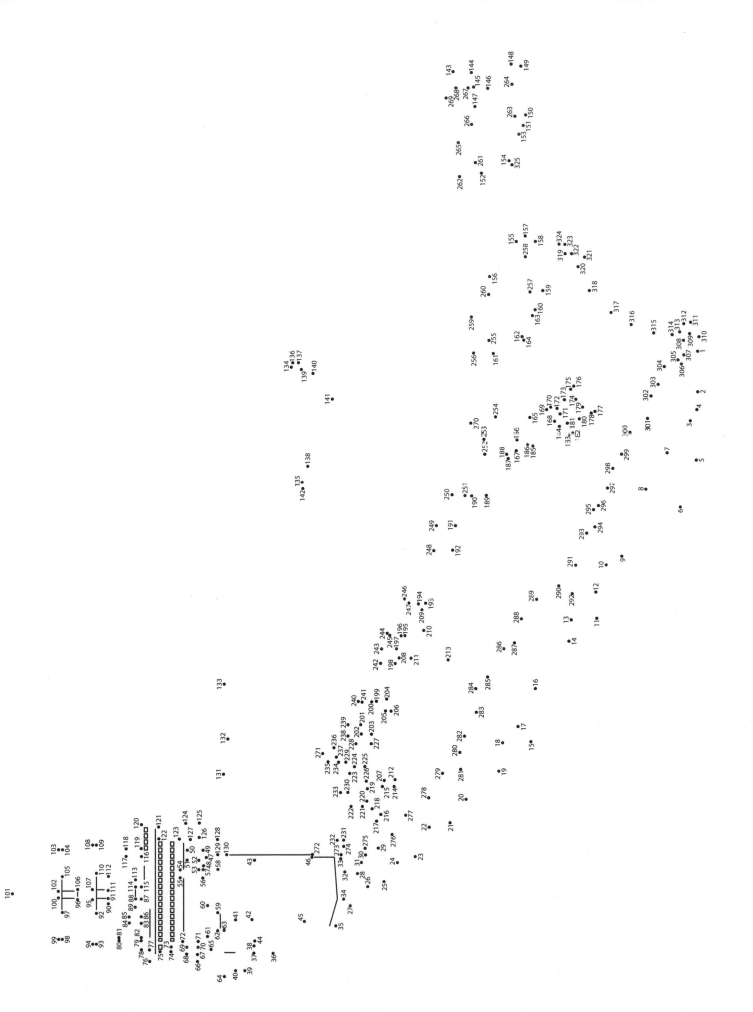

245

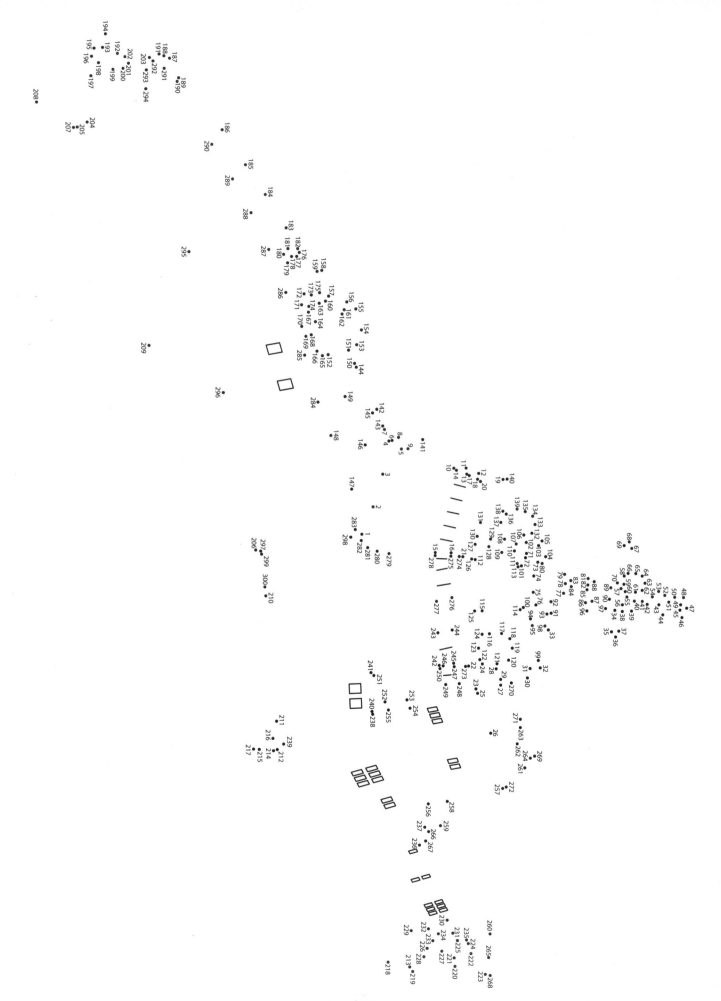

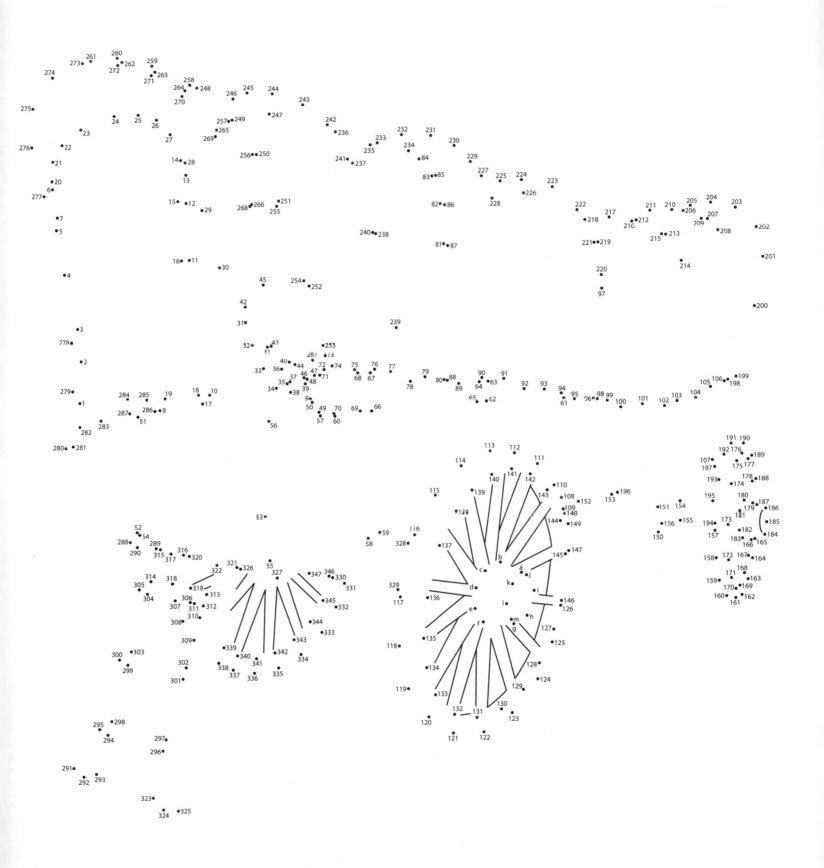

Scenes

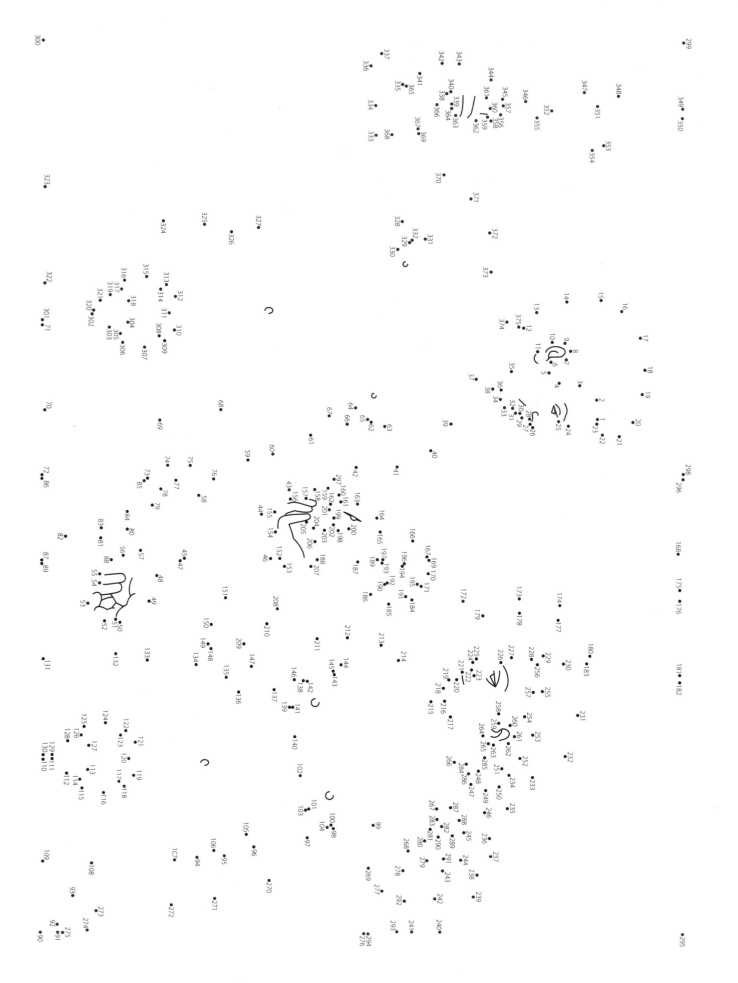

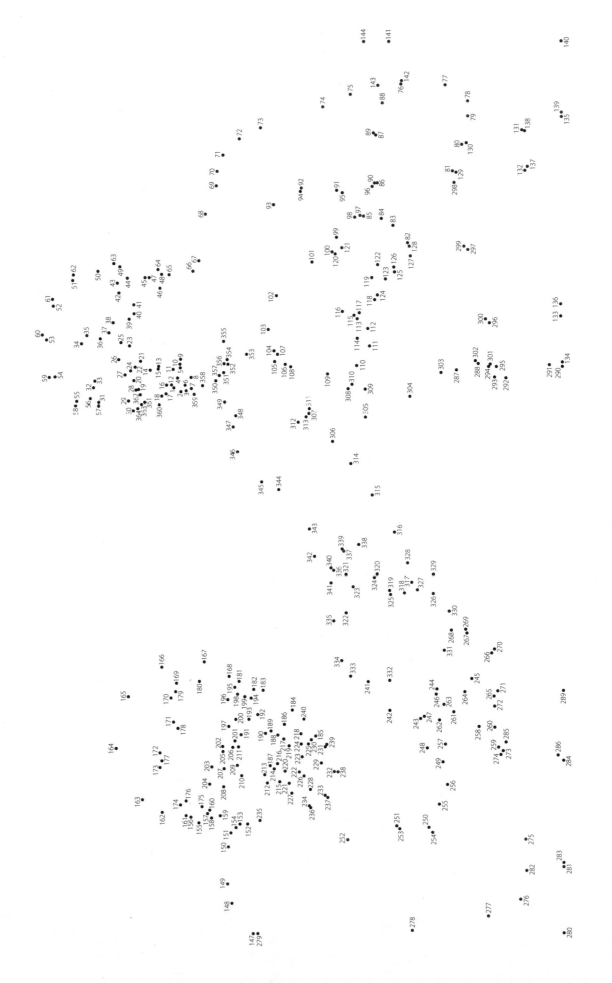

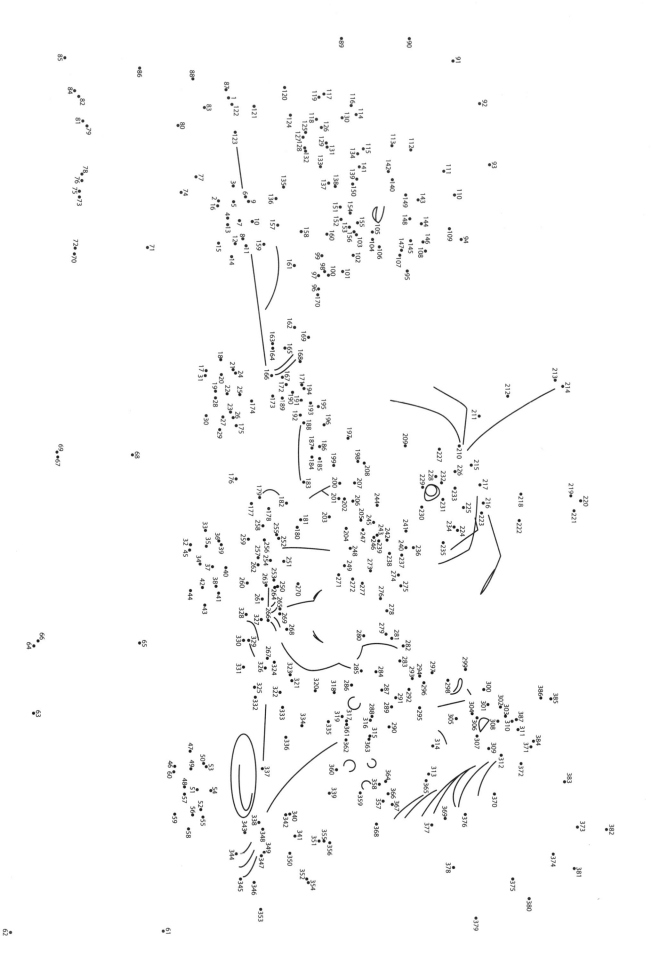

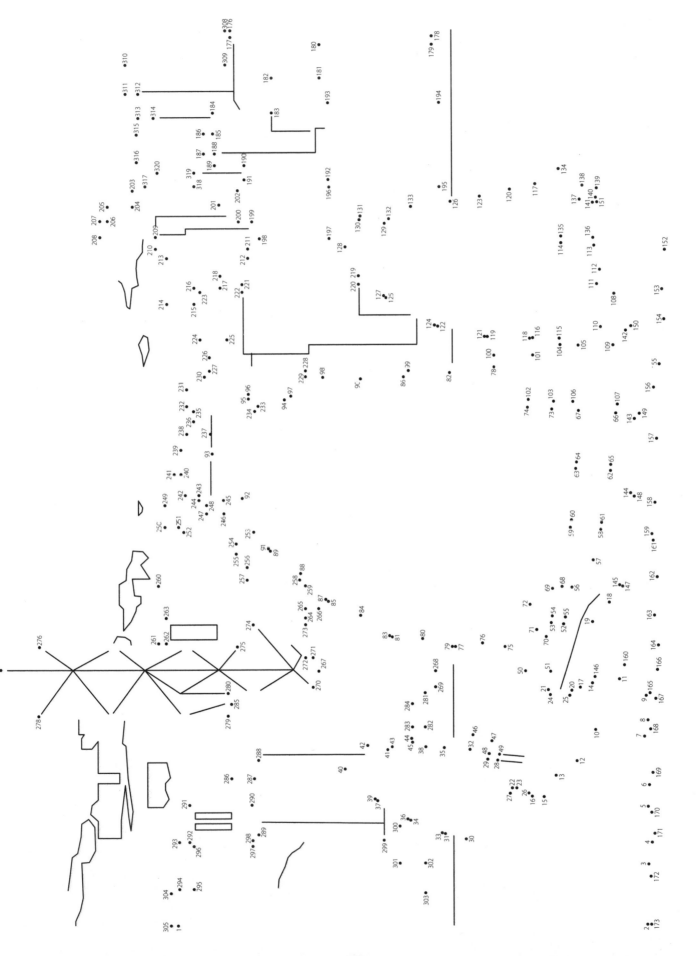

253

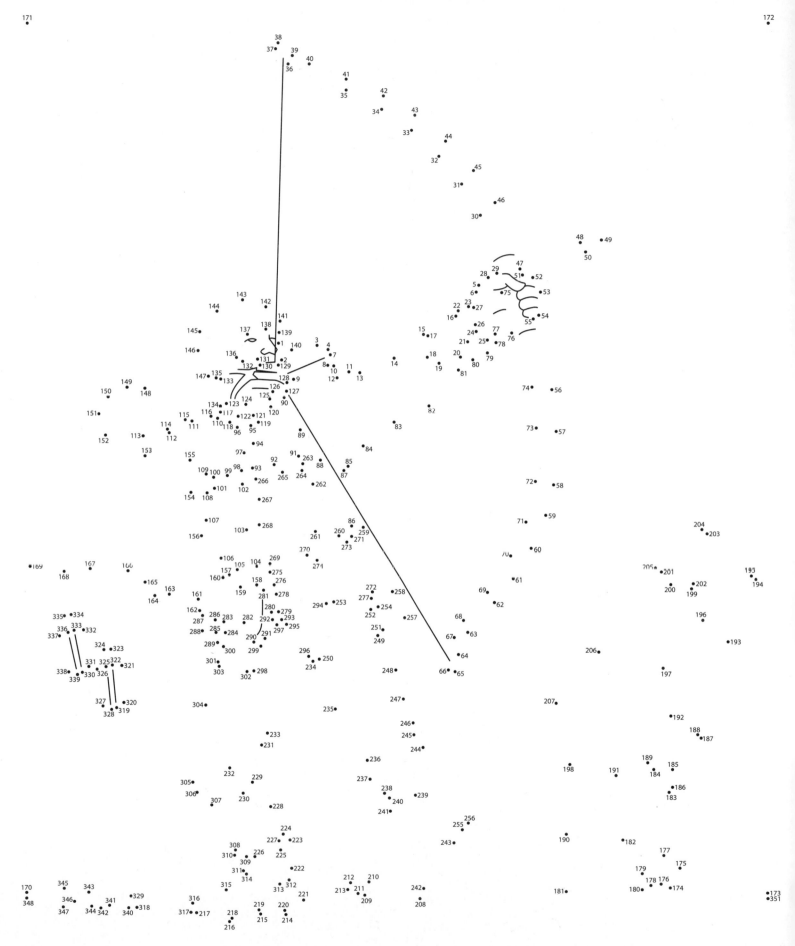

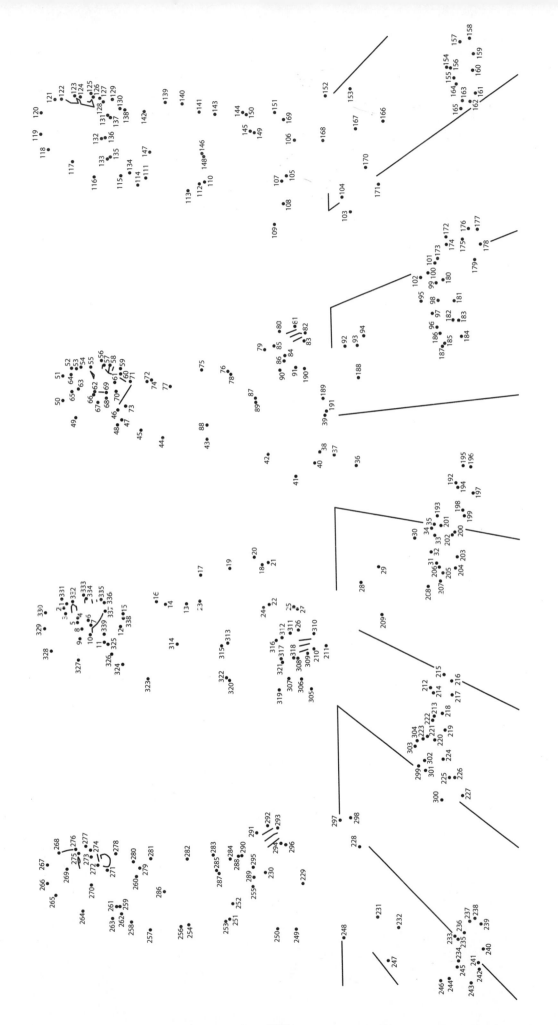

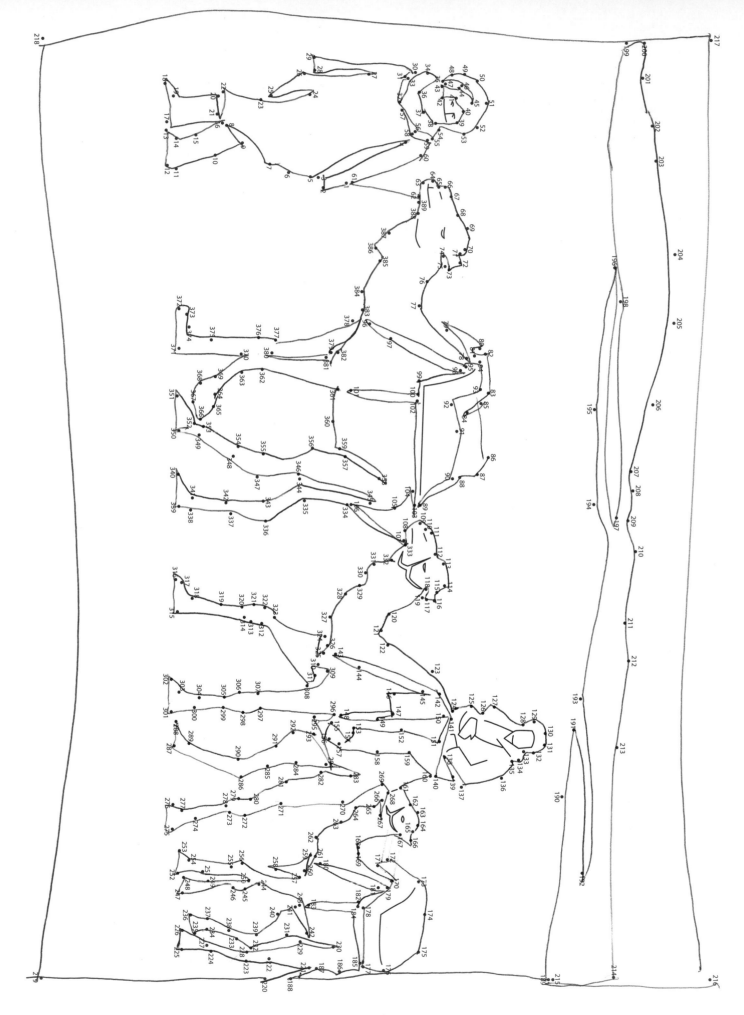

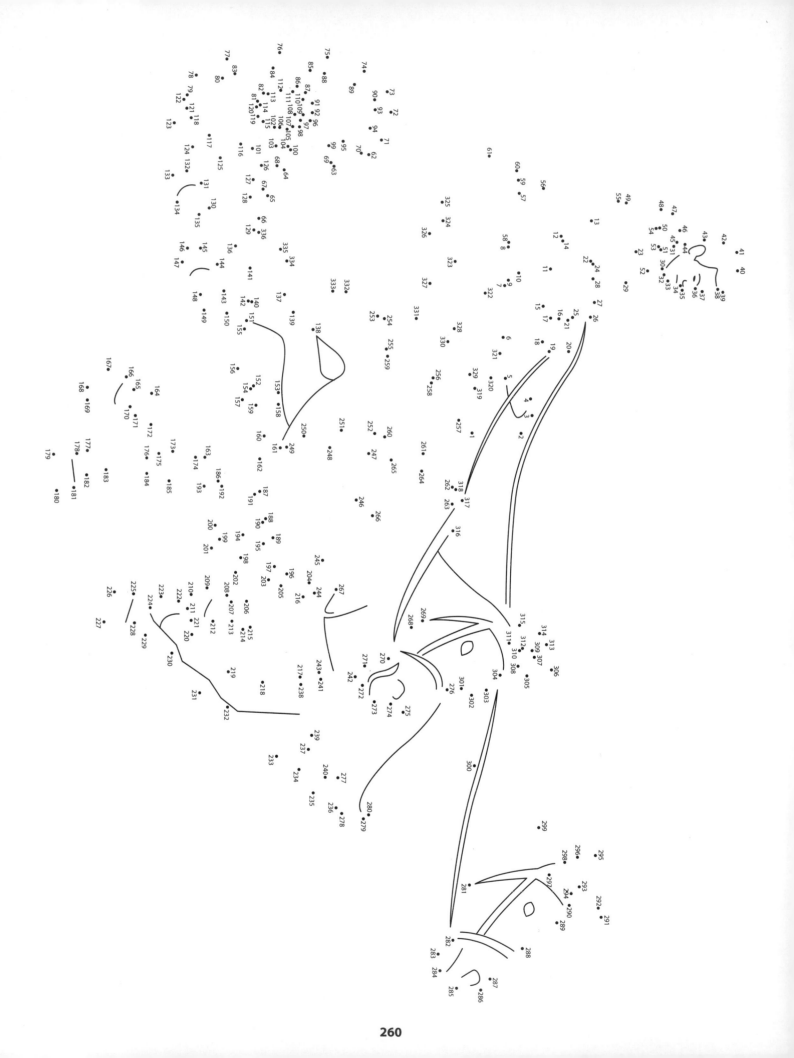

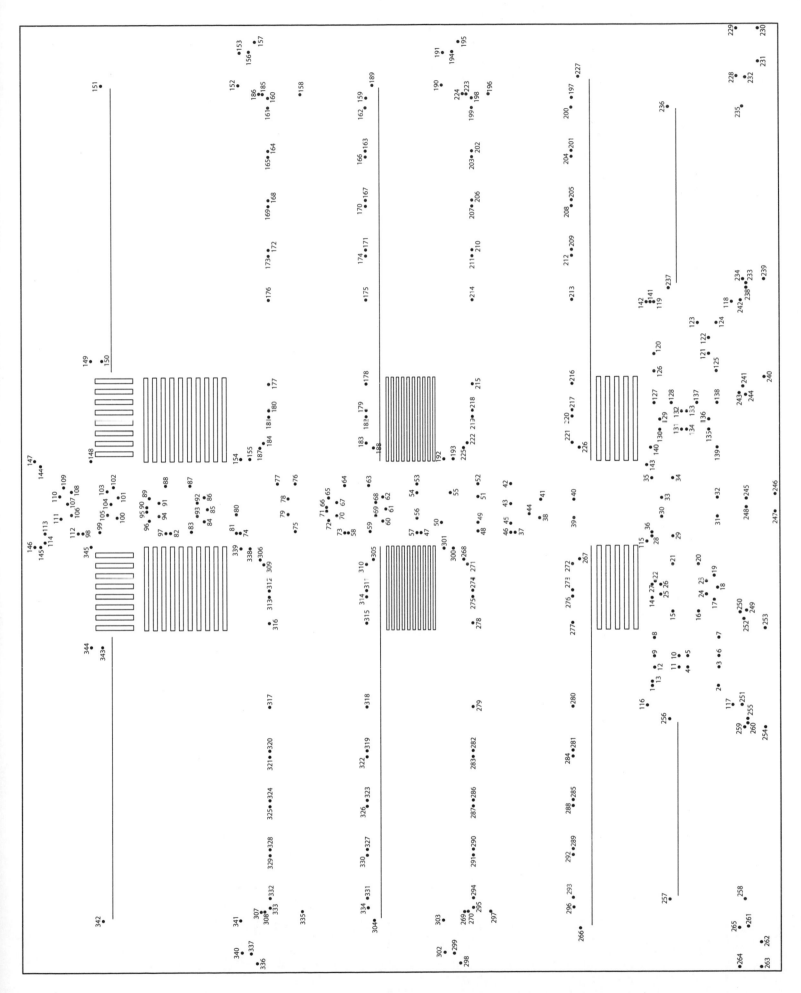

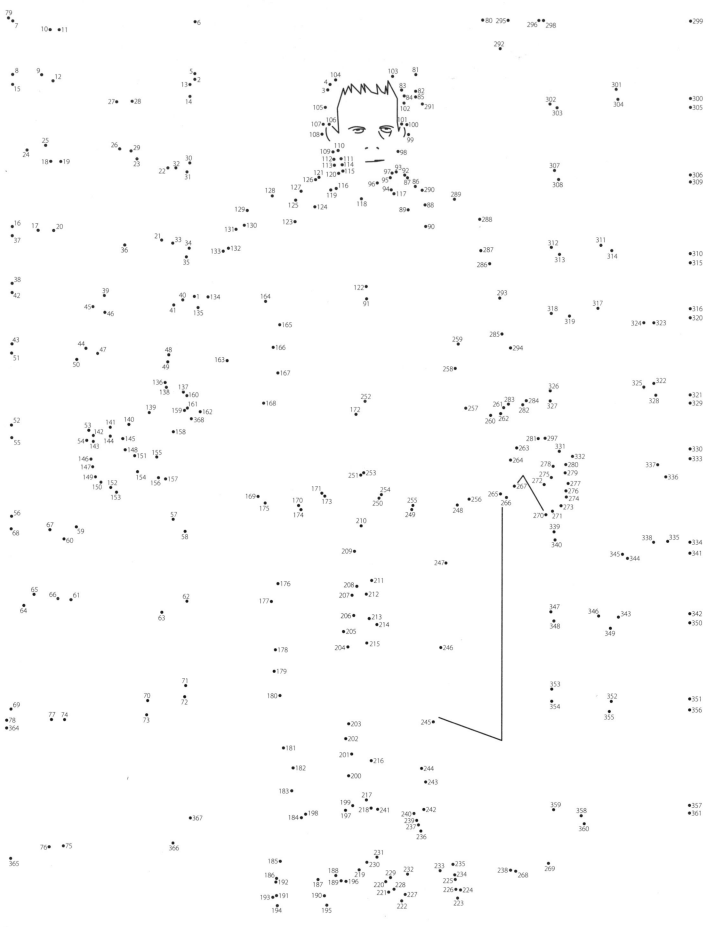

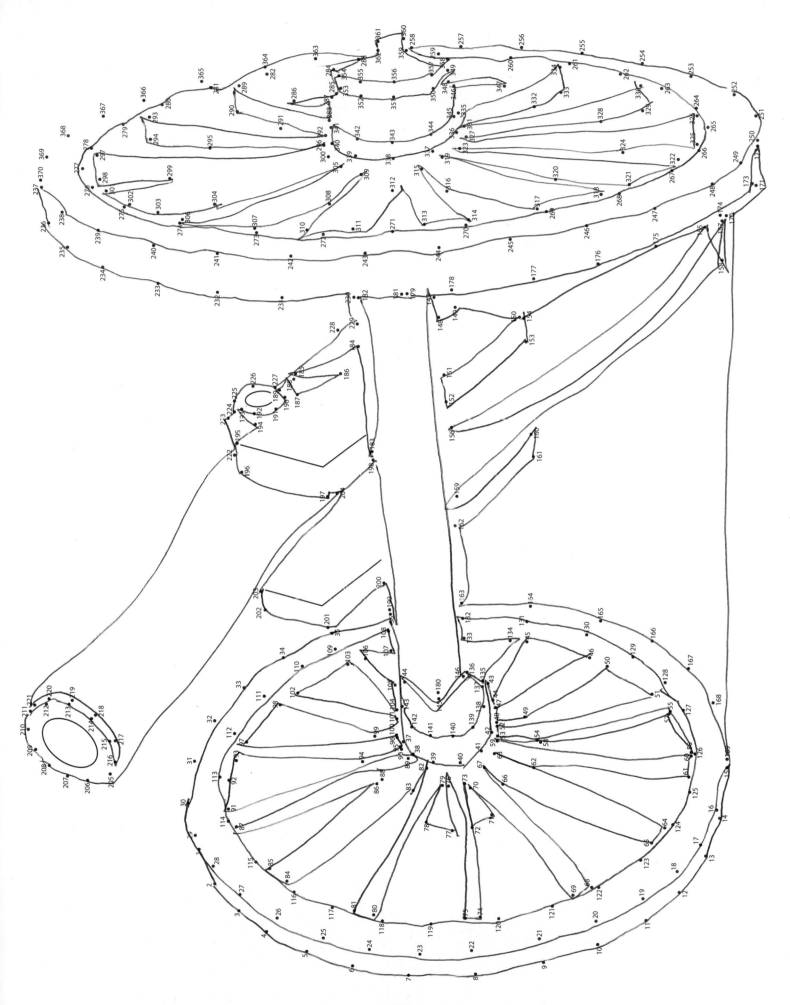

263

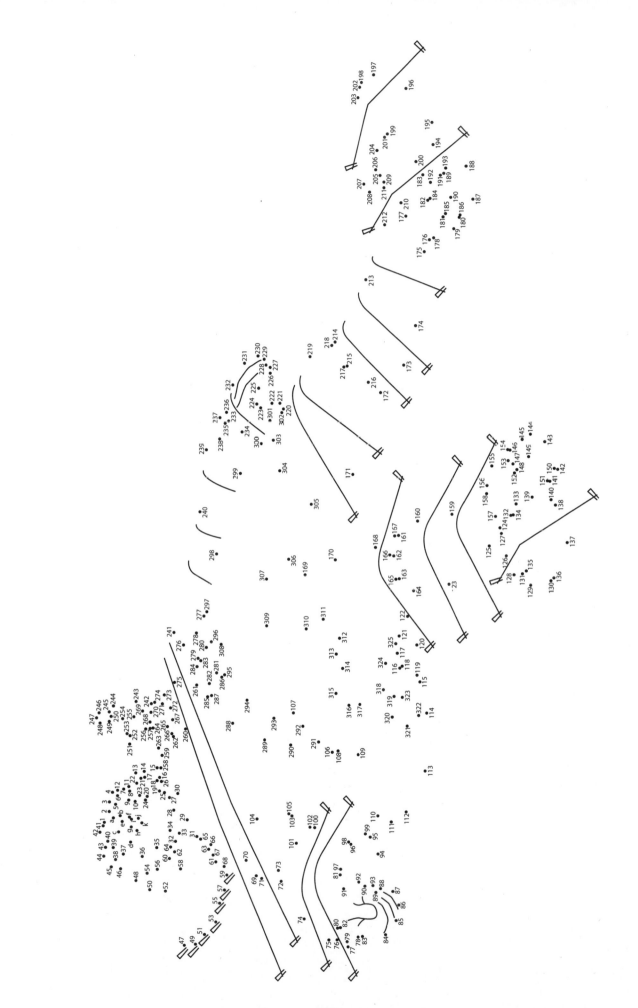

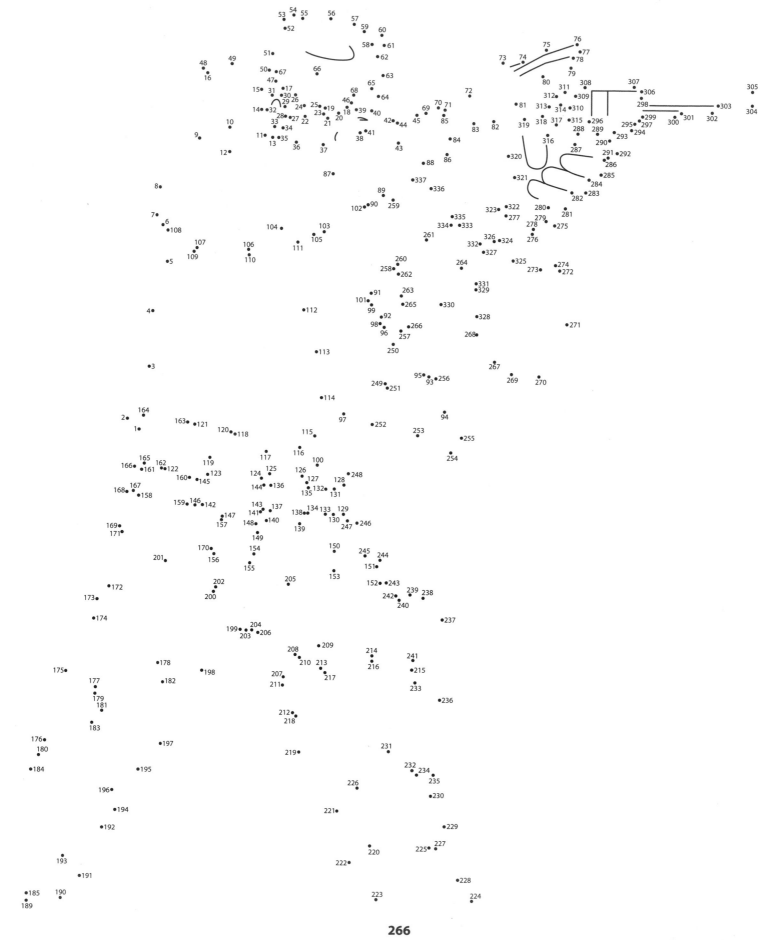

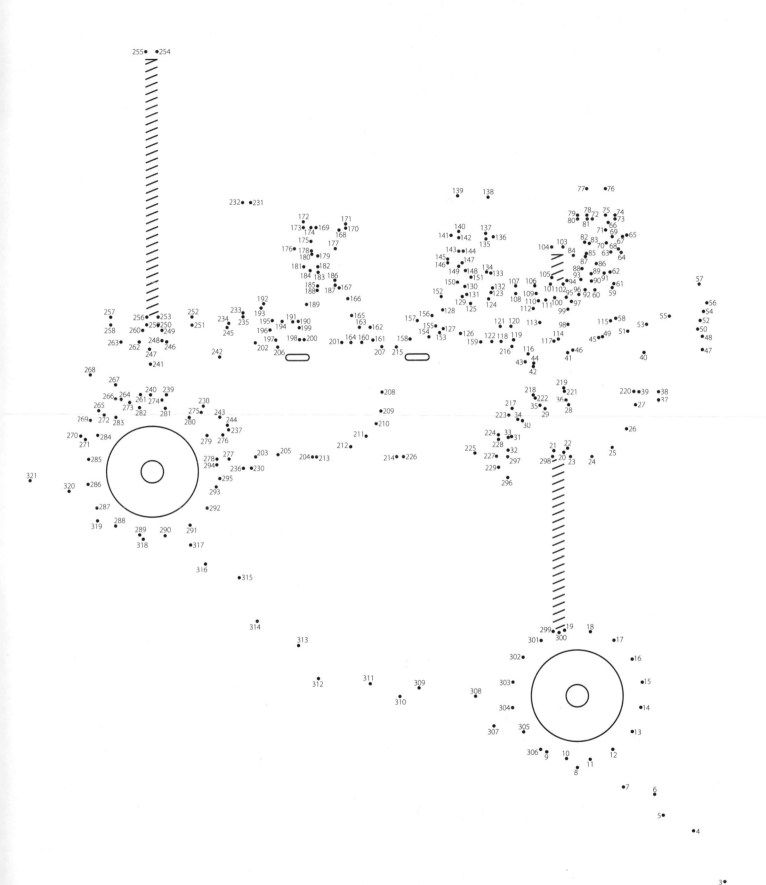

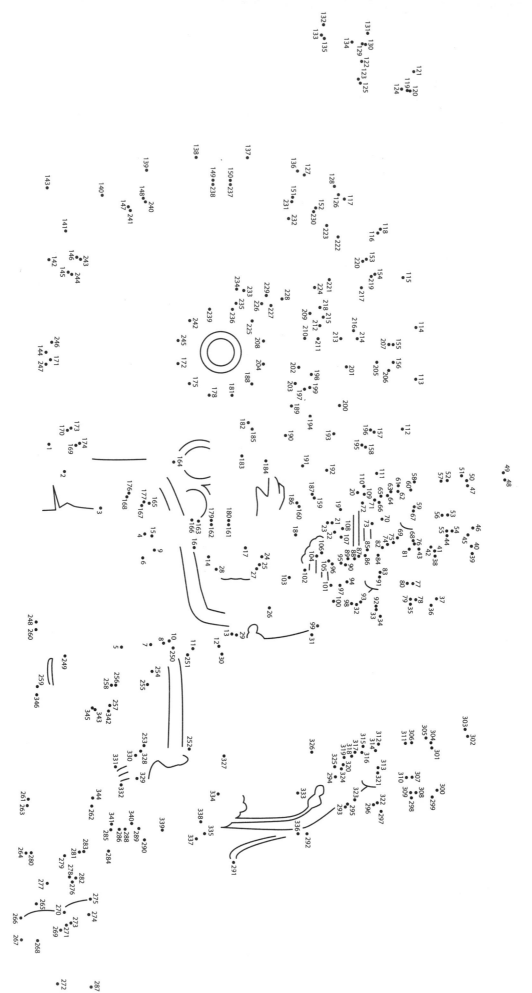

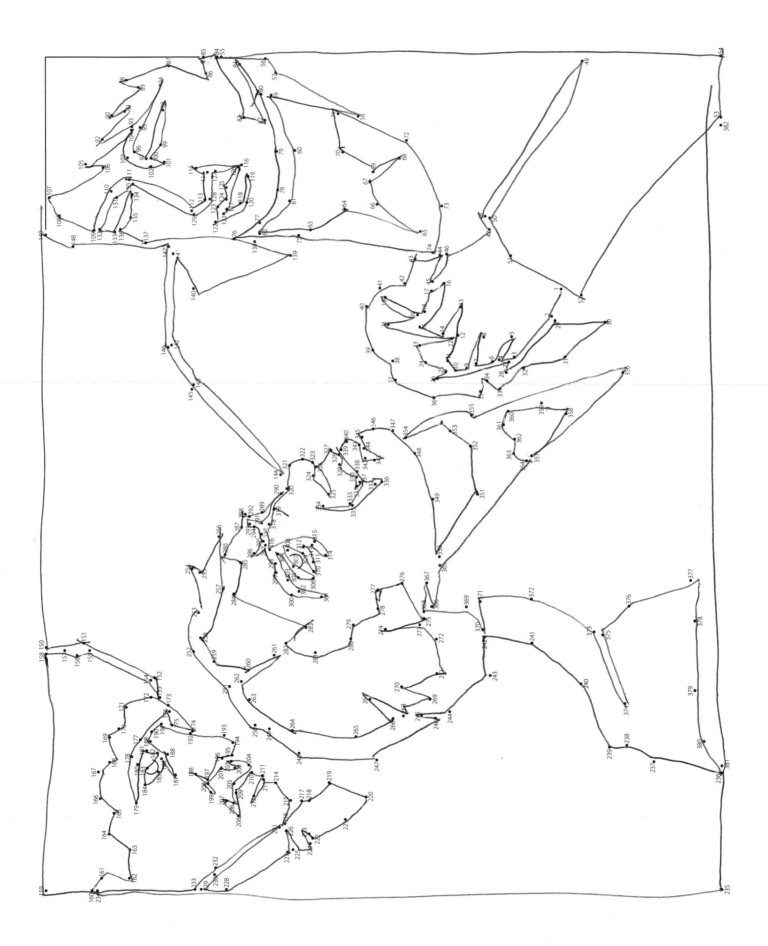

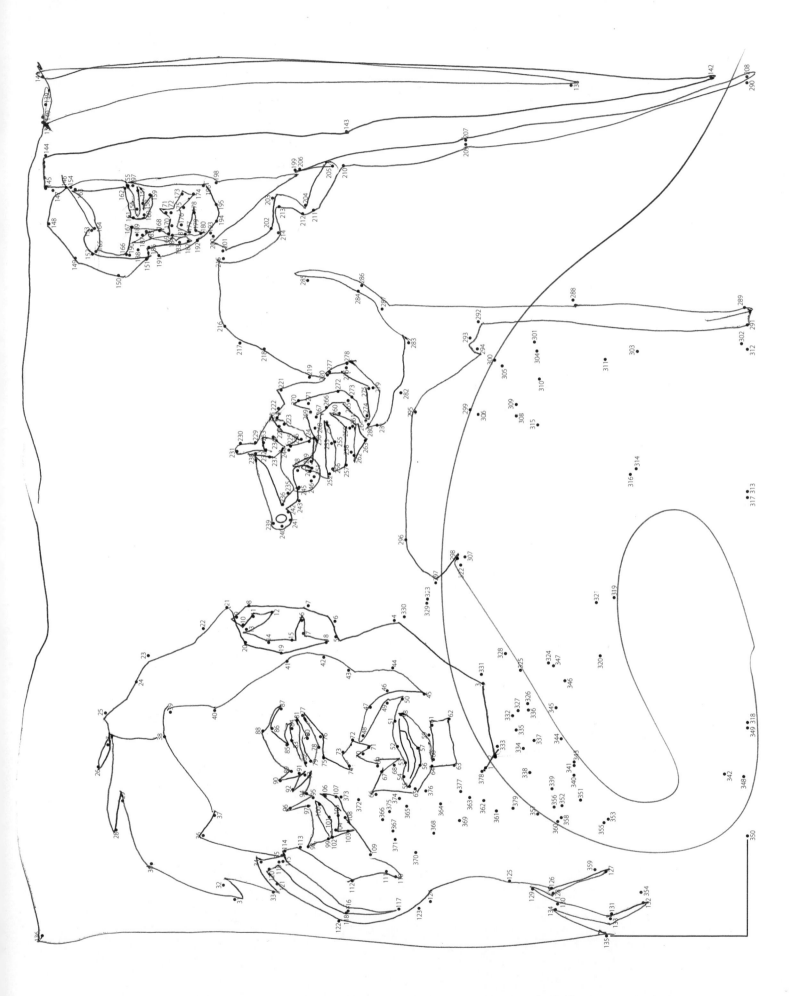

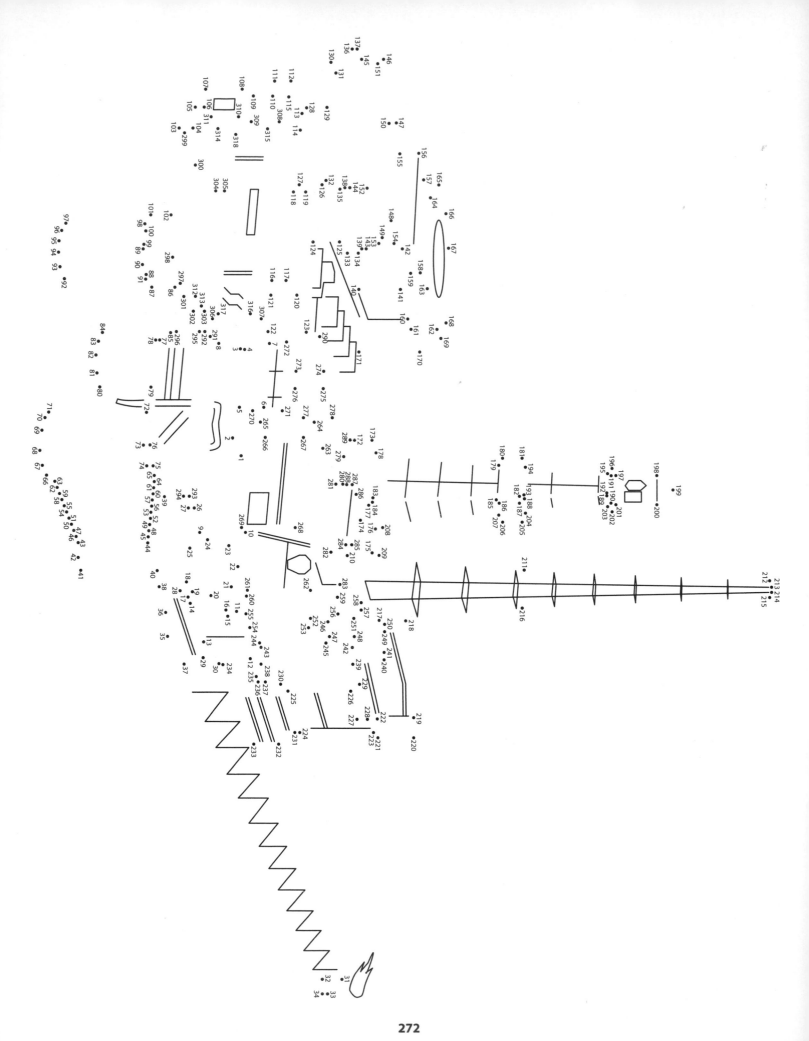

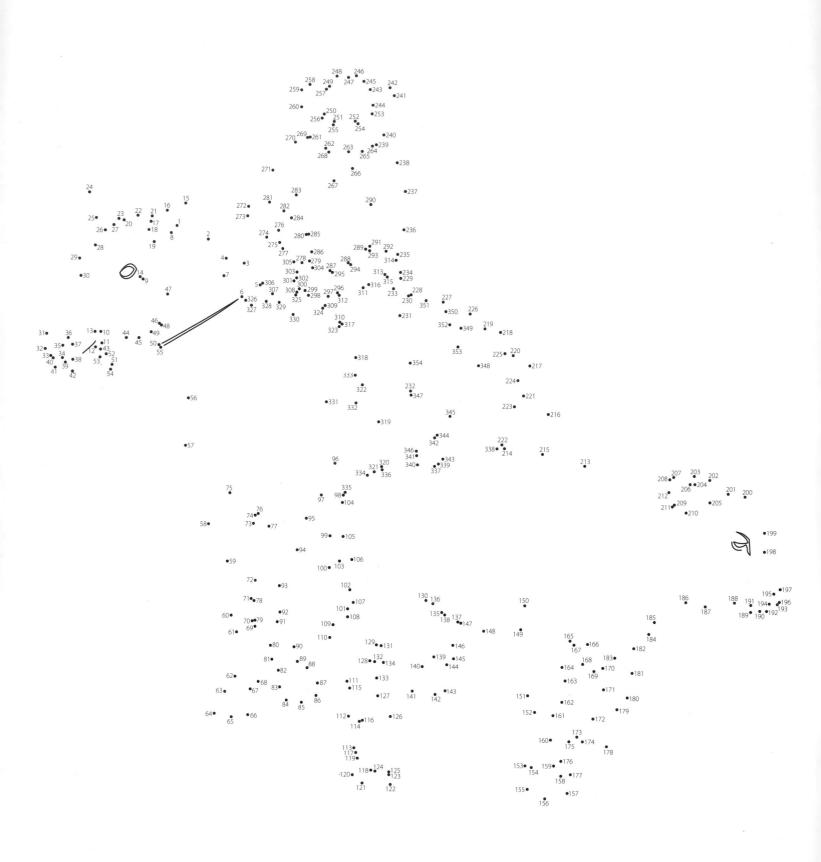

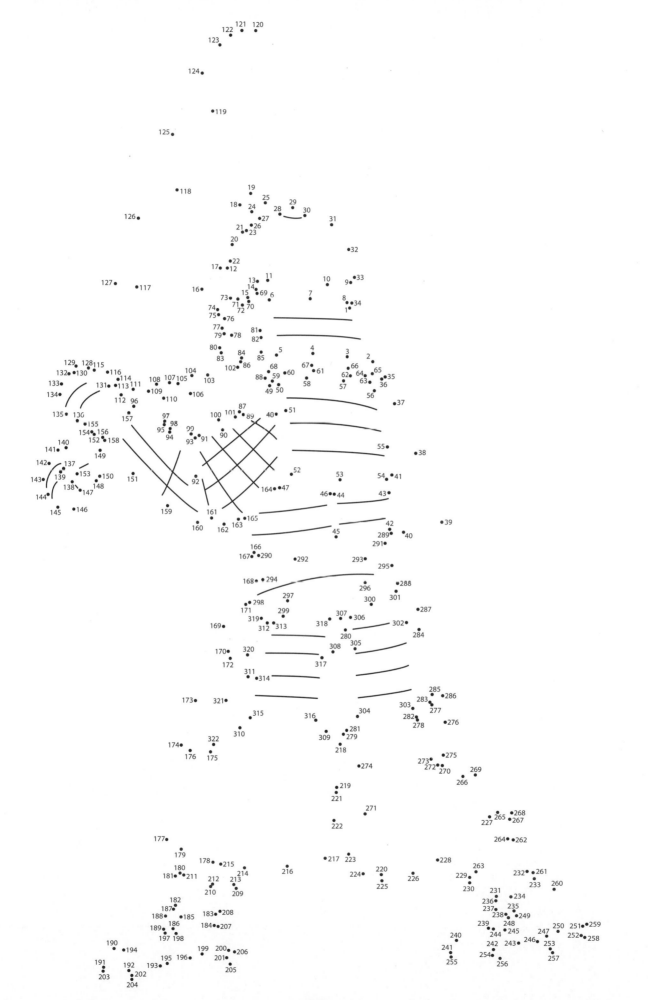

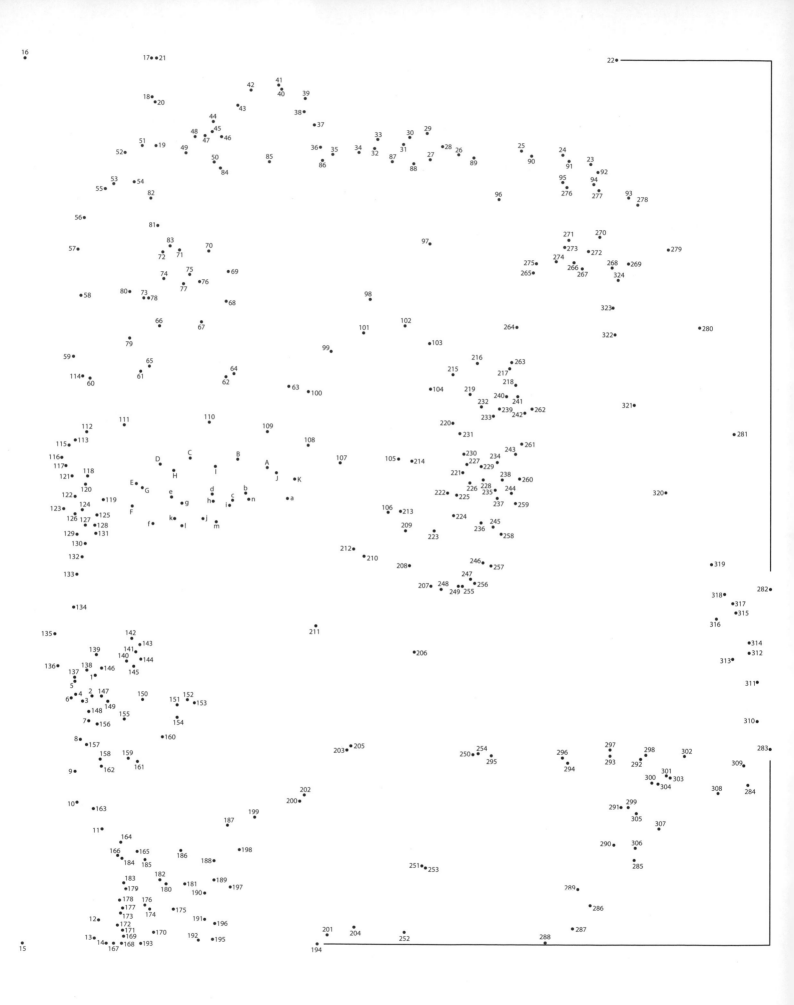

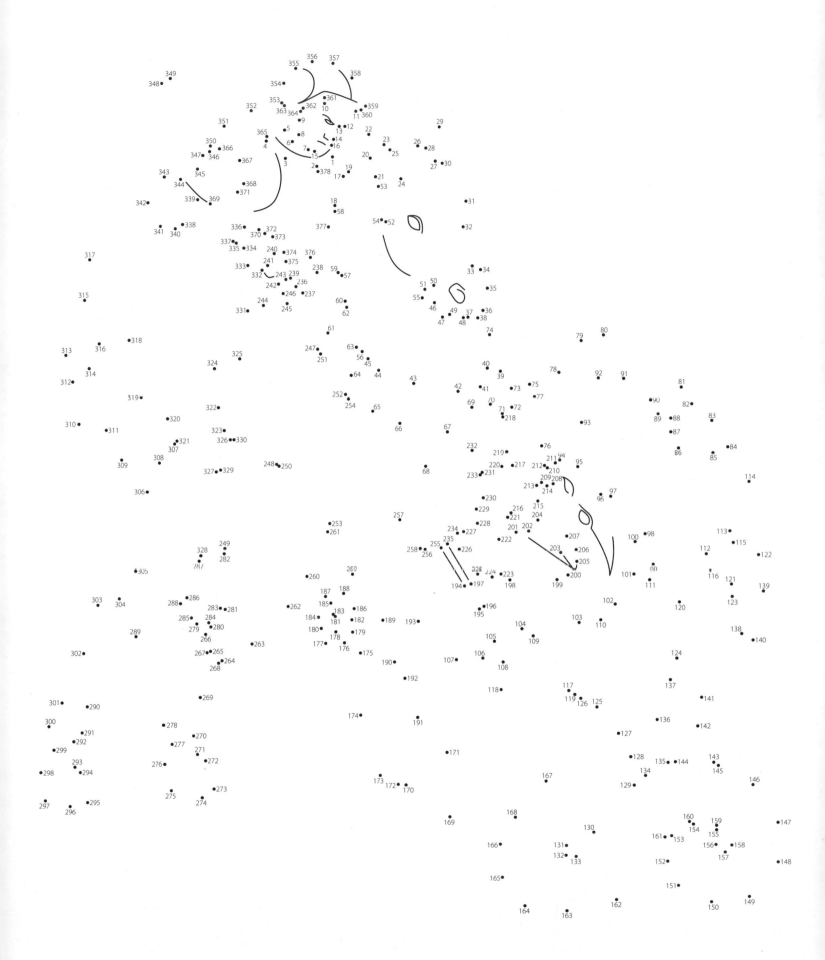

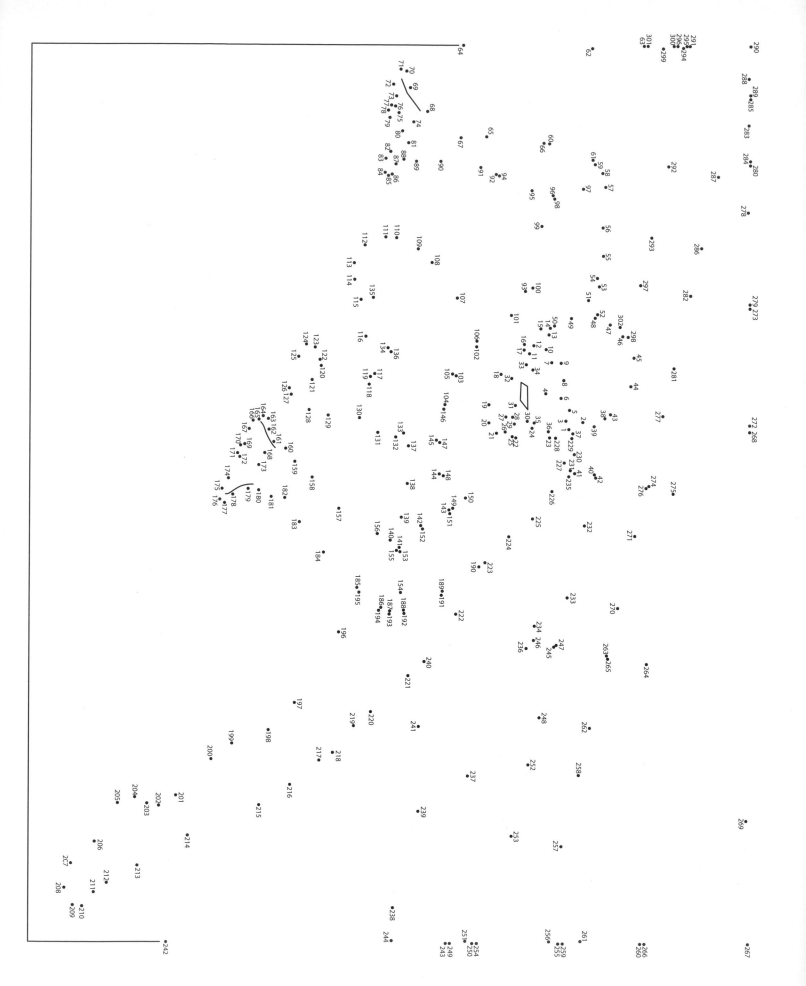

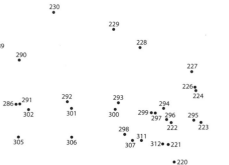

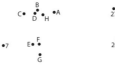
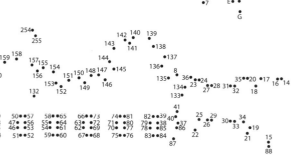
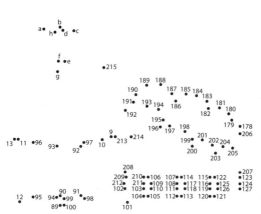

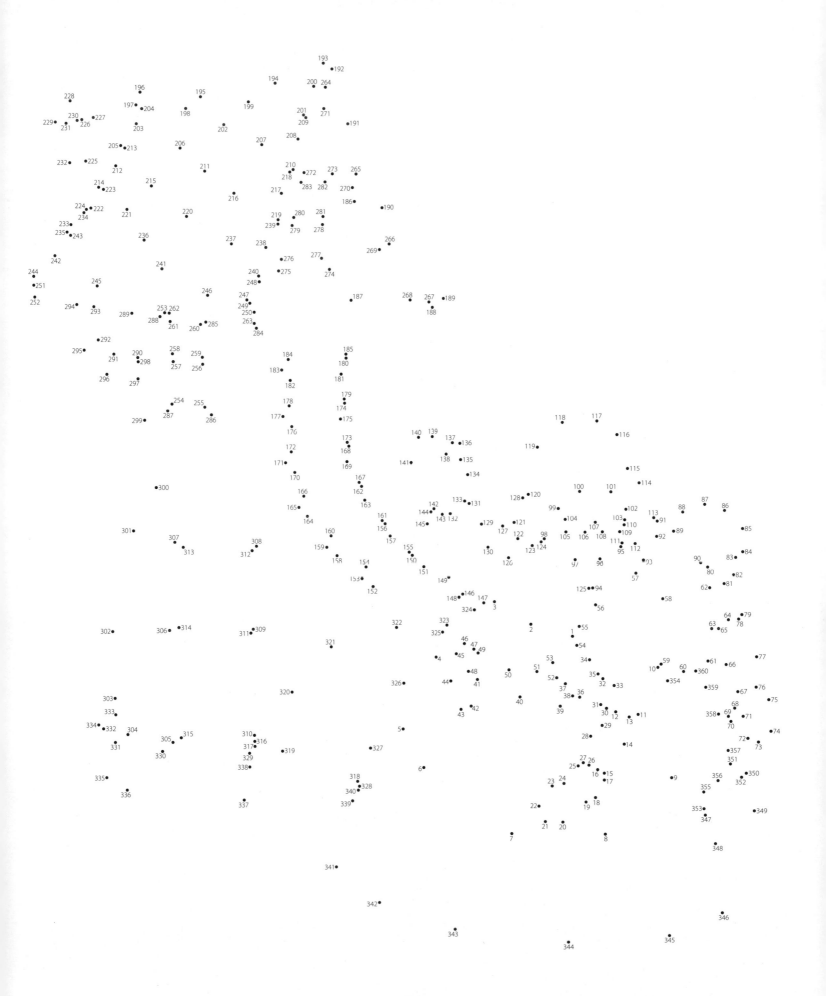

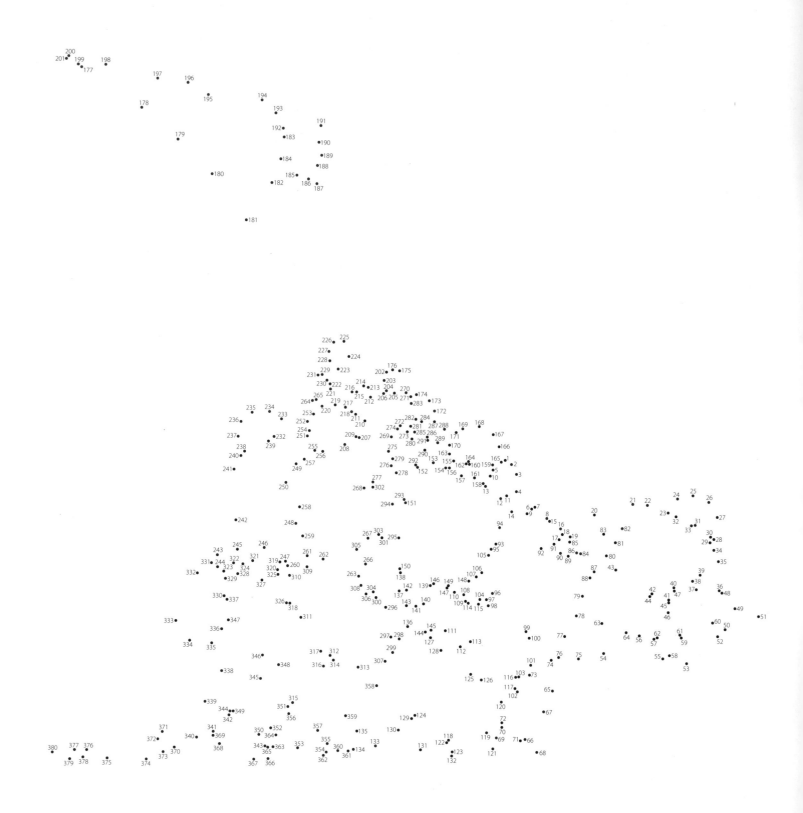

LIST OF ILLUSTRATIONS

WORKS OF ART

ROYAL FAMILY

SCENES